STUDY AND REVISE

AS/A2 Level

Business Studies

First published 2000
exclusively for WHSmith by

Hodder & Stoughton Educational
338 Euston Road
LONDON NW1 3BH

Text © Neil Denby 2000

All rights reserved. No part of this publication may be reproduced or
transmitted in any form or by any means, electronic or mechanical, including
photocopying, recording or any information storage and retrieval system,
without permission in writing from the publisher

A CIP record for this book is available from the British Library

Text: Neil Denby with Tony Buzan
Mind Maps: Jennifer Denby

ISBN 0-340-74331-X

      10 9 8 7 6
Year   2005   2004

Printed and bound in Great Britain for Hodder & Stoughton Educational by
The Bath Press, Bath

Contents

Revision for A Level success   v
by Tony Buzan

Section 1
Objectives and the business environment   1

1. Business strategy and objectives   2
2. Stakeholders and their objectives   8
3. The beginnings and growth of a business   13
4. External influences 1 – micro-factors   21
5. External influences 2 – macro-factors   28

Section 2
Marketing   37

6. Marketing objectives and planning   38
7. Market analysis and research   43
8. Marketing planning   50
9. Forecasting and predicting   55
10. The marketing mix – price   59
11. The marketing mix – product   63
12. The marketing mix – promotion   69
13. The marketing mix – place   74

Section 3
Finance and accounts   78

14. Management accounting   79
15. Break-even analysis   84
16. Investment appraisal   90
17. Financial accounting   95
18. Ratio analysis   101

Section 4
People in business   105

19. Management structure and organisation   106
20. Management styles   112
21. Employer/employee relations   117
22. Human resource management   124

Section 5
Operations management   130

23. Organising production   131
24. Controlling operations   136
25. Maintaining quality   143

Index   148

Each section begins with a summary of the **specification content** for that subject. Use this to help you plan your revision.

Study and Revise for A Level success — INTRODUCTION

You are now in the most important educational stage of your life and are soon to take exams that may have a major impact on your future career and goals. As one A Level student put it: 'It's crunch time!'

At this crucial stage of your life, the thing you need even more than subject knowledge is the knowledge of **how** to remember, **how** to read faster, **how** to comprehend, **how** to study, **how** to take notes and **how** to organise your thoughts. You need to know how to **think**; you need a basic introduction on how to use that super computer inside your head – your brain.

The next few pages contain a goldmine of information on how you can achieve success, both at school and in your A Level exams, as well as in your professional or university career. These pages will give you information on memory, thinking skills, speed reading and study that will enable you to be successful in all your academic pursuits. You will learn:

1 How to remember more *while* you are learning.
2 How to remember more *after* you have finished a class or a study period.
3 How to use special techniques to improve your memory.
4 How to use a revolutionary note-taking technique called Mind Maps that will double your memory and help you to write essays and answer exam questions.
5 How to read everything faster, while at the same time improving comprehension and concentration.
6 How to zap your revision.

How to understand, improve and master your memory

Your memory really is like a muscle. Don't exercise it and it will grow weaker; do exercise it and it will grow incredibly more powerful. There are really only four main things you need to understand about your memory in order to increase its power dramatically:

1 Recall during learning – you must take breaks!

When you are studying, your memory can concentrate, understand and remember well for between 20 and 45 minutes at a time. Then it needs a break. If you carry on for longer than this without one, your memory starts to break down. If you study for hours non-stop, you will remember only a fraction of what you have been trying to learn and you will have wasted valuable revision time.

So, ideally, *study for less than an hour*, then take a five- to ten-minute break. During this break, listen to music, go for a walk, do some exercise or just daydream. (Daydreaming is a necessary brainpower booster – geniuses do it regularly.)

During the break your brain will be sorting out what it has been learning and you will go back to your study with the new information safely stored and organised in your memory banks.

Make sure you take breaks at regular intervals as you work through your *Revise AS and A Level* book.

2 Recall after learning – surfing the waves of your memory

What do you think begins to happen to your memory straight after you have finished learning something? Does it immediately start forgetting? No! Your brain actually *increases* its power and carries on remembering. For a short time after your study session, your brain integrates the information making a more complete picture of everything it has just learnt. Only then does the rapid decline in memory begin, and as much as 80% of what you have learnt can be forgotten in a day.

However, if you catch the top of the wave of your memory, and briefly review back what you have been revising at the correct time, the memory is stamped in far more strongly and stays at the crest of the wave for much longer. To maximise your brain's power to remember, take a few minutes and use a Mind Map to review what you have learnt at the end of a day. Then review it at the end of a week, again at the end of a month and, finally, a week before the exams. That way you'll surf-ride your memory wave all the way to your exam, success, and beyond!

3 The memory principle of association

The muscle of your memory becomes stronger when it can **associate** – when it can link things together.

Think about your best friend and all the things your mind automatically links with that person. Think about your favourite hobby and all the associations your mind has when you think about (remember) that hobby.

When you are studying, use this memory principle to make associations between the elements in your subjects and to thus improve both your memory and your chances of success.

4 The memory principle of imagination

The muscle of your memory will improve significantly if you can produce big **images** in your mind. Rather than just memorising the name of an historical character, **imagine** that character as if you were a video producer filming that person's life.

In *all* your subjects, use the **imagination** memory principle.

Study and Revise for A level success

Your new success formula: Mind Maps®

You have noticed that when people go on holidays or travels they take maps. Why? To give them a general picture of where they are going, to help them locate places of special interest and importance, to help them find things more easily and to help them remember distances, locations and so on.

It is exactly the same with your mind and with study.

If you have a 'map of the territory' of what you have to learn, then everything is easier. In learning and study, the Mind Map is that special tool.

As well as helping you with all areas of study, the Mind Map actually *mirrors the way your brain works*. Your Mind Maps can be used for taking notes from your study books, taking notes in class, preparing your homework, presenting your homework, reviewing your tests, checking your and your friends' knowledge in any subject, and for *helping you understand anything you learn*.

As you will see, Mind Maps use, throughout, Imagination and Association. As such, they automatically strengthen your memory muscle every time you use them. Throughout this *Study and Revise AS and A2 Level* book you will find Mind Maps that summarise the most important areas of the subject you are studying. Study them, add some colour, personalise them, and then have a go at drawing your own – you will remember them far better! Put them on your walls and in your files for a quick and easy review of the topic.

Using Mind Maps

Mind Maps are a versatile tool – use them for taking notes in class or from books, for solving problems, for brainstorming with friends, and for reviewing and revising for exams – their uses are infinite! You will find them invaluable for planning essays for coursework and exams. Number your main branches in the order in which you want to use them and off you go – the main headings for your essay are done *and* all your ideas are logically organised.

Super speed reading and study

What happens to your comprehension as your reading speed rises? 'It goes down.' Wrong! It seems incredible, but it has been proved that the faster you read, the more you comprehend and remember.

So here are some tips to help you to practise reading faster – you'll cover the ground much more quickly, remember more *and* have more time for revision and leisure activities.

How to make study easy for your brain

When you are going somewhere, is it easier to know beforehand where you are going, or not? Obviously it is easier if you do know. It is the same for your brain and a book. When you get a new book, there are seven things you can do to help your brain get to 'know the territory' faster.

1 Scan through the whole book in less than 20 minutes, as you would do if you were in a shop thinking whether or not to buy it. This gives your brain control.

2 Think about what you already know about the subject. You'll often find out it's a lot more than you thought. A good way of doing this is to draw a quick Mind Map on everything you know after you have skimmed through it.

How to draw a Mind Map

1 Start in the middle of the page with the paper turned sideways. This gives your brain more radiant freedom for its thoughts.

2 Always start by drawing a picture or symbol. Why? Because **a picture is worth a thousand words to your brain**. Try to use at least three colours, as colour helps your memory even more.

3 Let your thoughts flow, and write or draw your ideas on coloured branching lines connected to your central image. These key symbols and words are the headings for your topic.

4 Next, add facts and ideas by drawing more, smaller, branches on to the appropriate main branches, just like a tree.

5 Always print each word clearly on its line. Use only one word per line.

6 To link ideas and thoughts on different branches, use arrows, colours, underlining and boxes.

How to read a Mind Map

1 Begin in the centre, the focus of your topic.
2 The words/images attached to the centre are like chapter headings; read them next.
3 Always read out from the centre, in every direction (even on the left-hand side, where you will have to read from right to left; instead of the usual left to right).

Study and Revise for A level success

3. Ask who, what, why, where, when and how questions about what is in the book. Questions help your brain 'fish' the knowledge out.

4. Ask your friends what they know about the subject. This helps them review the knowledge in their own brains and helps your brain get new knowledge about what you are studying.

5. Have another quick speed through the book, this time looking for any diagrams, pictures and illustrations, and also at the beginnings and ends of chapters. Most information is contained in the beginnings and ends.

6. Build up a Mind Map as you study the book. This helps your brain organise and hold (remember) information as you study.

7. If you come across any difficult parts in your book, mark them and move on. Your brain *will* be able to solve the problems when you come back to them a little bit later, much like saving the difficult bits of a jigsaw puzzle for later. When you have finished the book, quickly review it one more time and then discuss it with friends. This will lodge it permanently in your memory banks.

Super speed reading

1. First read the whole text (whether it's a lengthy book or an exam paper) very quickly, to give your brain an overall idea of what's ahead and get it working. (It's like sending out a scout to look at the territory you have to cover – it's much easier when you know what to expect.) Then read the text again for more detailed information.

2. Have the text a reasonable distance away from your eyes. In this way your eye/brain system will be able to see more at a glance and will naturally begin to read faster.

3. Take in groups of words at a time. Rather than reading 'slowly and carefully', read faster, more enthusiastically. Your comprehension will rocket!

4. Take in phrases rather than single words while you read.

5. Use a guide. Your eyes are designed to follow movement, so a thin pencil underneath the lines you are reading, moved smoothly along, will 'pull' your eyes to faster speeds.

Helpful hints for exam revision

To avoid exam panic, cram at the start of your course, not the end. It takes the same amount of time, so you may as well use it where it is best placed!

Use Mind Maps throughout your course and build a Master Mind Map for each subject – a giant Mind Map that summarises everything you know about the subject.

Use memory techniques, such as mnemonics (verses or systems for remembering things like dates and events or lists).

Get together with one or two friends to revise, compare Mind Maps and discuss topics.

And finally . . .

- *Have fun while you learn* – studies show that those people who enjoy what they are doing understand and remember it more and generally do better.

- *Use your teachers* as resource centres. Ask them for help with specific topics and with more general advice on how you can improve your all-round performance.

- *Personalise your **Study and Revise AS and A2 Level** book* by underlining and highlighting, by adding notes and pictures. Allow your brain to have a conversation with it!

Your amazing brain and its amazing cells

Your brain is like a super computer. The world's best computers have only a few thousand or hundred thousand computer chips. Your brain has 'computer chips' too; they are called brain cells. Unlike the computer, you do not have only a few thousand computer chips – the number of brain cells in your head is a *million million*! This means you are a genius just waiting to discover yourself! All you have to do is learn how to get those brain cells working together, and you'll not only become more smart, you'll have more free time to pursue your other fun activities.

The more you understand your amazing brain, the more it will repay and amaze you!

Objectives and the business environment — SECTION 1

Specification content

Advanced Supplementary (AS)

AQA

Module 3 is *'External Influences and Objectives and Strategy'*. It includes:

- Economic opportunities and constraints
- The market and competition
- Macro economic issues including business cycle; interest rates, exchange rates, inflation and unemployment
- Government opportunities and constraints including an outline of relevant UK and EU legislation
- Social opportunities and constraints including social responsibilities, business ethics, technological change
- Starting a small business
- Legal structures
- Business objectives
- Business strategy – SWOT analysis

OCR

Unit 2871 is *'Business: Objectives and Environment'*. It includes:

- The nature of business
- What businesses do
- What businesses need
- Accountability
- Classification of businesses by economic sector, size, legal structure and ownership
- Business objectives and planning
- Stakeholders
- External influences on business including the market, interest and exchange rates, taxation and the business cycle
- Other influences including technological, social and legal, political, environmental, moral and ethical

Edexcel

Unit 1 is *'Business Structures, Objectives and External Influences'*. It includes:

- Macro variables such as unemployment, inflation and economic growth
- The structure of business
- Business objectives and stakeholders
- Economic influences (including supply and demand)
- Legal, political and social influences
- Internal organisation (see Chapter 18)
- Communication in business (see Chapter 18)
- Motivation in business (see Chapter 19)

Advanced Level (A2)

AQA

Module 6 is *'External Influences and Objectives and Strategy'*. It includes:

- Economic opportunities and constraints
- Implications for business strategy of international competitiveness
- Economic growth
- EU and other emerging markets
- Government opportunities and constraints including policies affecting business
- Social opportunities and constraints including social responsibilities, business ethics, environmental factors
- Business objectives, growth and changes in ownership
- Business strategy and decision making

OCR

Module 2880 is *'Business Strategy'*. It includes:

- Setting corporate objectives
- Tools for corporate planning
- External influences including the market, market failure, economic growth and technological change
- Macro influences including interest and exchange rates, taxation, unemployment and inflation
- Technological change
- Social, legal, environmental, moral and ethical influences
- Devising and reviewing strategies
- Managing strategic change

Edexcel

Unit 6 is *'Corporate strategy'*. It includes:

- Responding to external influences
- Developing a global strategy
- Responding to social responsibilities and ethics
- Business strategy and decision making
- Corporate and organisational culture
- Management of change

Unit 5 is *'Business Planning'*. It includes:

- The planning process
- Business planning
- Human resources, marketing and financial planning

CHAPTER 1 Business strategy and objectives

PREVIEW

- This chapter looks at the way in which businesses decide on aims and objectives, and the strategies they may use to achieve those aims. This section draws on all elements of the specification and on all areas of the subject that you have studied. The skill of synthesis is most likely to be tested here.
- You need to be aware of the ways that businesses set aims and targets and how they plan to reach them.
- You need to recognise that objectives are interrelated and you should be able, from case study material, to devise possible strategies for a business and comment on their effectiveness.
- You need to understand the nature of decision-making in a business.
- You will be expected to know how a business collects, analyses and acts on internal and external information.
- See if you can answer at least four of these five questions before continuing with the rest of the chapter.

Questions

1. What is the difference between a firm's mission, targets and objectives?
2. Can you say what the difference is between satisficing and maximising targets?
3. What is a SMART target?
4. Name four of Drucker's eight possible objectives.
5. What are SWOT, PEST and gap analyses?

Check your answers before continuing with the chapter. Try the questions again once you've finished the chapter.

FACTFILE

- Strategy is defined in terms of war; it is 'the art of a commander-in-chief; the art of projecting and directing the larger military movements and operations of a campaign' (OED).
- Managers can therefore be seen as being like generals, they have targets and use strategies to reach those targets.

Mind Map

Start a Mind Map similar to the one shown here. Put a central image of your own in the middle. This image works for me – it makes me think of targets and attempting to reach them; it reminds me that businesses operate within a framework. You need to draw an image that works for you! The first 'legs' of the Mind Map have been started for you. Add points to your map as you work through the chapter. At the end of the chapter is an example of what a finished Mind Map might look like. Don't forget, you can – and should – use colour!

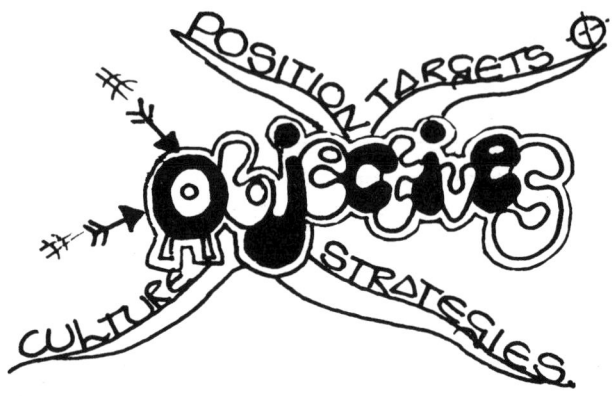

Definition

All business activity takes place within a context. Business objectives are set by management who then use strategies – or plans – to try to achieve these targets.

The context of business

Can you swim? Swim a length of a swimming pool. Now put what you have done in business terms:

Mission

Your 'mission' might have been to keep fit, or to enjoy yourself, or to be faster than anyone else. This could be embodied in your 'mission statement'. For example, First Direct, the telephone banking subsidiary of HSBC has a mission 'to create harmony between the services it provides and the way people live their lives with simple, straightforward products'. Coca-Cola wants to become the 'beverage of choice'. Your mission statement outlines your general aims and gives an idea of the context in which your organisation operates. It provides the framework for your business activities.

Objective

Your 'objective' may have been more precise and probably more short-term – to get to the other end of

Business strategy and objectives

the pool. You may be able to set a target – one that is quantifiable or measurable – taking a particular time to reach the other side; beating a previous time. A business will have certain objectives and shorter term targets that can be measured.

Strategy

Your 'strategy' is the method you have employed to reach your objective. In the case of your swim, it might be training or the development of a skill, or it might be the use of flippers! A business will look at all the possible ways to bring about the desired result.

Your swim could not, however, take place without the assistance of others – the building of the pool, the filtering of the water, the lifeguard – or without certain rules and regulations. This is the 'environment' and the 'constraints' in which your swim took place. Businesses operate in an environment, much of which they have no control over, and are constrained by many factors; these are outlined in Chapters 4 and 5.

Businesses need to be set in a context for you to understand how strategy and objectives work. They operate in an environment which affects them and on which they too can have an effect. The mission statement says 'this is what we do; this is why we are in business'; the objectives are the steps on the way to achieving that target; strategies are the methods used.

Objectives

Business objectives can, broadly speaking, be put into three categories.

- **Satisficing objectives** are those where a business says 'I have done enough; I have reached a particular point; 'I am satisfied'. Satisficing objectives may include:
  - survival
  - breaking even
  - making a certain level of income.
- **Maximising objectives** are those where a business wants to reach the maximum – the most – of something.

Many theorists and commentators have made the assumption that firms are profit maximisers. There are, however, a number of other areas that they might prefer to maximise. Peter Drucker, a management theorist, suggests that there are eight possible areas in which firms may have objectives, including the obvious one of profit maximisation. They are shown in the following table with an idea of what the firm may wish to maximise under each objective.

Objective	Maximisation
Profit	The difference between costs and revenues
Productivity	Efficiency of workers and machines and combinations of them
Innovation	The use of new technology or introduction of new products or ranges
Management	Efficiency, knowledge, training and loyalty of managers
Marketing	Market share, market penetration or market domination
Manpower	Recruitment of the best employees – education, training, experience
Resources	The most reliable sources; the best value for money
Social responsibility	Reputation

- **Minimising objectives** are those where a business wants to make the least, rather than the most, of something. A firm might, for example, want to minimise labour turnover or the damage to its reputation caused by the building of a new plant.

Research activity: What has Peter Drucker's influence been on the theory of management by objectives?

SMART targets

- Objectives should be set so that they are SMART. This stands for:
  SPECIFIC – you should know when an objective has been reached by making it as definite as possible
  MEASURABLE – it should, where possible, be quantifiable
  ATTAINABLE – it should be a target that is possible to achieve
  RELEVANT – it should form a logical part of the business's overall strategy
  TIME-RELATED – a time for the achievement of the target should be set
  NB: You may find other versions of SMART!

- Targets or objectives may be either short-term, or long-term. Short-term targets are often called 'intermediate' targets and are seen as milestones on the way to achieving the long-term target.

- Objectives may conflict with each other.

Study and Revise AS and A2 Level Business Studies

Objectives and the business environment

> **Questions**
> 1. What is a firm's 'mission'?
> 2. What is a firm's 'strategy'?
> 3. What are a firm's 'objectives'?
> 4. What areas might a firm want to maximise?
> 5. What is a SMART target?
>
> Add these points to your Mind Map.

Corporate culture

Organisational or corporate culture means the way in which an organisation works – the commonly held beliefs and accepted patterns of working within an organisation. Some companies will have a culture which is based on the ethos of their owner or founder. Anita Roddick's Body Shop is seen as being caring and environmentally sensitive; Richard Branson's Virgin Group is seen as entrepreneurial and exciting; Rupert Murdoch's News International is seen as acquisitional and competitive. These are examples of a corporate culture that has arisen because of the high profile nature of the owner.

In other organisations, corporate culture may be developed as a team approach (many Japanese companies encourage uniforms and a company song, for example) or as a 'valued person' approach. The corporate culture will determine the way in which the company operates and how it interacts with both its employees and other companies with which it deals.

Types of culture are generally recognised as the following:

- power – typically owner-managers
- role – senior managers with power due to their function
- task – 'finish the job' is the imperative
- person – emphasises the people in the organisation

Strategic planning

This involves a business asking itself a number of key questions:

- Where are we? What is the market position of the business? What are its strengths and weaknesses?
- How did we get here? What paths or routes did we take that have contributed to present successes (or failures)?
- Where are we going? What path are we going to lay out for the future of the business?
- How will we get there? What tactics or methods will take us forward towards our objectives?
- What are our operational considerations? What is it possible for us to do? What planning will be necessary? What amount or calibre of staff do we need? What machinery do we need?

Positional analysis

A business has a number of ways to analyse its position in the market. The main methods used are SWOT, PEST and GAP.

SWOT analysis

SW stands for *internal*

- **S**trengths – this could include items such as the product or product range, or the firm's reputation.
- **W**eaknesses – this could include poor employee relations, high staff turnover, or product problems.

Internal strengths and weaknesses can be found out by a business doing an internal audit (a management consultancy may be used for this). The business will then be able to recognise – and build on – its strengths and remove or minimise its weaknesses. Internal factors are those which the business has control over.

OT stands for *external*

- **O**pportunities – this could include new methods of production or distribution, new materials or methods of communication over which the business has no control.
- **T**hreats – this could include threats from local, national or international governments or bodies. (For example, in the tobacco industry governments have imposed more and more restrictions on tobacco and cigarette advertising, forcing tobacco companies to respond in different ways in order to try and maintain their sales.) Other threats may come from competitor firms, new entrants to the market, new products, or from factors that have affected consumer demand. Recent food scares, for example, have included eggs, beef and genetically modified crops.

A SWOT analysis is usually presented as a diagram:

	Strengths	Weaknesses
INTERNAL		
	Opportunities	Threats
EXTERNAL		

Business strategy and objectives

> **FACTFILE**
>
> In some cases it is up to the business to ensure that an external factor turns into an opportunity rather than a threat. The growth of the Internet, for example, is obviously external – outside the control of individual businesses – but can be turned into an opportunity (the growth and success of Freeserve, the free Internet Service Provider launched by the Dixons group is an example) or seen as a threat – for example, to traditional methods of communication and information gathering.

> **FACTFILE**
>
> Sharing best practice
> 'Best practice' is the optimum way to achieve a particular outcome. This may be in, for example, production or labour relations, distribution, or any area of the firm's activities. Businesses will observe best practice in competitors and adopt it themselves. For example, Japanese methods of labour relations are now in widespread use (see Chapter 22). Firms in some industries, recognising that this is a more efficient approach, actually share best practice with competitors to make the whole industry more efficient (see Chapter 25).

PEST analysis

These are all external factors, i.e. outside the control of the business. PEST stands for:

- **P**olitical factors – local, national or international government factors that affect the firm; legislation, regulations; constraints
- **E**conomic factors – changes in consumer demand; changes in macro-factors such as interest rates and the value of a currency; changes brought about by the economic or business cycle
- **S**ocial factors – changes in consumer demand brought about by changes in attitudes or in society; small changes (e.g. white weddings going out of fashion) will have effects as will large changes (e.g. demographic structure changing to an ageing population)
- **T**echnological factors – changes in technology either in the form of threats or opportunities (see Fact file above)

Later versions of PEST include both legal issues (making SLEPT) or environmental issues (making PEEST).

- **L**egal factors – changes in the law that might affect a firm (usually included in **P** (Political))
- **E**nvironmental factors – green factors are becoming increasingly important to firms; a firm's environmental credentials will be linked to it's reputation and corporate image

Acronyms like PEST and PEEST are not set in stone; often a different commentator will devise a different acronym. You could devise a mnemonic of your own so that you can remember the factors.

Gap analysis

A business can look at where it hoped to be at a particular point in time and at where it actually is and see what the gap between expected and actual outcome is, and what factors could have caused the gap. For example, a firm might have aimed for 10% growth in a particular market and achieved 7%. Managers would seek the reasons for the gap and devise strategies to close the gap. If such strategies could not be devised, the firm might have to revise its objectives.

Making decisions

It is the role of managers within a firm to make decisions. There are three main types of decision:

- **Strategic decisions:** these are taken at the highest level of management and will affect the overall structure or direction of a company. The decision to acquire a competitor is an example of a strategic decision.
- **Tactical decisions:** these are made by senior managers and involve major changes, such as buying new plant or deciding on which products to promote.
- **Operational decisions:** these are made by junior or middle managers and involve the day-to-day running of the firm.

Remember, in a smaller business – a sole trader or partnership, for example – all of these decisions may be taken by the same person. There will still, however, be a distinction between strategic, tactical and operational decisions.

Conflicts between targets need to be resolved by management. It is part of the managerial role to ensure that decisions on objectives do not lead to conflicting targets or, if they inevitably do, to resolve the conflict.

Objectives and the business environment

Financial implications of decisions

These can be estimated by:

- **Investment appraisal:** this uses 'what if?' questions to measure the likely effects of a new investment in terms of
  - quantity: will the investment ever pay for itself (payback)? If so, when?
  - quality: are there non-quantifiable benefits, e.g. to the firm's reputation?
- **Decision trees:** a decision tree puts a monetary value on each possible decision and outcome, using probability percentages to estimate likely costs and benefits. The further away from the 'trunk', the more the branch possibilities become 'guesstimates'.

The planning cycle

Managers

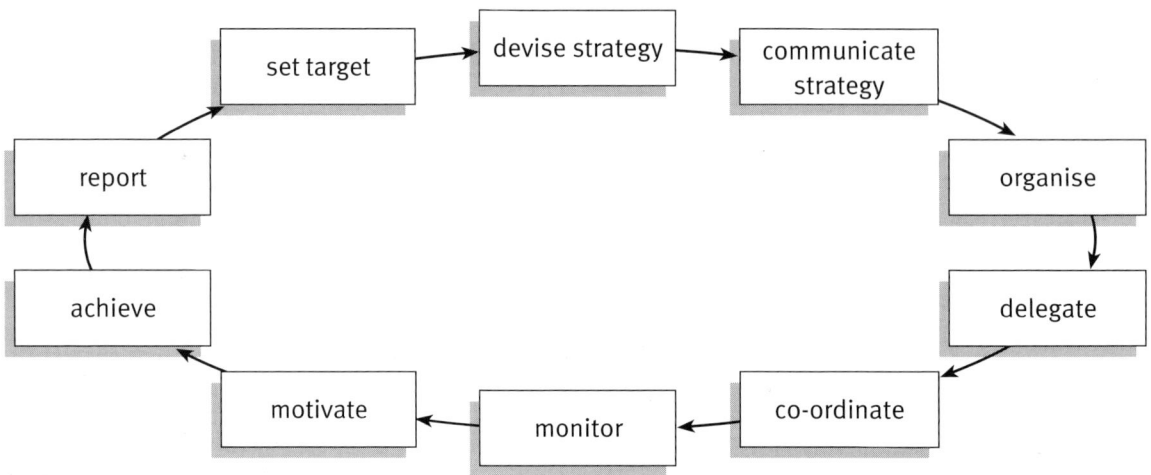

See Chapter 20 on management styles for more detail on decision-making.

Mind Map

Finish off your Mind Map by adding these points. You can return to it later to add any other points that you think are relevant. Don't forget to add some visual reminders of your own, like the wasps round PEST analysis.

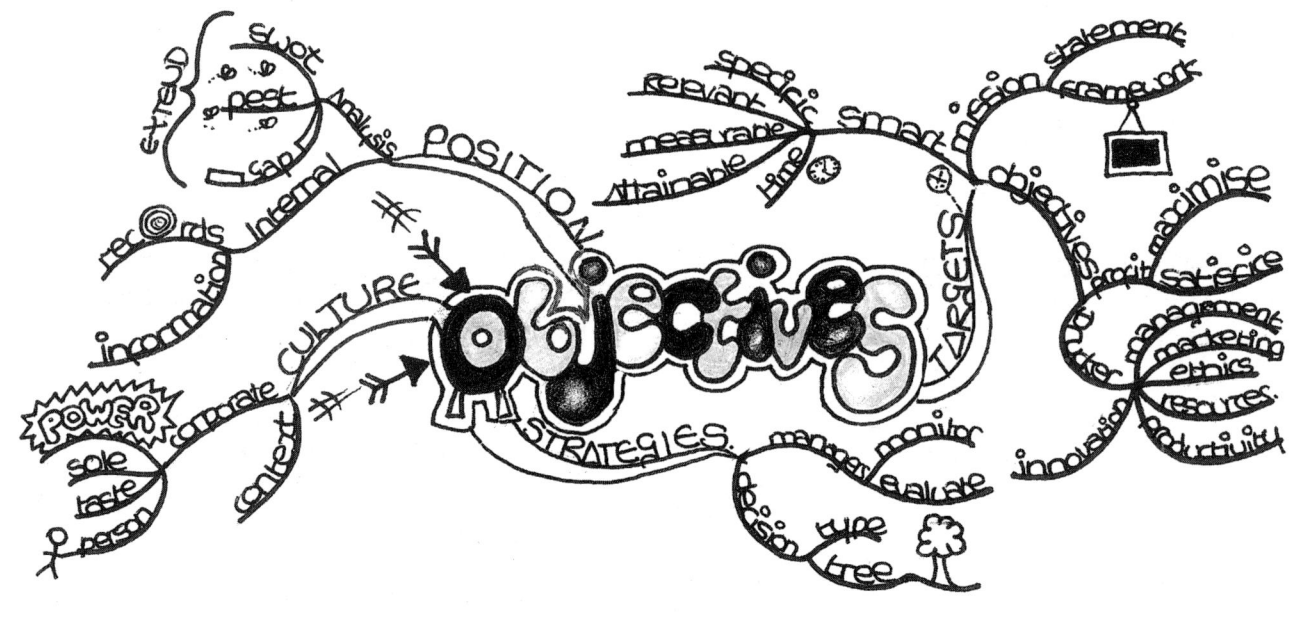

Business strategy and objectives

CHECKLIST

- ✓ All firms operate in a business context and within constraints.
- ✓ A firm plans to reach objectives by having a strategy and targets.
- ✓ Its mission and objectives will be linked to its corporate culture.
- ✓ It establishes 'where it is' through market analysis tools such as
  SWOT analysis
  PEST analysis
  Gap analysis.
- ✓ It establishes 'where it is going' through strategic planning.
- ✓ It sets up a managerial role for decision-making.

TEST YOURSELF

Use your Mind Map to see if you can answer the following questions.

AS
1. What is the purpose of a mission statement?
2. Outline the possible short-term and long-term objectives of a medium-sized frozen food distributor.
3. Suggest strategies to achieve these objectives.

A2
1. In what circumstances might a mission statement be seen as ineffective?
2. How would a corporate culture affect a firm's objectives?
3. What are the main ways in which a firm analyses its current position?

Sample question and answers

Gremlins Ltd have analysed their current position. They expect their turnover next year to be £1m. Profit is forecast to fall, resulting in a loss of £100,000. What actions do you suggest Gremlins management takes?

You could plan your answer using a mini Mind Map.

1. What is the aim/objective of the firm? State what is possible – satisficing, maximising or minimising? All could apply; assume they want to stay in business and maximise profits. For next year they may wish to minimise losses.
2. Managers must find out where the problem lies if they are to find a solution. Possibilities are increasing costs or falling revenues. Investigate what might cause either:
   - **Increasing costs**: internal due to increased fixed costs? Variable costs? External due to market conditions? Suppliers?
   - **Falling revenues**: are sales falling? Has price fallen? Has competition taken market share?
3. Is it short-term or long-term? If short-term, the firm might decide to 'ride' it (if they can afford to). If long-term, measures must be taken to combat problem or change strategic objectives.
4. If internal costs are increasing, cut by rationalisation; increased efficiency; increased productivity . . .
5. Increase revenue by increasing sales, increasing price (this could have the opposite effect)
6. Conclusion
   Conclusions should offer solutions by saying 'If . . ., then . . .'. For example, '**if** the problem is rising costs, **then** the solution could be . . . **if** the problem is long-term, **then** the following is suggested . . .'. Because you don't have the analysis you cannot be more certain than this.

Summary

- Businesses operate within a context which includes constraints and their own corporate culture.
- All businesses will be seeking to achieve certain targets – these could be satisficing, maximising or minimising.
- Strategic planning is used by a firm to establish 'where it is'; 'where it wants to be'; how to get there'.
- Various analytical tools can be used to help the firm answer these three questions.
- The decision-making function within a business is managerial.

Study and Revise AS and A2 Level Business Studies

CHAPTER 2 — Stakeholders and their objectives

PREVIEW

- In this chapter we look at the fairly new concept of stakeholders. Stakeholders are the people who have a stake or interest in the success of a business. They include groups both within the organisation and groups outside it. Within the organisation there are owners, managers and employees. Outside the organisation are suppliers, creditors and, of course, customers.
- Even further removed from the organisation, but still with an interest in its success, are bodies such as the neighbours of the organisation and the government.
- You need to know who the stakeholders in an organisation are likely to be, what their objectives are likely to be, and where those objectives might conflict.
- You need to be able to suggest solutions to possible conflicts within an organisation. You need to be able to put stakeholders' objectives in order of priority.
- See if you can answer at least four of these five questions before continuing with the rest of the chapter.

Questions

1. From a business's point of view, which stakeholders would be most important; which least? Draw up a list of stakeholders putting them in order of priority.
2. Can you put the major objective of each stakeholder next to their name?
3. Look at the objectives that you have listed. Pair them up to show which might conflict with which.
4. What can an organisation do to try to avoid conflicts?
5. What can an organisation do to try to solve conflicts if they arise?

Check your answers before reading the rest of the chapter. Try answering the questions again when you've finished the chapter.

Mind Map

Start a Mind Map similar to the one shown here. Put an image of your own in the middle (the image here reminds me that all stakeholders have a claim in the success of the firm). Remember to use a different colour for each 'leg' of your map.

FACTFILE

H.I. Ansoff, in his book *Corporate Strategy*, (1965) coined the term 'stakeholder'. He said that 'the objectives of top management can and frequently do come in conflict with objectives of other stakeholders in the firm.'

FACTFILE

The Body Shop International plc include a list of its stakeholders in its mission statement. Part of it reads: 'To creatively balance the financial and human needs of our stakeholders – employees, franchisees, customers, suppliers and shareholders.'

Definition

A stakeholder is any individual or group of people that affects or is affected by a business organisation.

Stakeholder groups (inside the organisation)

Stakeholders exist within an organisation; these people are likely to share the common objective of success for the firm. Their interpretation of success may, however, be different from each other.

Owners

In a small business the owners may also be the workers (especially in a sole tradership) and conflicts are unlikely to arise. As soon as there is more than one owner, however, there can be disagreement. For example, a partnership or joint stock company with many owners may have problems with differing objectives.

Stakeholders and their objectives

Sole traders are likely to have satisficing targets – making enough income, survival, a modest profit.

Partnerships may have more ambitious aims but these should be regulated by the Partnership Agreement. However, as any partner can make a decision – without consultation – that is then binding on the other partners, there exists the possibility of real conflict. If one partner has a satisficing aim and another a maximising one, then conflict will occur.

Shareholders in a joint stock company are all likely to want the same thing – success for the company measured in terms of profit. The profit motive is seen as the single most usual reason for people to become shareholders and, while there may be other reasons, it is likely to be paramount. As early as 1936, the economist John Maynard Keynes in his 'General Theory' stated that 'the quantity of aggregate investment is determined by the profit motive alone'.

Profit maximisation, as an aim, may come into conflict with many other aims.

The divorce of ownership from control may mean that the organisation is owned by one group of stakeholders yet controlled by another. In this case, the owners, wanting profit maximisation, may have little regard for the aims and objectives of the managers.

A further aim of owners might be shareholder value. This means trying to maximise the value of shares. An organisation's share price should improve if it is doing well. However, it could be an organisation that is doing badly in a sector that is otherwise doing well, or an organisation whose share values have increased for other reasons – perhaps it is subject to a take-over bid. However, this is still a target sought by shareholders as it maximises the paper value of the company and therefore the paper value of their shareholdings.

Managers

Senior managers in a joint stock company are appointed by the directors; the directors are elected by the shareholders, but does everyone share the same set of aims? Managers' success may not be measured in terms of profit but either in satisficing terms – aiming for a particular status within a company, or in maximising terms that conflict with profit. A plant manager may have the aim for his/her plant to be the most productive within a group, however, this may not accord with maximising profit.

Some companies link management success to profit through profit sharing or incentive schemes. At senior management level, such perks are often viewed with envy by junior managers and employees and may, therefore, be counter-productive. For example, large salaries and other benefits were what gave rise to the phrase 'the unacceptable face of capitalism'.

Junior managers may not be party to such benefits but, again, may seek status or promotion as aims that do not necessarily fit in with the objectives of the company.

Managers may also seek to maximise the power or influence that they have within an organisation. This could be more important than any of the other factors.

Employees

Employees are likely to want a number of things:
- safe and healthy working conditions
- a decent wage or salary
- promotion or advancement prospects
- job satisfaction
- a feeling of being valued and not exploited

At some time or other each of these will take priority over the others. An employer may find that objectives such as these come into conflict with their own desire to maximise profit, or production, or efficiency.

Teamworking

One way of trying to avoid possible conflicts – and employee/employer conflicts can be of the most damaging sort to a business – is to involve the workers in decision-making. Traditional management techniques have involved 'top down' communication, where management set out objectives and tell the workers what to do. New methods of working involve cell or teamworking, where each task or series of tasks requires a team for completion. The team is given the tools to do the job and the power to make decisions and is encouraged to be independent. This is seen as 'workers with power' and is called 'empowerment' (see diagram on following page). Good ideas and new ways of solving problems are said to 'filter' or 'bubble up' through the organisation.

Stakeholder groups (outside the organisation)

Stakeholders also exist outside the organisation. These people are likely to have their own objectives;

> **FACTFILE**
>
> Employees do not always have the interests of their employer at heart. Disgruntled employees have been known to introduce foreign bodies to pre-packed food on a production line or deliberately complete a job poorly, hoping to damage the company's reputation.

Objectives and the business environment

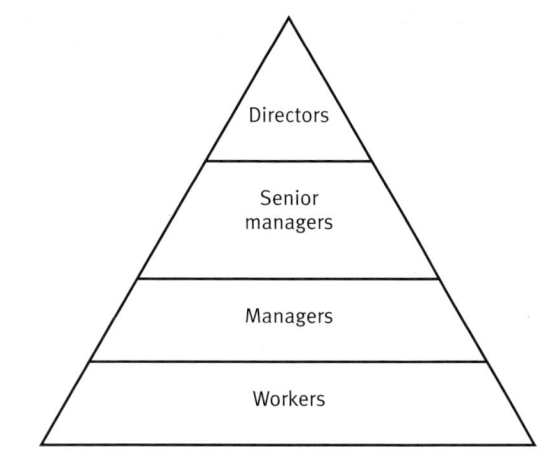

A traditional 'tall' organisation

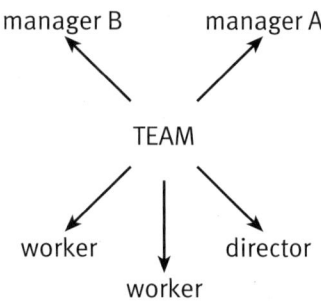

Teamworking

such objectives may well come into conflict with those of the internal stakeholders.

Suppliers

Suppliers will seek a regularity of trade and a reliability of payment. They are also businesses and are therefore likely to share aims such as profit maximisation, meaning that they would like to sell as much of whatever they are supplying at as high a price as possible. Suppliers will be particularly keen to ensure that payments are both reliable and on time. They are especially vulnerable to late payments and will often be the first to suffer if a business is facing a cash flow problem. Often suppliers will have special discounts for early payers and penalties for those who pay late.

Creditors

Any organisation or individual that lends money to a business organisation will, of course, have an interest in the success of that organisation. Creditors will want regular payments and may well have control over the future direction of an organisation if such payments are not forthcoming or look threatened.

Customers

To most firms, customers are probably the most important group of stakeholders. Finding out what customers actually want can be a major part of a businesses function. (For example, Nokia, the global telecommunications company, sets out as one of its core values 'customer satisfaction'. Nokia seeks to identify, anticipate and satisfy customer requirements.) Most customers want reliability, good after-sales service, variety and, above all, value for money. It is this last that business organisations seek to provide.

Social responsibilities

Many organisations now take into account their 'social responsibilities'. These are their obligations towards all the stakeholders in the company. This includes the public at large, the environment and other groups – not just the direct stakeholders in a business. One example of this is that of Lever Brothers and Procter and Gamble, the major manufacturers of soap powders. They have decided on policies to 'green' their products. As one-time targets of environmental groups for their use of packaging and bleaches, they introduced a range of 'eco-friendly' products and cut down on packaging by introducing concentrates, reusable containers and promoting the recycling of all paper and card waste. Taking their social responsibilities into account in this way also made extremely good business sense. Social responsibilities may take into account reputation, all groups of stakeholders and external bodies such as pressure groups and the state.

- **Reputation:** a good reputation can be priceless; a bad one hard to recover from. The Virgin group of companies has maintained its good reputation for most of its products, but this is currently being undermined by the under-performance of Virgin Rail. Companies such as Barclays bank are still struggling to regain their reputation after the long-term damage that their involvement with apartheid in South Africa caused.

- **Stakeholder auditing:** also known as a social audit, this involves questioning a large section of stakeholders to see where a business is doing well for its stakeholders and where it is perceived to be doing badly. Audits should be carried out by external, independent bodies to ensure that they are honest and unbiased, and should include all groups of stakeholders. The Body Shop audits some 5000 people in its social audit, including employees, franchisees, customers, suppliers, Fair Trade partners and shareholders. The reputation and impact of the company in the areas where it trades (including community projects where local Body Shop volunteers are involved) is also audited.

Stakeholders and their objectives

- **External bodies:** these include pressure groups, the most well known being national and international environmental bodies such as Friends of the Earth and Greenpeace. There will also be local pressure groups who, for example, are opposed to a new development.

They also include the state, which has a stake in the success of organisations both in the interests of the good of the economy and in its role as a collector of taxation from income and profits. It also has a 'duty of care' to the population at large to ensure that organisations do not exploit workers or the environment.

Avoiding conflict

Rather than solving the conflicts between the different aims of stakeholders, organisations can try to avoid them through:

- teamworking
- social audits
- inclusion (including local people in business decisions, for example)

It is more efficient to recognise possible conflicts and avoid them than it is to wait for conflicts to arise and then try to solve them.

Solving conflicts

If conflicts do happen the main ways to solve them are through:
- communication
- consultation
- negotiation

Mind Map

Finish off your Mind Map to include all the points that have been mentioned. An example of what it might look like is shown here.

> **CHECKLIST**
>
> Stakeholders are groups of people or individuals with a stake or claim in the success of an organisation from:
>
> ✓ Inside the organisation
> - employees: job security, a decent wage, to be valued
> - managers: status, profit, power
> - owners: satisficing targets, profit maximisation, maximum share value.
>
> ✓ Outside the organisation
> - customers: value for money, reliability, quality
> - suppliers: regular orders, reliable payments
> - creditors: a return on their investment
> - pressure groups: various targets including environmental ones.
> - the state: taxation of income and profits, legal trading practices.

> **TEST YOURSELF**
>
> Choose an organisation with which you are familiar and, using your Mind Map, say:
> 1. Who are the stakeholders in an organisation?
> 2. What are their likely objectives?
> 3. How do they conflict with each other?
> 4. How can conflicts be avoided?
> 5. How can conflicts be solved?

Objectives and the business environment

Summary

- **Stakeholders are any person or group of people who affect or are affected by an organisation.**
- Some groups – employees, owners, managers, franchisees – are within the organisation. Other groups – creditors, suppliers, customers, the state, pressure groups – are outside the organisation.
- Each group will have its own objective or set of objectives.
- These objectives may often conflict with each other.
- It makes good business sense for an organisation to:
  - find out what it is doing well for its stakeholders
  - find out what it is doing badly for its stakeholders
  - try to build on the former and reduce the latter

  This is called a social audit and is a way of avoiding conflict.
- In order to avoid or reduce conflict, organisations may also try to involve stakeholders in decision-making through:
  - consultation
  - teamworking
  - focus groups.
- If conflicts do arise, then they need to be solved by negotiation before they become too damaging.

Sample questions and answers

The move of the Royal Armouries – which houses the national collection of arms, armament, weapons and armour – to a specially designed site in Leeds from the Tower of London, under a private finance initiative, has been full of problems. The museum was opened by the Queen in 1996 and projections were that it would attract 750,000 visitors a year. There has not been the projected number of visitors to the complex, about 400,000 in any one year, and admission charges are seen as being too high with tickets at £7.95 plus a minimum of £2 for parking. A family ticket costs just under £25.

With debts of over £20 million in August 1999, it was the museum's main creditor, the Bank of Scotland, that put pressure on the Armouries to come up with a successful strategy to reduce the debt or to close, thus 'cutting their losses'. The Bank of Scotland put up much of the original investment for the museum and expects to get their returns over a number of years from a proportion of the fees which people pay to enter.

Royal Armouries is run by a set of trustees, appointed by the government, who have to make the decision in the best interests of the national collection. The manager of a local attraction was quoted as saying: 'If the Armouries close, it will be a disaster. We will be back to square one.' Royal Armouries was the lead building in a series of developments which have provided jobs and boosted tourism in the region.

AS level questions

1 Identify the stakeholders who may be affected by any decisions made regarding Royal Armouries.
2 What is meant by 'social responsibilities'?
3 Write a report recommending the actions that the Bank of Scotland should take if its aim is to meet its social responsibilities.

A2 level questions

1 How could the Royal Armouries use its social responsibilities to increase the number of visitors?
2 Imagine the Bank of Scotland believed that its duty was purely to its shareholders, rather than any other stakeholders. Outline what you think its decision in this case would be and how it would affect the other stakeholders.
3 Write a report to advise the Bank of Scotland as to whether this would be a good business decision in the short-term; in the long-term.

AS

1 Businesses in Leeds; Bank of Scotland; trustees; government; visitors.
2 The obligations towards all the stakeholders in an organisation. In this case, obligations to create jobs in Leeds as well as obligations to people who wish to view the collection.
3 To meet its social responsibilities you would probably recommend that prices were lowered to make the attraction more accessible; publicity was increased and better. The government could be encouraged to take on the debt as it, too, has social responsibilities.

A2

1 The Royal Armouries could decide that its function was not to make a profit, but to provide a service. In this case, it could lower prices to attract more visitors. Alternatively, the Trustees might decide that their obligation to the collection would be better served by moving it back to the Tower of London.
2 If the bank believed that its duty was solely to shareholders, then its intention would be to maximise profits. Either the Armouries would have to devise a strategy to move from loss into profit, or the bank would, in the best interests of its shareholders, pull out of the project. Other stakeholders would not benefit – in particular the businesses in Leeds and the Trustees.
3 Your answer should pivot on whether you think the short-term-gains made by removing pressure on the bank's profits could/would be outweighed by harm to their reputation in the long-term. It is unlikely that they would suffer any loss of reputation or business.

The beginnings and growth of a business — Chapter 3

PREVIEW

- In this chapter we look at how a business might be established and what the aims of its owners are likely to be. Why should the business grow and, if it does decide to grow, what sort of direction might it take. You need to be able to evaluate different types of business organisation and be able to suggest what sort of growth might be the most suitable for a particular organisation.

- You will need to know how a business can be started, where its finance can be raised from, and what factors are likely to mean that an entrepreneur is successful. You will need to be able to analyse the factors that lead to the success or failure of a new business venture including possible sources of borrowed funds. You will need to know the different ways that businesses can be classified and the different types of legal structure that a business can have. You will need to understand that the organisational structure of a firm will have an effect on the targets and aspirations of its owners and stakeholders.

- You will need to know why a firm might decide to grow and what reasons there may be for its staying small. You should be able to analyse the possible growth or other changes within an organisation and recommend paths for an organisation to take.

- See if you can answer at least four of these five questions before continuing with the rest of the chapter.

Questions

1. Some new businesses are successful. List the factors that are likely to have contributed to that success.
2. Explain the difference between limited and unlimited liability.
3. What is meant by a business having continuity?
4. What is an economy of scale? Suggest four possible economies.
5. Label the diagram below with the correct types of integration.

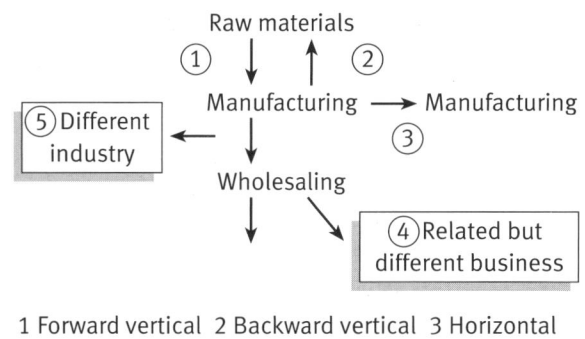

1 Forward vertical 2 Backward vertical 3 Horizontal
4 Lateral 5 Conglomerate

Check your answers before reading the rest of the chapter. Try answering the questions again when you've finished the chapter.

Mind Map

Start a Mind Map like the one shown here. Choose a graphic of your own for the middle – mine reminds me that we are talking about beginnings and growth. Don't forget to use a different colour for each branch.

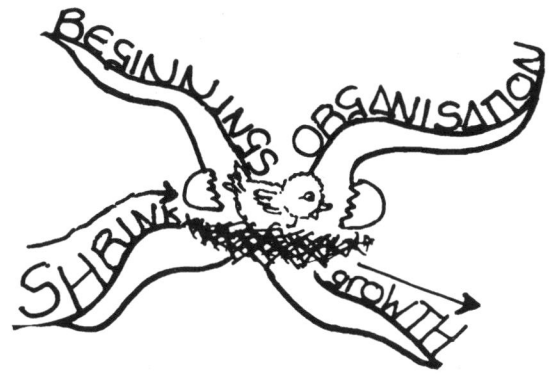

Definition

In economic terms, to produce any good or service requires four factors: land, labour, capital and enterprise. In business terms the most important of these is enterprise.

Starting up

The person who provides the enterprise is called the entrepreneur. An entrepreneur is basically a risk-taker and any profit that they make is their reward for taking the risk.

New businesses may have their own personal sources of start-up capital – savings, family, friends – but most will usually need some help in sharing the risk and will turn to lending institutions for finance. Lenders have their depositors' interests to consider and will be keen to protect any investment. Thus,

Objectives and the business environment

getting finance for what lenders see as a high-risk operation may be difficult and lenders will probably require some sort of security e.g. a charge on the assets of the business or the entrepreneur. Lending from banks and financial institutions could be in the form of:

- **loans**: a fixed amount of money lent and repayable in regular instalments over a pre-set term
- **overdraft**: permission to take more out of a current account than you currently have in it, a much more flexible arrangement where interest is only paid on what is borrowed for as long as it is owed.

The government have established a number of bodies to help small businesses, in particular providing security through the Loan Guarantee Scheme which ensures that if businesses do fail, banks are guaranteed to receive 80% of their money back.

Other schemes include the:

- **Enterprise Investment Scheme:** provides income tax relief for investors in smaller companies
- **Business Start-Up Scheme:** gives some financial help to long-term unemployed who are trying to get back into work by setting up in business.
- **SMART** (Small Firms Merit award for Research and Technology): gives financial help to small firms developing new technology.

Other help includes bodies such as The Princes Trust, which helps young people under 30 to set up in business, and local chambers of commerce.

Will it survive?

Over half of small businesses fail within the first two years of their operation, many do not even survive their first six months. There are a number of factors that are likely to lead to a business enterprise being successful:

- Identifying a gap in the market. Careful market research should be undertaken to ensure that there really is a gap in the market for the product or service which the business intends to supply.
- Creative thinking. 'Would people like to be able to listen to music whilst they travel about?' is a classic example of a creative thought that led to a mass market in a new concept, branded by Sony as the 'Walkman'. Good or innovative ideas are not always successful, however. 'Would people like a cheap and reliable electrical car for town visits?' sounds like an equally good idea but development work has yet to convince people to leave petrol motors behind.
- Financial planning. Many firms fail because they do not make an accurate assessment of the finance that they will need in the early months of their operation.
- Protecting your invention. The Patent Office can be used to protect a new product for a period of 20 years. However, protecting a patent which a small firm thinks has been breached can be a long and costly legal process. The idea for the 'walkman' was actually patented long before Sony developed the concept. They, however, declared that they had come to the same conclusions through independent research. The idea itself caught on to the extent that many companies produce versions of the design. All that is really protected is the trade name 'Walkman'.

FACTFILE

Some of the most famous success stories come from business start-ups that grew into large and successful businesses:

- Michael Marks and Tom Spencer became partners in 1894; Marks and Spencer plc now has almost 300 stores both in the UK and Europe.
- Forrest Mars (who died in 1999) founded the Mars (chocolate) Company, one of the largest privately owned businesses in the world.
- In 1950, Bernard Matthews set up in business with 20 turkey eggs and an incubator, costing £2 10s 0d (£2.50).

Types of business organisation

Businesses fall into two categories: those that are established in the private sector and those in the public sector. Public sector businesses are those owned or controlled by government, national or local, on behalf of the public. Private sector businesses are those owned by private individuals or bodies.

Public sector businesses

These include bodies established by government such as The Post Office, government departments such as The Stationery Office (the government's publishers) and the CSO (Central Statistical Office) and nationalised industries (industries that were once privately owned but were then taken into government ownership). Almost all of these have now been returned to private ownership through privatisation.

The beginnings and growth of a business

Government has also established partnerships with private industry such as the PFI (Private Finance Initiative) where private capital is used for a government sponsored scheme with the capital providers then getting a return through returns on the project (e.g. tolls on roads or bridges, museum charges).

Private sector businesses

These have liability that is either unlimited or limited.

- **Unlimited liability** means that the responsibility of the owner/s for debt is limited only by the extent of their personal wealth. Almost everything that they own can be taken and sold to pay the debts of their business.
- **Limited liability** means that the responsibility for the debts of the business is limited to the amount of money which the owners have invested.

Definition

Liability is a debt that has not been paid. In business terms it means the responsibility of the owners for the debt.

The legal structures which businesses can take are outlined in the table below. This also includes the major features and problems of the organisation and the likely objectives of stakeholders.

Franchises

It is worth treating franchises separately so that you remember that they are not a form of business ownership. Buying a franchise is a way of buying into an established firm's name, brand and success. The franchisee may be organised as a sole trader, partnership, co-operative or limited liability company. Franchisees:

- pay a fee for the franchise
- pay royalties to the franchiser
- benefit from the franchisers market position and advertising
- may get help, advice and training from the franchiser

Organisation	Main features	Main problems	Stakeholder objectives
Sole trader	Easy to set up Single owner Takes all decisions Takes all profit	Stands all losses Takes all risk Unlimited liability Lack of capital Lack of continuity	Self-employment Satisficing
Partnership	Easy to set up Two to twenty owners* Shared decisions Shared risk	Disagreements Unlimited liability Shared profit Lack of continuity	Self-employment Satisficing
Co-operative	Joint ownership by producers consumers or workers	Lack of agreement Lack of capital Lack of management expertise	Providing employment Providing income Social targets
Private limited company	Shares not on sale to public Limited liability Separate legal identity Legal formalities of establishment Continuity	Owners could lose control Accounts must be produced and made public	Maximising targets (usually profit)
Public limited company	Shares on sale to public Limited liability Separate legal identity Legal formalities of establishment Continuity	Divorce of ownership from control Accounts must be produced and made public Complex management structure may be needed	Maximising targets (usually profit)

*except in specific circumstances such as banking and the stock exchange

Objectives and the business environment

Questions

1. What do you understand by the terms:
   - Entrepreneur?
   - Start-up capital?
2. What government schemes are in place to help entrepreneurs?
3. Why do you think so many new firms fail?
4. What elements help new firms to succeed?
5. What is the difference between private and public sector firms?
6. What do you understand by 'limited liability'?

Add these points to your Mind Map.

Growth of organisations

In terms of size, the smallest business units are sole traders; the largest are public limited companies. Only 3% of businesses in the UK have a turnover of above £1m. Less than three quarters have a turnover of above £100,000. Other measures of size include the number of employees and the share the business has of a market.

Businesses often want to grow because they can gain certain advantages from being larger. Some of these advantages may come from:

- buying competitors
- buying into closed markets (buying a UK firm, for example, gives entrance to the EU market)
- buying suppliers
- buying distributors
- buying technology

Economies of scale

In particular, firms will look to gain economies of scale. An economy of scale is a benefit gained through increased size. Economies of scale may be:

- **financial:** it is easier for a large company to borrow money and they are likely to get better rates
- **technical:** companies can afford mass production techniques and large or expensive machinery
- **strategic:** some businesses have to be big. For example, the amount of investment needed for a railway, airport, or underground transport system is so large than no one company could manage it
- **risk bearing:** companies can take risks on new projects while other parts of the organisation support initial growth
- **managerial:** bigger companies can afford the best managers and will often 'head hunt' them

FACTFILE

Sky TV was launched in February 1989. It reached operational break-even in March 1992, 17 months after its merger with British Satellite Broadcasting (BSB). In the previous year it made a loss of £47 million. However, profits from other divisions of News International, the parent company, meant that the venture could be supported until it went into profit. A smaller company could not have achieved this.

Why are there so many small businesses?

- They may be just starting
- They may be serving small (niche) markets
- They may be providing a personal service (hairdressers, taxis)
- They may have no desire to expand

There may, also, be diseconomies of scale:

- Organisational diseconomies can arise if the business organisation grows to be too complex and if it is not clear where decision-making and responsibility should lie.
- Geographical diseconomies are linked to organisational ones in that different offices in, for example, different countries, may be operating to different agendas.
- Communications diseconomies can occur in any large organisation.
- Diseconomies of diversification. Sometimes, if a firm is trying to grow in too many directions at once, it becomes weakened on all fronts.

Acquisition and integration

Businesses that wish to expand will do it through:

- **Organic growth**, where a business grows from within by ploughing back its own profits into growth. They may use funds to take on more employees, open new outlets, open new plants etc. This type of growth tends to be slow but does not carry a lot of risk.

The beginnings and growth of a business

> **FACTFILE**
>
> 'Sticking to the knitting'. Business writer Tom Peters uses this phrase to describe a company that decides to expand by concentrating on its lead products – those where it has its strengths – and off-loading its less successful lines. This is the opposite approach to that of diversification and can be seen in many growing companies. The Finnish telecommunications company Nokia is one such example. In 1986 17% of the business was telecommunications based. Ten years later this figure had risen to over 90%.

- **Acquisition or integration:** this is joining together with or taking over another company.
- **Mergers**, where the two companies are equal partners and agree to join together.
- **Take-overs**, where one company buys out another. This may be an agreed bid or it may be a hostile take-over, involving the company buying shares in its target acquisition. The buying company must make a bid for its target once it has 30% of the shares. Shareholders can accept or reject the bid. Often the price of shares will rise on the expectation of a bid and the buying company will have to increase its offer several times before being successful. Fighting off a hostile bid can often weaken a company and leave it vulnerable to other bids.
- **Integration** can take place in several directions, depending on which way along the chain of distribution the coalition takes place.

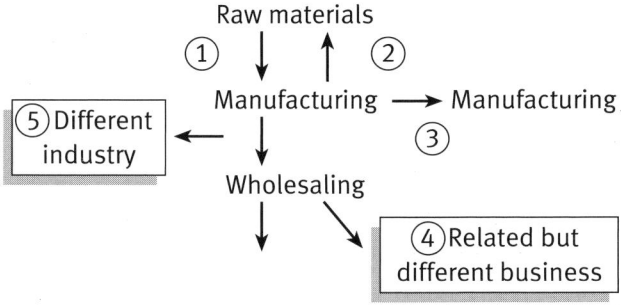

1 Forward vertical 2 Backward vertical 3 Horizontal
4 Lateral 5 Conglomerate

Types of integration

Downsizing

When one company mergers with another this often means a duplication of staff at many levels. One of the advantages that the company can gain is by reducing this duplication. Staff may be made redundant as a company restructures its organisation. This is often called 'downsizing',

Synergy

Remember what Tony Buzan says about synergy in the introduction? That the two halves of the brain, working together, are more efficient. In other words that 1 plus 1 is greater than 2. The same is often applied to companies whose operations seem to fit particularly well together. For example a bank joining with an insurance society or pension fund where each can benefit from the other's markets and particular expertise and acumen.

MBOs and MBIs

The ownership of a business can change if the management decide to buy the company. An MBO (Management Buy-Out) occurs when managers buy the company that they are working for. These are often successful as managers are the ones who know the strengths and weaknesses of the company in the most detail. Denby pottery, initially bought by wallpaper manufacturers Coloroll, was one of Coloroll's assets for sale when that company failed. It was bought by its management team for £5.3 million. MBIs (Management Buy-Ins) are where the management of a company decides to buy into the ownership of another company.

Getting smaller

Some firms might seek to concentrate on their core business by off-loading peripheral businesses or, where two or more distinct areas of operation have developed, by demerging, as ICI did with Zeneca in 1992.

Management of change

Organisations go through periods of evolution (slow growth and consolidation) followed by short periods of revolution (when rapid changes may take place).

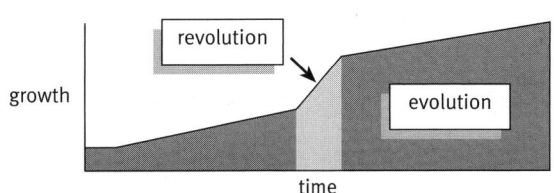

Graph to show growth of a company

Objectives and the business environment

The process of strategic management means setting a target or objective and then putting into place the policies that will achieve that objective, in other words, deciding how change is to take place and then managing the process of that change. This is done by a process which involves asking three questions:

- Where are we now?
- Where do we want to be?
- How will we get there?

The process involved is:

- recognising that change is needed, agreeing on its direction
- auditing the organisation – what is it good at, what could be improved?
- analysing possible routes (SWOT analysis may be used, see Chapter 1)
- agreeing on key personnel
- agreeing on which are the most important obstacles
- setting intermediate targets for when these obstacles are overcome
- setting measures for success
- analysing and evaluating the completed process

The Sigmoid curve

Charles Handy suggests that firms need to recognise their position on what he calls the 'Sigmoid curve' (see below). This is in the shape of a Greek sigma or 'S' on its side. Organisations that appear to be successful are currently on the upward sloping part of the curve but need to realise that they are near their peak. (Remember, the organisation can only predict past 'now', not actually see it.) Intelligent organisations need to recognise this point on the curve and develop strategies to ensure that they don't fall victim to the downturn.

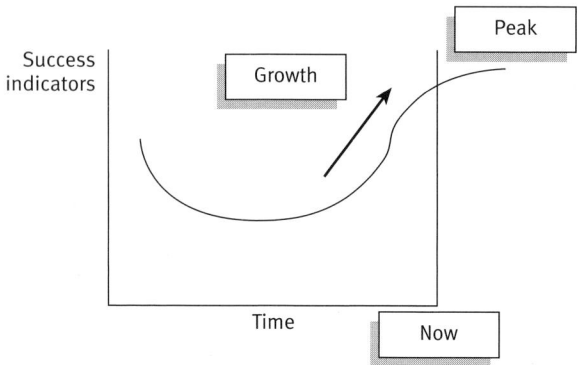

The Sigmoid curve

> **FACTFILE**
>
> **Globalisation**
> This is the process by which a company decides to focus on global markets rather than on domestic ones. Coca-Cola, for example, has expanded into Eastern Bloc countries and Russia, seeing itself as a global concern. It seeks to have a majority share of the global market and competes on a global basis, not just in its home territory.
>
> Many companies that operate on a global basis are multinationals or trans-national companies, with plant and operations in many countries. This allows them to move investments to keep both costs and taxation low and often puts them outside national laws.

CC

The Competition Commission (CC) is a government-backed body that looks into intended mergers to decide whether or not they will be in the public interest. Sometimes permission for mergers is refused if the CC thinks that the new company would be in a position to exploit consumers or employees because of its monopoly power.

The shrinking world

The vast improvements that have taken place in Information and Communications Technology – the advent of the PC, mobile telephones, the move from analogue to digital signals – mean that many companies can now operate in a global environment. New technology has, as a result of the instant formation of a mass market (which continues to grow) also fallen in price in real terms. (The cost of a transatlantic telephone call, for example, is less than one per cent of what it was 50 years ago, and the cost of travelling to America, about ten per cent in real terms; the cost of a PC continues to fall while specifications rise.) A business can set up on the Internet for a very low outlay and is immediately trading in world markets. Certainly any business that calls itself an e-commerce or e-business (in other words, one which trades from and through the Internet) is by definition a global concern. Air travel has become global and, having conquered international markets, is now beginning to home in on local markets (check with your local airport: you may be surprised to find that it is often cheaper to fly than

The beginnings and growth of a business

to take an alternative form of transport, even over fairly short distances).

Global concerns, such as e-commerce companies, may access world markets via global sales. True transnationals will have production or distribution in many countries worldwide. Global distribution is usually achieved by promoting a global brand. This means ensuring that the same product, service etc. is available in the same format across the globe. Sometimes this may mean a name change – as in the case of the 'Marathon' bar, which became 'Snickers' – but more often than not global brands are linked to particular images or life styles – Hugo Boss or Levi, for example. In other cases, the brand may provide an 'umbrella', for a variety of different products – Sony, for example. Transnationals that produce globally may have different reasons for doing so. It may be to take advantage of lower labour costs, less organised labour or lower taxation. Global concerns can sometimes decide where to pay their taxes to take advantage of different rates. Sometimes such production is so that producers can access markets that would otherwise be protected from them – this has brought several firms to within the EU.

CHECKLIST

✓ **Organisations grow to: consolidate market share; acquire new market share; acquire suppliers or customers; gain economies of scale.**

✓ **Organisations grow by: acquisition; integration; organic growth.**

✓ **Some businesses – just starting, satisfying, niche markets – don't want to expand.**

Mind Map

Finish off your Mind Map with all the points shown. Use word pictures where these will help. 'Growth' of firms is one example on the example Mind Map shown.

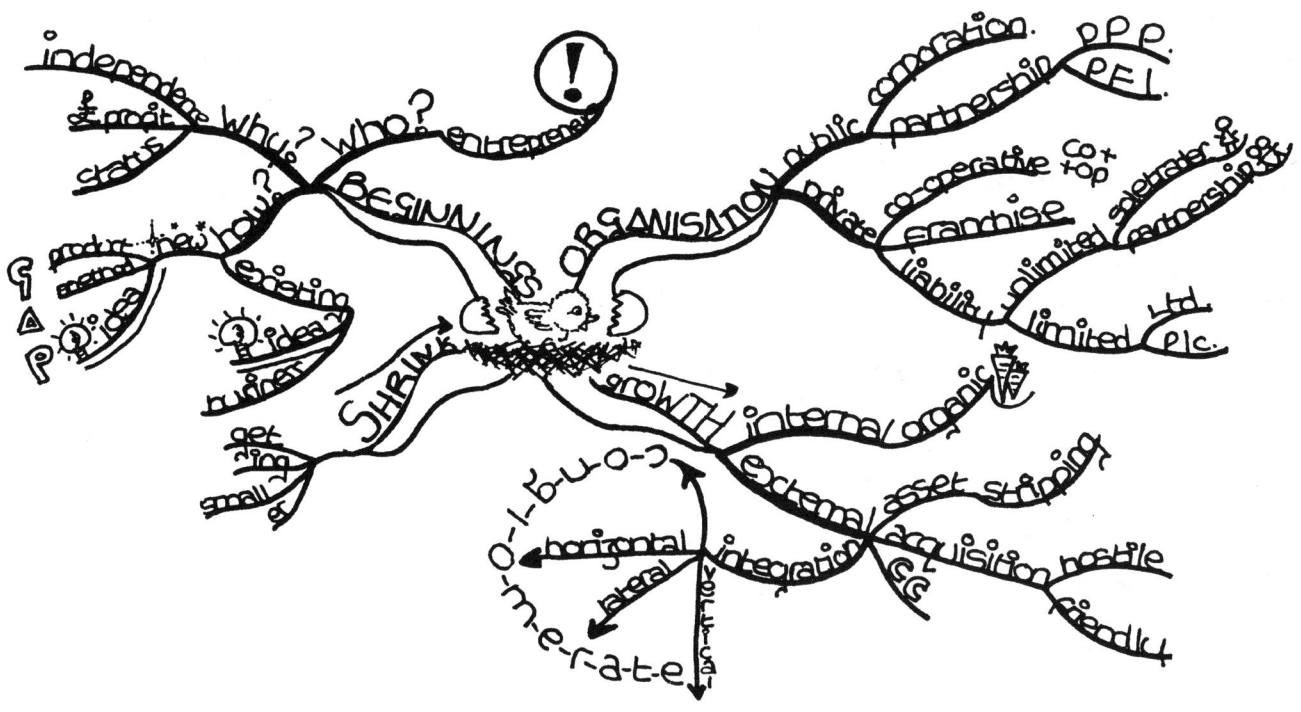

Objectives and the business environment

Sample question and answer

Global-link plc, a large communications company, has bid to take over Tiny TVs Ltd, a small communications company. Discuss the advantages and disadvantages of this move for:
a   Global-link
b   Tiny TVs

Make sure you balance possible advantages against possible disadvantages. You could plan your answer as a seven paragraph essay as follows. The mini Mind Map will give you guidance on how to plan this.

1   Global-link: advantages
2   Global-link: disadvantages
3   On balance . . .
4   Tiny TVs: advantages
5   Tiny TVs: disadvantages
6   On balance . . .
7   Conclusion

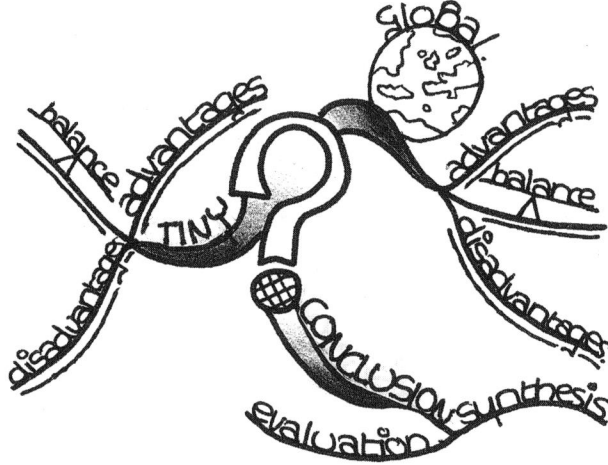

1   Global-link: horizontal take-over therefore should gain economies of scale as operating in the same market; can therefore share marketing costs; buys market share therefore removing competition; increased monopoly power.
2   Cost of take-over could outweigh benefits, especially if there are rival bidders; could suffer diseconomies of scale, especially if management is duplicated; could damage reputation if it looks like 'corporate bullying', especially if management or employees of small company are rationalised
3   Balance the likelihood of benefits against problems.
4   Future of company secure; opportunities for advancement for managers and workers; possible cash incentives to agree to take-over
5   Small company loses identity; could be asset stripped and closed down; could be rationalisation of workforce and management.
6   Balance the likelihood of benefits against problems.
7   Conclusion. Again, it depends. As long as it is well argued, there is no right or wrong answer.

TEST YOURSELF

Test yourself with the questions from the beginning of the chapter again. Can you complete them all correctly? Use your Mind Map to see if you can answer the questions below.

AS
1   What is meant by unlimited liability?
2   List the main forms of finance for a new business.
3   What is the difference between the public sector and the private sector?

A2
1   Explain why, in spite of its disadvantages, many businesses still have unlimited liability.
2   What government help is available to new businesses?
3   How do organisations grow in size? Why do they grow?

Summary

- Starting up in business requires land, labour, capital and enterprise. The most important of these is enterprise.
- The entrepreneur will need to borrow money to acquire the other factors.
- Many businesses fail due to lack of market research and lack of financial planning.
- There are different types of legal organisation for private sector business ranging from sole trader to public limited company.
- Liability is the owner's responsibility for the debts of the firm. It can be limited.
- Organisations may have reasons to stay small.
- Organisations may have reasons to grow.
- Growth can be internal (ploughing back profits) or external (acquisition).
- Types of integration categorise the direction of growth.
- Growth and change should be carefully planned and managed.

External influences (1) micro-factors — CHAPTER 4

PREVIEW

- This chapter looks at the way in which the various external influences on business affect it. Important factors are the influences of market forces and how firms both try to affect these forces and react to changes in them. You will need to have an awareness of how the external influences on a business provide opportunities and impose constraints on the actions of a business.

- Other major external factors which influence business include the state of the economy, the environment. ethics, the law, social and technological factors. These are 'macro' factors and are separated from 'micro' factors by being factors which occur at a national level rather than at the level of an individual consumer or a firm in the market.

- You will need to understand the nature of markets, and what makes a market. You will need to understand clearly how the forces of supply and demand interact to produce a price equilibrium, how the mechanism can fail, and what governments may attempt to do if it does fail.

- Above all, you need to understand that business does not operate in a vacuum, but in an ever changing scenario that means decisions are taken on the basis of many different factors.

- While there may be a specific section in your specification for external factors, you should realise that these are factors which affect all parts of business decision-making and cannot, therefore, be kept in isolation.

- See if you can answer at least four of these five questions correctly before reading the rest of the chapter.

Questions

1. What is the difference between a 'micro' and a 'macro' factor?
2. Define what is meant by the *ceteris paribus* assumption.
3. Write out the demand function. Briefly describe what each part means.
4. Label the diagram below to show where equilibrium lies.

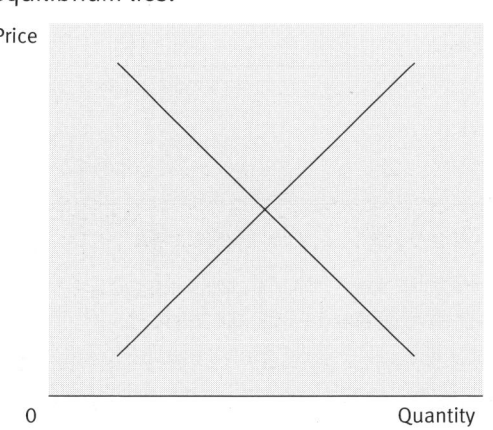

5. What is meant by elasticity of demand?

Check your answers before reading the rest of the chapter. Try answering the questions again when you've finished the chapter.

Mind Map

Start a Mind Map similar to the one shown. Don't forget to use colour on the separate 'legs' and to start with an image of your own in the centre of the page. The image I have chosen reminds me that there are a large number of external influences that businesses must take into account.

Micro-factors

These are those factors which happen at the 'micro' or individual person or firm level. While they may be very influential, they do not involve national or 'macro' factors. The biggest single micro factor is opportunity

Objectives and the business environment

cost. When a consumer or an organisation makes a decision to do something – chooses to do something – then they have chosen, at the same time, not to do all the other alternative things that they could have done. Opportunity cost is the cost of the next best of those alternatives. For example, you have decided to study Business Studies. To do so, you have decided not to study something else, e.g. watch television. As you can see, *any* decision you make involves an opportunity cost and the way in which you decide has an enormous effect on business.

> **FACTFILE**
>
> As demand in a market changes, a firm will have to 'reposition' or 're-launch' products to maintain their market share. As demand moved away from Boots No. 7 cosmetics in the 1990s, Boots responded by altering the image of the range so that it would appeal to a wider market sector. The successful re-launch in 1995 lifted sales by over 40% and, in particular, gained a foothold in the 20–30 age group, where 27% of women bought the brand in 1995/6.

The market: market forces of demand and supply

Businesses **supply** goods and services to meet the **demands** of consumers. These two words have a special meaning in the economics of business. Between them they determine what price levels are and therefore help to determine whether a business can stay in business or not!

Demand

If you can remember what economists call the 'demand function', you will be able to remember the main forces acting to change demand. You should also remember that the rule of *ceteris paribus* applies: to be able to study a change in demand, we have to assume that there is only one factor – the one we wish to study – changing at any one time. *Ceteris paribus* is the Latin term used to mean 'other things equal'.

Demand is a function of (P, P1−n, Y, t)

- P = price. As price falls, so demand for a good will rise and vice versa.
- P1−n = the price of other goods and services. These fall into the main categories of:
  - **a** complements – goods or services bought with something else, e.g. fish and chips
  - **b** substitutes – goods or services bought instead of something else, e.g. cod or haddock
- Y = income. As incomes rise, so will demand, but the pattern of demand will also alter, e.g. higher levels of income mean greater demand for luxury goods.
- t = taste or fashion. As tastes change, so will the pattern of demand. This could be as a result of a change in fashion, for example, or of a more permanent change, such as in the structure or size of population (an ageing population means greater demand for nursing homes and hospital care; a young population means greater demand for music and entertainment).

Supply

Supply is the willingness and ability of producers to supply goods or services at a particular price. In general, the higher the price, the higher the amount of product the supplier will be willing to supply.

Drawing graphs

Both demand and supply measure the amount or quantity that will be demanded or supplied at a particular price. They can therefore be plotted on a graph.

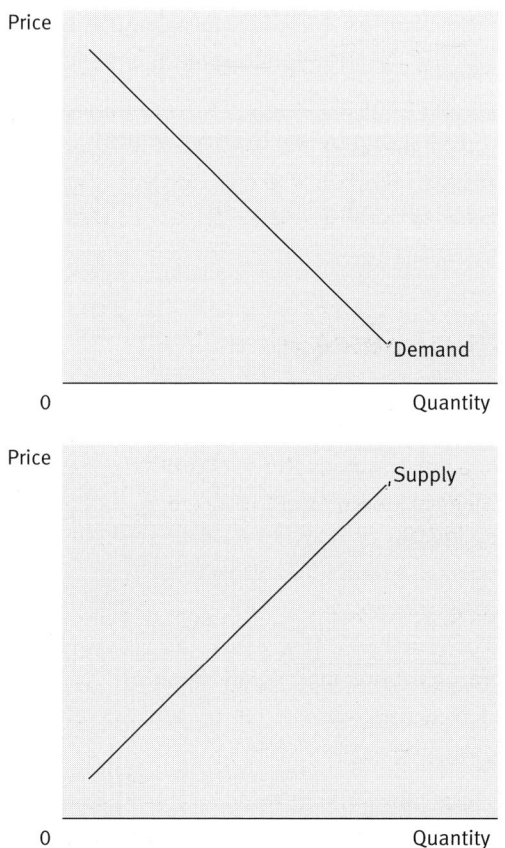

External influences (1) micro-factors

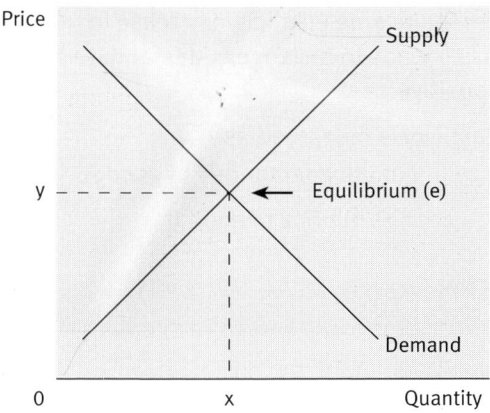

'e' shows the equilibrium position. This is the point where there is no pressure on price to move in either direction. Suppliers are willing to supply x amount at y price, consumers willing to buy x amount at y price.

Market adjustments

If the market is not in equilibrium it should adjust by always moving towards equilibrium. If there is excess demand, then consumers are demanding more than the market can currently supply. The market will therefore increase price to cut off the excess demand, or suppliers will move to increase the amount supplied.

If there is excess supply, then producers are producing more than consumers are willing to buy. The result should be that price will fall to remove the excess, or producers will produce less. See if you can work out the movements of the demand and supply curves the case of both excess supply and excess demand.

Elasticity of demand

Sometimes there is a big movement in demand if there is a change in price, or income; sometimes there is only a small move. The extent of the change – the responsiveness of demand to a change in another factor – is called elasticity. There are three main types:

- **Price elasticity of demand:** if a large change in demand is caused by a proportionately small change in price then the product is said to be price elastic. This will be the case if the product is not a necessity or has many and close substitutes.
- **Income elasticity of demand:** if a large change in demand is caused by a proportionately small change in income then the product is said to be income elastic.
- **Cross elasticity of demand:** if goods are complements or substitutes then a change in the demand of one will affect the demand for the other. The closer the relationship, the higher the cross elasticity. Two different brands of petrol, for example, will have extremely high cross elasticity as consumers can switch from one brand to another easily.

Measuring elasticity

- Price elasticity is measured as:

$$\frac{\% \text{ change in quantity demanded}}{\% \text{ change in price}}$$

Because a positive change in quantity means a fall in price, the two signs (+ and −) mean that the answer will always be negative. Elasticity ranges from (−) infinity to 0.

(−) infinity is perfectly elastic.

› (−)1 means demand is elastic

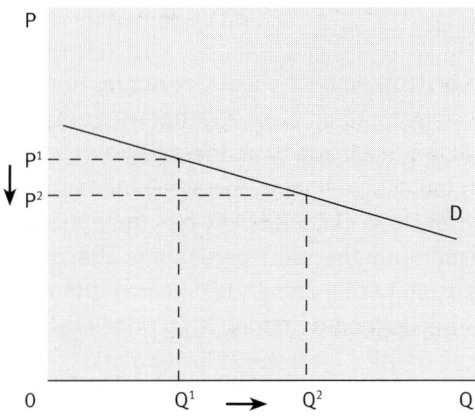

(−) means unit elasticity – exactly the same percentage change

Study and Revise AS and A2 Level Business Studies

Objectives and the business environment

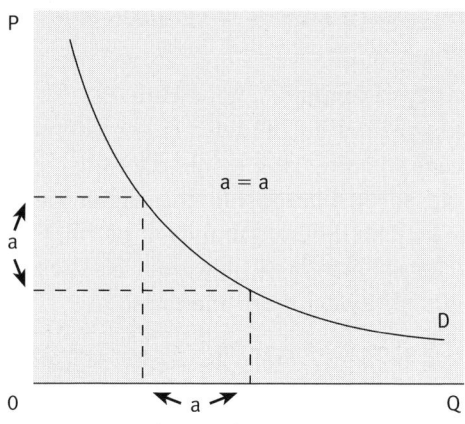

< (−)1 means demand is inelastic

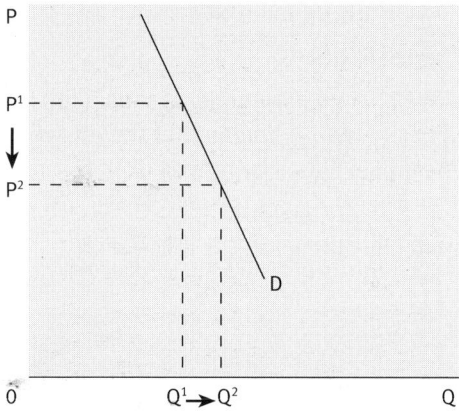

0 means demand is perfectly inelastic

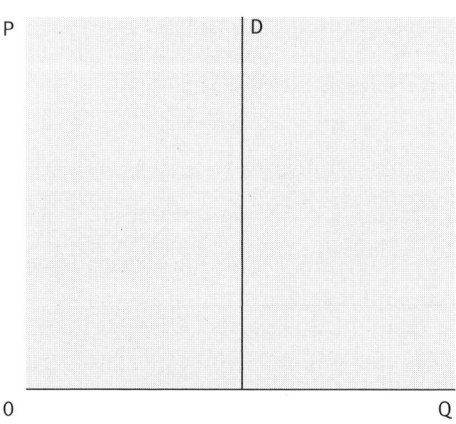

Elasticity can be worked out by using revenue. Note in the diagrams above and on page 23, that with elastic demand, a fall in price leads to an increase in revenue; with inelastic demand, the same fall leads to a decrease in revenue. Unit elasticity has to be drawn as a curve to maintain the same percentage change. Remember, a straight line demand curve has different elasticities along its length ranging from price elastic at higher prices to price inelastic at lower ones.

- Income elasticity is measured as:

$$\frac{\text{\% change in quantity demanded}}{\text{\% change in income}}$$

Note the sign for income elasticity (increase in income) (+) leads to increase in demand. (+) is usually positive.

- Cross elasticity is measured as:

$$\frac{\text{\% change in quantity demanded of good A}}{\text{\% change in price of good B}}$$

Questions

What do you understand by:
1. Market forces?
2. Demand and supply?
3. Equilibrium?
4. Elasticity of demand?

Add these features to your Mind Map then test yourself on the questions at the start of this chapter again, to see if you can answer them.

Market organisation

There are a number of different types of market ranging from one extreme – pure monopoly to the other – perfect competition.

Pure monopoly

There is only one firm in the industry; the firm is the industry. There are no close substitutes and the product of the industry is a necessity. A monopoly is a price-maker – it sets the price in the market and consumers have to pay that price, however high. A single supplier of water or power could be seen as a pure monopoly.

Monopoly

An ordinary monopoly is defined as having control over 25% of the market for a good or service. In fact, much less than this is necessary to control a market if all the other firms in it only have a small percentage of the market each. A monopoly is, again, a price-maker. Additionally, the business can prevent entry of competitors into the market by erecting barriers (such as limiting access to technology) to entry.

Oligopoly

This is where the market is dominated by a few firms. Again they are price-makers. Supermarket chains in the UK are a good example, and some of the features of oligopoly can be seen by looking at these chains. The major companies compete with each other but not always on the basis of price. Because firms are

External influences (1) micro-factors

facing very similar cost structures, it is not always possible to compete on price and still remain profitable. Firms therefore tend towards non-price competition, competing on differentiated or branded products, using advertising, promotion, convenience, service, loyalty cards etc.

Sometimes firms are forced to compete on price and this will lead to a 'price war' with companies willing to make a short-term loss in order to gain or protect a share of the market. Price wars have the effect of lowering prices in the short-term. However, one result of a price war can be that the smallest player goes out of business – at least in that segment of the market – and consumer choice is reduced. Prices will then have a tendency to rise to recoup losses made in the price war.

Oligopolies can put up barriers to entry – for example, the start-up costs for an out-of-town supermarket development might be prohibitive. Firms in an oligopoly will often collude agreeing, privately, to fix prices or supply at particular levels. Each firm in an oligopoly depends on the other firms to stay in business. They will watch what other firms are doing and generally follow suit. Oligopolies have a tendency towards price stability. If a firm lowers price, other firms follow suit and all can end up making losses. If a firm raises price, then consumers will go to the other firms in the market.

Monopolistic competition

This is when there are many firms in the market selling differentiated products. Generally competition is on the basis of one brand versus another. Firms are price-takers, in that the market sets price. There is free entry and exit into the market, although companies will try to erect barriers through, for example, advertising and brand loyalty. Trainer shoe manufacturers cannot, for example, stop a new brand of trainer from being marketed, but can counter it with expensive advertising and promotion campaigns.

Imperfect competition

This is the usual condition of markets in that the features that would be needed to make it perfect are not present. For example, consumers seldom have information as to exactly what prices are being charged and where, and will take other (non-price) factors into account, such as convenience and service.

Perfect competition

The theoretical opposite of pure monopoly. There are many sellers in the market, the product is exactly the same, and consumers have perfect information. As a result, prices are set by the market and no one individual firm can influence them – all firms in the market are price-takers. Imagine visiting a market that sold only eggs. On what basis would you make the decision as to which trader to buy from?
See if you can plot these changes on a demand and supply diagram.

> **FACTFILE**
>
> Before privatisation, the Central Electricity Generating Board produced all the electricity that people needed. When privatised, it was split between Powergen, National Power and Nuclear Electric. Other competitor firms were also encouraged to enter the market. Electricity is a product that cannot be differentiated – it is homogeneous, meaning that one supplier provides exactly the same product as any other. Consumers can now choose which firm (and there are now around 30 of them) will provide their electricity. Firms can only really compete on price as there is no difference in the service or product offered. Powergen maintained its market share by lowering costs and by adding extra areas of activity to the company's business. Consumers benefit from lowered prices.

Market failure

This is when markets fail to 'clear', i.e. they stick at a point other than the equilibrium with surpluses or shortages in the market. Sometimes shortages can be such that some goods and services that are needed are not produced at all.

In a competitive market, profits are the signal for firms to enter the market whilst losses are signals for them to leave. If continuing excessive profits (or losses) are being made then this is a sign of market failure.

Two types of market failure are monopoly and oligopoly, where firms can keep prices high artificially and make excess profits. Another type of failure is where external costs are not taken into account. Costs such as pollution and environmental damage should be reflected in the cost structure of the firm but often are not, with society left to pick up the cost.

Government action to correct market failure includes:

- monitoring monopoly prices and power through the Monopolies and Mergers Commission (MMC)
- monitoring the fairness of prices and practices through the Office of Fair Trading

Objectives and the business environment

- appointing various watchdogs to oversee the privatised utility industries which have tended towards an oligopolistic structure (Ofgas, Oftel, Ofwat respectively watch the gas, water and telecommunications industries)
- legislation to control pollution and 'make the polluter pay' are in place
- minimum wage legislation stops firms from keeping wages at very low levels
- goods that the market would not produce (public goods like streetlights and merit goods like education) are provided by local or national government

TEST YOURSELF

AS
1. What are the two extreme positions of market organisation?
2. What is the difference between a price-maker and a price-taker?
3. What are 'barriers to entry' and who might use them?

A2
1. Explain why we use the two extreme positions of market organisation if neither of them actually exists.
2. How would you measure elasticity? Who would use the measurements?
3. In what ways do governments try to counteract market failure?

CHECKLIST

- ✓ A market is formed by a combination of supply and demand.
- ✓ Supply is what suppliers are willing to supply at a particular price. This usually means more the higher the price.
- ✓ Demand is what consumers are willing to buy at a particular price. This usually means more the lower the price.
- ✓ Elasticity is the responsiveness of demand to changes in another variable – price, income or other goods.
- ✓ Markets should clear at equilibrium.
- ✓ Markets are organised on a scale ranging from perfect competition to pure monopoly.
- ✓ Sometimes markets fail.
- ✓ When this happens governments can intervene.

Mind Map

Finish off your Mind Map by adding all the points above – an example of what your finished Mind Map might look like is shown below. Test yourself using your Mind Map.

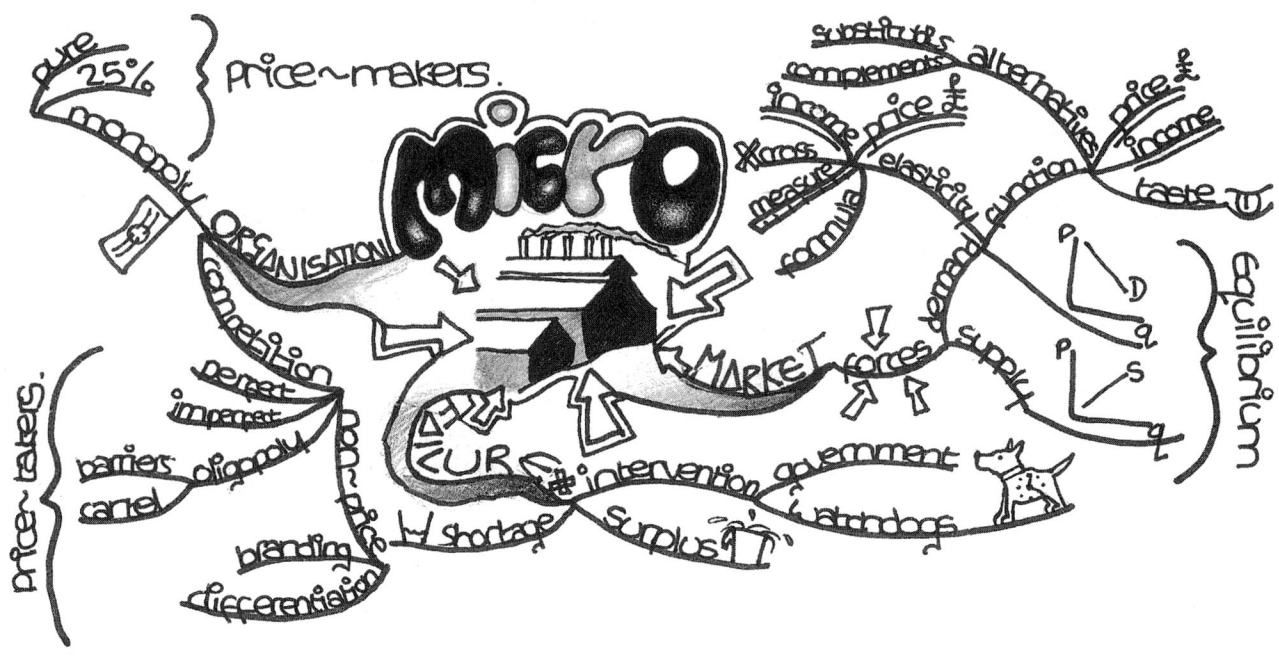

External influences (1) micro-factors

Sample question and answer

In the mid 1990s, BSkyB had a virtual monopoly of satellite broadcasting in the UK. By 2000, competition in the form of cable and digital television is affecting their market position. Using demand and supply diagrams, show what changes have occurred.

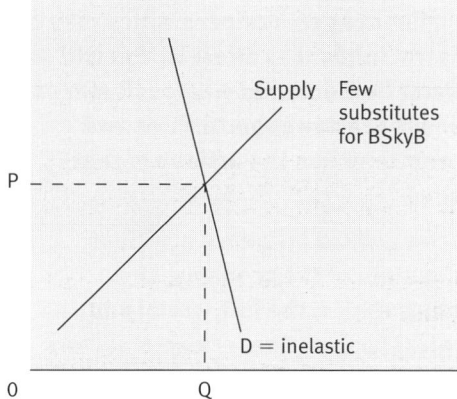

1. You need to point out that the market being considered is important. Is it the market for entertainment? Television channels? Satellite broadcasting? The important market is the one for television channels (and advertising revenues).
2. BSkyB as a monopoly would have certain features, the main ones being control over supply and inelastic demand (due to the lack of substitutes). Of course, it faces competition from terrestrial operators and from satellite operators based abroad. Its near monopoly position means that it could control price and supply. It is able to keep prices high, to make excess profits, and to deny other firms entry to the market by erecting barriers (such as deals with satellite suppliers and installers). You could explain what this means and give more detailed examples.
3. Increased competition has come from other forms of television – not satellite broadcasting – and this has effectively broken BSkyB's monopoly. The result should be a shift in the supply curve to the right – an increase in the supply of television channels and the demand curve should become more elastic. As a result, there should be a reduction in the price and an increase in the quantity demanded. Demand and supply curves similar to these could be used to underline your argument:

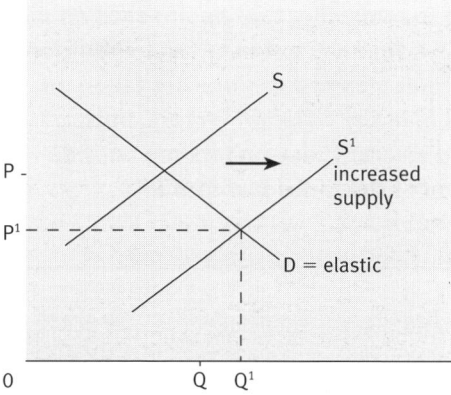

Summary

- **External factors will apply to every part of your course specification.**
- **Micro-factors that affect business are those at the level of individual consumer or company decision-making.**
- **Prices are set and supply allocated on the basis of what people are willing to buy at any one time – demand – and what firms are willing to sell at any one time – supply.**
- **The demand function $D = f(P, P1-n, Y, t)$ shows the main forces acting on demand: price, the price of other goods, income, and taste or fashion.**
- **The interaction of supply and demand should produce an equilibrium price for the market.**
- **Elasticity of demand measures the responsiveness of demand to changes in another factor.**
- **Market organisation ranges from the extreme of pure monopoly – one producer only in a market, to perfect competition, many small producers with no one firm able to influence market price.**
- **These two extremes do not actually exist but are used as measures, or parameters, against which to measure actual forms of market organisation.**
- **Markets can fail to allocate efficiently.**
- **When markets fail, government may need to step in to correct the market failure.**

Study and Revise AS and A2 Level Business Studies

Chapter 5: External influences (2) macro-factors

PREVIEW

- This chapter looks at the way in which the external influences on business which may be called 'macro' influences affect it. You will need to know how external macro influences on a business provide opportunities and impose constraints on the actions of that business.

- Macro-factors which influence business include the state of the economy, the environment, ethics, the law, social and technological factors. These 'macro' factors are separated from 'micro' factors by being factors which occur at a national level rather than at the level of an individual consumer or a firm in the market.

- You need to remember that businesses do not operate in a vacuum, but in an ever-changing scenario that means decisions are taken on the basis of many different factors, both micro and macro. These factors are outside the control of the individual firm or consumer.

- Political factors may well alter according to the 'colour' of the incumbent government. Right-wing parties (Conservatives in the UK, Republicans in the USA, for example) traditionally favour free enterprise and market forces. Left-wing parties (Labour in the UK, Democrats in the USA) traditionally favour tighter control over businesses and some government intervention to provide necessities for those who cannot afford them. Successful governments seem to be at neither extreme but to advocate a 'third way' which is a mixture of private enterprise and social legislation.

- While there may be a specific section in your specification for external factors, you should realise that these are factors that affect all parts of business decision-making and cannot, therefore, be kept in isolation.

- See if you can answer at least four out of the following five questions before continuing with the rest of the chapter.

Questions

1. What is the difference between a 'macro' factors and a 'micro' factor?
2. Can you describe the main features of a free market system and compare this with a planned economic system?
3. In what ways has the government moved assets from the public to the private sector?
4. What are the four aims of national government?
5. What is the difference between fiscal and monetary policy?

Check your answers before reading the rest of the chapter. Try answering the questions again when you've finished the chapter.

Mind Map

Start a Mind Map similar to the one shown. Remember to put an image of your own in the middle. The image I have chosen reminds me that these factors will all be pulling in different directions. Use colours for the central image and a different colour for each 'leg' of your Mind Map.

Definition

Macro-factors are those external factors that can be said to happen on the 'wider' stage – factors that occur at national and international level rather than at the level of an individual firm or organisation.

Free market system

Economic systems are strongly linked to political systems. In a free market system, resources are allocated by the market forces of supply and demand.

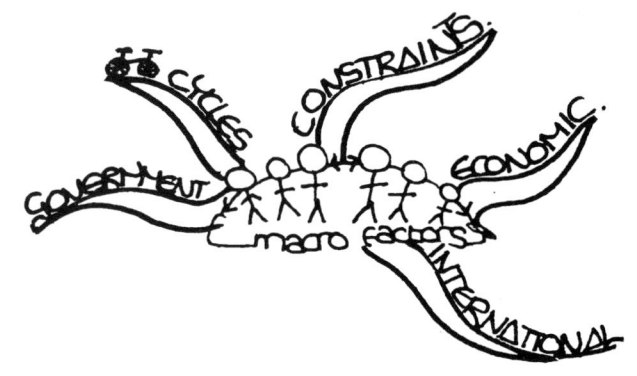

External influences (2) macro-factors

Advantages

- **Profit** is seen as an incentive for producers to be efficient and innovative.
- **Market forces** are seen as being impersonal (and fair) by responding to consumer wants.
- **Competition** is seen as leading to greater choice for consumers.

Disadvantages

- **Market systems** will not provide unprofitable goods and services, e.g. public goods such as street lighting, merit goods such as education and health services.
- **External costs** such as pollution are not taken into account.
- There is a tendency towards **inequality**, a wide gap between the richest and the poorest.
- Markets can **fail**.

Controlled or planned economy

In a controlled or planned economy resources are allocated by government on the basis of perceived need.

Advantages

- All sections of society are catered for **equally**.
- **Employment** is kept at a high level.
- **Resources** can be directed to where they are most needed.

Disadvantages

- Governments decide where resources are needed, this can be **politically biased**.
- There is no **profit motive** and therefore no incentive to improve.
- The system will tend towards **inefficiency** as there are no rewards for being better.

In practice, neither of these extremes exists but most economies are mixed – tending towards one extreme or the other with major state intervention in the market system or as little intervention as possible. The extremes of the completely free market economy and the totally state controlled or planned economy can be used as parameters to judge how 'mixed' a real economy actually is.

FACTFILE

Sometimes intervention in markets is necessary. The Health Service is an example of an organisation where market forces will not cause markets to 'clear'. Because there is no price for the services offered (consultations with a doctor, hospital treatment and operations), there is no mechanism for adjustment. Supply (of hospital beds and trained staff) is limited and demand is not. The only way to control the market is either through rationing (e.g. limiting the number of heart bypass operations available) or by queuing (making people wait their turn for treatment). Internal markets in Health Authorities were meant to try to introduce competition but, in practice, this just meant that the level of care in each authority was different as they decided on different routes to balance the budget.

Don't forget, an alternative market to the Health Service does exist, in the form of private medicine. Governments have encouraged the growth of this sector as one way of introducing a price mechanism. If those who can afford to pay do so, privately, then this should take pressure from the health service waiting lists.

Government policies

The UK government has moved, in recent years, to a position of less government influence in industry. A number of policies have been followed:

Privatisation

This is where the government moves an asset from the public sector into the private sector by:

- **privatisation:** the sale of shares in a previously state-owned industry
- **competitive tendering:** making local services (such as school catering or refuse collection) subject to bidding from private groups; this is also part of the strategy of allowing services to be 'contracted out'
- **sale of assets:** for example, council houses
- **deregulation:** removing artificial restrictions on competition
- **internal markets:** people are allowed to compete within particular public services, with the intention of bringing prices down.

Study and Revise AS and A2 Level Business Studies

Objectives and the business environment

Fund or budget holding

This is where organisations are given control of their own funds. Schools, for example, have their own budgets and have to manage them themselves rather than let the Local Education Authority do it (as they used to in the past). GP doctors (General Practitioners) in the health service have been given their own funds to run their practices. They therefore have a responsibility to try to become more efficient and to keep costs at a minimum.

Private Finance Initiative (PFI)

The government signs what amounts to a 'hire purchase' agreement with private companies. The company pays for a piece of major investment (e.g. roads, bridges, museums) and the government pays them back over an extended time period. Sometimes these payments are taken from the public in the form of fees or tolls.

> **FACTFILE**
>
> PFI projects include the Royal Armouries Museum in Leeds, the computerisation of the passport office, the building of 13 new hospitals at a cost of over £1billion, and the building of the M1–A1 link road.

Local government

Revenue is raised through the 'council tax' – a tax levied on people according to the value of their houses – and through the single business rate. Central government also provides a grant to local authorities. Major areas of expenditure are on education, road maintenance, environmental services, social services and recreation.

National government

This influences the economy through trying to reach the four main aims of government:

- full employment
- favourable balance of payments
- stable prices (i.e. low or no inflation)
- economic growth

Government influence extends through:

- expenditure on goods and services (e.g. motorways, hospitals, defence) plus indirect expenditure (e.g. on pensions, benefits etc.)
- taxation: direct taxation on earnings and profits; indirect taxation on goods and services
- regional policy: help in the form of expenditure, grants and tax breaks in areas of high unemployment or deprivation
- laws to regulate the conduct and actions of business

Policies and practice

Government policies to reach these targets by affecting the total demand in the economy (aggregate demand) are either fiscal or monetary:

Fiscal policies involve variations in government spending and in taxation in order to reach targets:

- expenditure changes can be directed to where they are most needed
- taxation changes can be in direct taxation or indirect taxation. Direct taxes are on income or company profits. Indirect taxes are on goods such as VAT or duty on tobacco and alcohol.
- the Public Sector Borrowing Requirement (PSBR) is how much money governments have to borrow to make up any shortfall between income in the form of taxes and duties and expenditure. The size of the PSBR is often seen as a measure of how well a government is handling the economy. (The use of tactics, such as the PFI, help to keep PSBR down as governments do not have to fund initial high investment costs for new projects)

Monetary policies involve controlling the supply of money in the economy. The tool of altering interest rates has now been given to the Bank of England so that interest rates are only altered for economic reasons, not for political ones.

Exchange rate policy

Governments can also use exchange rate policy – changing the value of the currency – to influence the price of imports and exports. In the UK this is not done directly: the currency is allowed to find its own level as a reflection of the strength of the economy and the level of interest rates. Governments can deliberately intervene in money markets in order to affect the price of a currency by buying or selling it.

Examples

Some examples of what might happen to illustrate how hard it is for governments to control the economy ($\rightarrow$ = 'leads to'):

increase in direct taxation $\rightarrow$ less expenditure $\rightarrow$ less demand $\rightarrow$ less employment OR $\rightarrow$ less pressure on prices $\rightarrow$ lower inflation OR $\rightarrow$ more

External influences (2) macro-factors

expenditure on cheap imports → less favourable balance of payments

increase in public expenditure → increased demand → more employment OR → higher PSBR → higher interest rates → lower demand

fall in interest rates → higher demand → higher prices → inflation OR → less saving → less available for borrowing → less investment OR a reduction in capital coming into the country and an increase in capital leaving (seeking higher interest elsewhere) → weakening of currency

an increase in the value of the £ → imports cheaper → less expenditure at home → less employment

Questions

1. What do you understand by:
   - free market economy?
   - planned economy?
   - mixed economy?
2. Outline the methods the UK government has used to put public sector firms into private ownership.
3. Give an example of a PFI project.
4. List the four aims of government.
5. Explain the difference between fiscal and monetary policy.

Add these points to your Mind Map.

FACTFILE

Aggregate demand is the total of all the demands in the economy less expenditure that 'leaks' out of the economy. It is consumer expenditure plus firms investment spending (on machinery, plant, equipment etc.) plus government spending plus exports (money coming in from people abroad) minus expenditure taken out of the economy. This is saving (future expenditure), taxation (which will return as government expenditure) and spending on imports (which goes to a foreign countries economy).

Business or trade cycle

The economy is said to go through a cycle of ups and downs – recession and recovery. This is called the trade or business cycle.

In a recession:
- demand is falling
- this in turn leads to increased stocks and reductions in production
- unemployment is likely to be increasing
- prices will be stable or falling
- interest rates will be increasing

At the bottom of the cycle:
- there is high unemployment
- demand is low
- expectations are that the situation has 'bottomed out' – things can't get any worse

In the recovery:
- stocks have fallen so low that firms need to restock
- extra employment is created
- demand increases
- interest rates are low
- investment increases

At the top of the cycle:
- demand has outstripped supply
- prices are high
- wage rates are high
- unemployment is low – there is no spare labour
- expectations are that things can't get any better
- the economy is said to be 'overheating'

Governments can try to counter the cycle by ensuring that their own patterns of expenditure – in the public sector – run counter to those in the private sector. This is called Keynesian demand management after the economist John Maynard Keynes. This is very difficult to achieve and was abandoned as policy in the early 1980s. It was replaced with monetarist policy and supply side policies in the belief that, for example, lower income tax would encourage people to work; lower benefits would keep people at work rather than on benefit, lower interest rates would encourage investment.

Objectives and the business environment

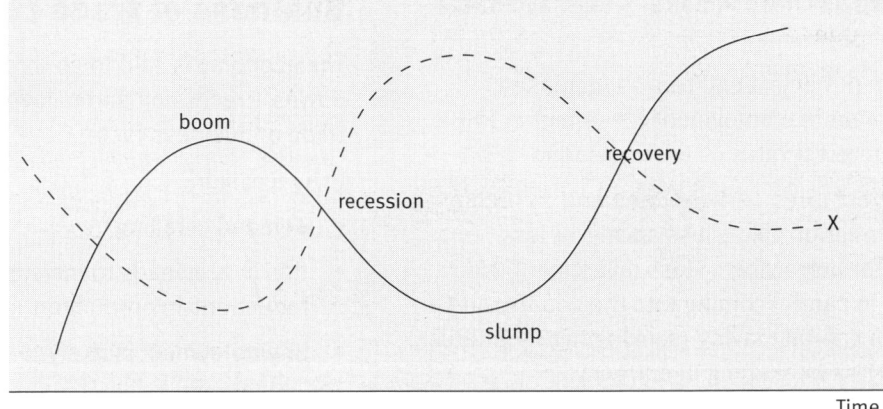

Keynesian fiscal policy would have government expenditure following the dotted line 'X'

The business cycle

> **FACTFILE**
>
> It is believed that there is a possible trade-off between inflation and unemployment. This means that an economy can't sustain both high employment levels and low levels of inflation. High employment means that most people have income to spend and this extra demand will push prices up. Low employment (high levels of unemployment) mean that demand is dampened down and prices are kept in check. Some governments have been accused of deliberately creating unemployment as a weapon against inflation.
>
> High interest-rate policies can also be used to 'choke off' inflation by encouraging people to save rather than to spend.

> **FACTFILE**
>
> If a frog wants to cross the lily pond to visit his lady frog friend, but can only ever jump half the remaining distance, when does he get there? The answer is 'infinity' as he must cross increasingly tiny increments until it is an infinitesimal distance to cross. He thus travels one jump plus half a jump plus a quarter of a jump and so on or $1 + 0.5 + 0.5^2 + 0.5^3 + 0.5^4 \ldots + 0.5^n$. This is equal to 2 (1 over 1 minus the marginal propensity to jump, which is a half). The multiplier is calculated in the same way. Each additional income receiver spends a proportion of that additional income. The size of the multiplier depends on the size of that marginal propensity to consume $(1/1-mpc)$.

Business cycle factors

Three factors have a major effect on the business cycle.

Multiplier

Any increase in injections into an economy (consumer spending, government spending, export sales or investment spending) will have a multiplied effect on the economy. Imagine the government spends £1m on a project. This expenditure has been paid as someone else's income. They will spend some of it and save some of it. The amount that they spend is, again, part of someone's income. The original injection is thus multiplied. The higher the proportion of extra income is spent (called the marginal propensity to consume), the higher is the multiplier.

Accelerator

This says that for increased production in an economy there has to be accelerated investment. For example, a firm using machines which produce 100 units which wishes to increase production by 1 must buy excess capacity of 99 units in order to be able to increase production at all. Investment is thus accelerated.

Expectations

This is what people think is going to happen or expect to happen. Expectations are generally self-fulfilling. If people expect a recovery then they will invest, spend, be confident and a recovery will happen. If they expect a recession then they will save and put off investment, causing the slump.

Time-lags

Problems are caused by the gap between planned investment or government expenditure and actual expenditure taking place. A business may decide to invest to increase capacity now, but it could be several months before capacity can actually be increased, by which time it may no longer be needed.

External influences (2) macro-factors

The lag between government planning and actual expenditure – due to the huge nature of some of the capital projects involved – can be even longer.

Add these points to your Mind Map

> **FACTFILE**
>
> The government's introduction of the minimum wage can be seen as a policy which is ethically correct yet economically incorrect. Ethically, the government is ensuring that many people actually earn a living wage. Economically, they are interfering with the mechanism of the market and therefore could be creating unemployment.

International influences

Countries trade with each other according to who can produce what most efficiently. Comparative advantage means that one country can produce goods at a lower opportunity cost than another. It is therefore sensible for countries to specialise in what they produce best and trade their surpluses.

Barriers to trade

Countries will sometimes try to protect their home industry by erecting barriers to trade. These include:

- **tariff:** placing an extra tax on imported goods
- **quota:** limiting the amount of a particular good allowed into a country
- **regulations:** special rules or technical regulations making it hard for importers to compete
- **embargo:** total ban on the import of certain goods
- **currency restrictions:** limiting the amount of currency that can be exchanged to buy imports

Exchange rates

This is the worth of a currency in terms of other currencies. It will fluctuate according to the strength of the country's economy, interest rates and through speculators buying and selling for profit. Political changes will also affect the currency.

Balance of payments

This is the balance between money earned from abroad by exports and money spent on imports. A balance of payments deficit is when more is spent on imports than is earned from exports. A balance of payments surplus vice versa.

GATT and WTO

The General Agreement on Tariffs and Trade was an organisation that aimed to bring as much free trade to the world as possible. Member countries meet regularly to try to solve trade disputes and reduce the barriers to trade. It has now been replaced by the World Trade Organisation, which has similar aims.

The pattern of trade

The UK has traditionally conducted a lot of its trade with Commonwealth countries and receives favourable trading terms. Thus trade with New Zealand, Australia and the Indian sub-continent forms the basis for much of the UK's trade. Since joining the European Union, Britain's main trading partners are now within Europe, making up 60% of UK trade.

The European Union (EU)

Originally the EU was just a customs union – member states encouraged free trade between their countries and allowed free movement of labour, capital etc. This was finalised with the Single Market (1992) within which there is complete freedom of movement for goods, people and capital. Countries outside the EU pay a tariff to trade with countries inside it.

Further harmonisation has taken place with many EU laws becoming part of UK law, such as the Social Charter which guarantees workers' rights, the advent of the single European currency and the possibility of monetary union.

Criticism of the Union has often centred on:

- **Common Agricultural Policy:** keeping farm prices high through subsidies is the major part of the Union's expenditure
- **EU directives:** instructions from the EU to alter or change something so that it is harmonised – often to the detriment of some member countries

The Union is governed by its institutions:

- **European Commission** takes an overview, proposes policies; it is appointed by members
- **European Council of Ministers** is made up of ministers from member countries who meet to formulate policy (defence ministers for defence, prime ministers for major decisions etc.). This is effectively the cabinet of the EU.
- **European Parliament** made up of directly elected members and forms the legislative body of the EU

Objectives and the business environment

European Monetary Union

Previously, the amount of trade within the EU made it essential that the minimum of currency transactions took place. There were two policies – a unit so that all transactions could be expressed as a single currency (the European Currency Unit or ECU) and the Exchange Rate Mechanism (ERM) which linked the value of all member state currencies. The ERM was replaced by the Euro on 1 January 1999 when member countries exchange rates were locked together. The Euro will replace domestic currencies in 2002.

Britain has not yet joined the single currency as the government is not yet convinced that the good points outweigh the bad ones.

Advantages

- no exchange rate costs or fluctuations
- comparisons of prices are easier
- no movement of capital to seek different interest rates
- inflation is kept under control

Disadvantages

- loss of control over your own currency
- a feeling of loss of sovereignty
- costs of transition and dual pricing
- much of Britain's trade is outside the EU – these businesses will bear the costs of transition but gain no benefits
- some regions will benefit more than others; some may not benefit at all

Legal constraints

The government sees itself as paternalistic when it comes to preventing or encouraging business to do certain things. Legislation governs:

- conditions of employment
- the rights of consumers
- competitive behaviour
- health and safety
- ethical considerations

Bodies also 'self regulate' – policing their own actions in the hope that the government will not feel it necessary to intervene. These areas are covered in detail in the relevant chapters.

Social environment

These are long-term factors that will affect business and include:

- the size and structure of population (demography) and whether or not it is growing
- skill and education levels
- changes in technology leading to changes in firms' employment needs
- changes in working patterns – more women working, early retirement, more young people in further education
- increasing interest in seeing businesses as environmentally and ethically responsible

Ethical constraints

Ethics is the study of what is 'right' or proper. An example of an ethical problem in business is the use of animals for testing. One argument would say that such practices are ethically wrong, as the animals are made to suffer unnecessarily. The counter argument would be that such testing is ethically right, as it may lead to great advantages for humans. Sometimes it depends on the nature of the problem – animal testing for cosmetics might be seen as unnecessary, but for life-saving drugs it could be argued as being essential.

What other ethical dilemmas can you think of in business? Which businesses have taken an 'ethical stance' and included it in their mission statements?

CHECKLIST

External factors apply to all sectors of business studies. These include:

- ✓ economic systems
- ✓ government policy
- ✓ international trade
- ✓ exchange rate fluctuations
- ✓ the state of the economy
- ✓ international bodies and agreements such as GATT and the European Union

Constraints on the operation of business may be:

- ✓ legal
- ✓ political
- ✓ social
- ✓ ethical

External influences (2) macro-factors

Pressure groups

Pressure groups are groups of people who will join together in order to try to influence opinion and policy. Best-known are national and international environmental groups such as Friends of the Earth and Greenpeace. There are also single-issue groups – 'Stop the Bypass'; 'Keep the Railway Open' – that will exist only for the life of that issue.

Mind Map

Finish off your Mind Map by adding all the rest of the points mentioned. An example of a finished Mind Map is shown below. Don't forget to use word pictures where appropriate e.g. you could use the word 'Pressure group' appearing on a demonstrator's placard. Test yourself by using your Mind Map.

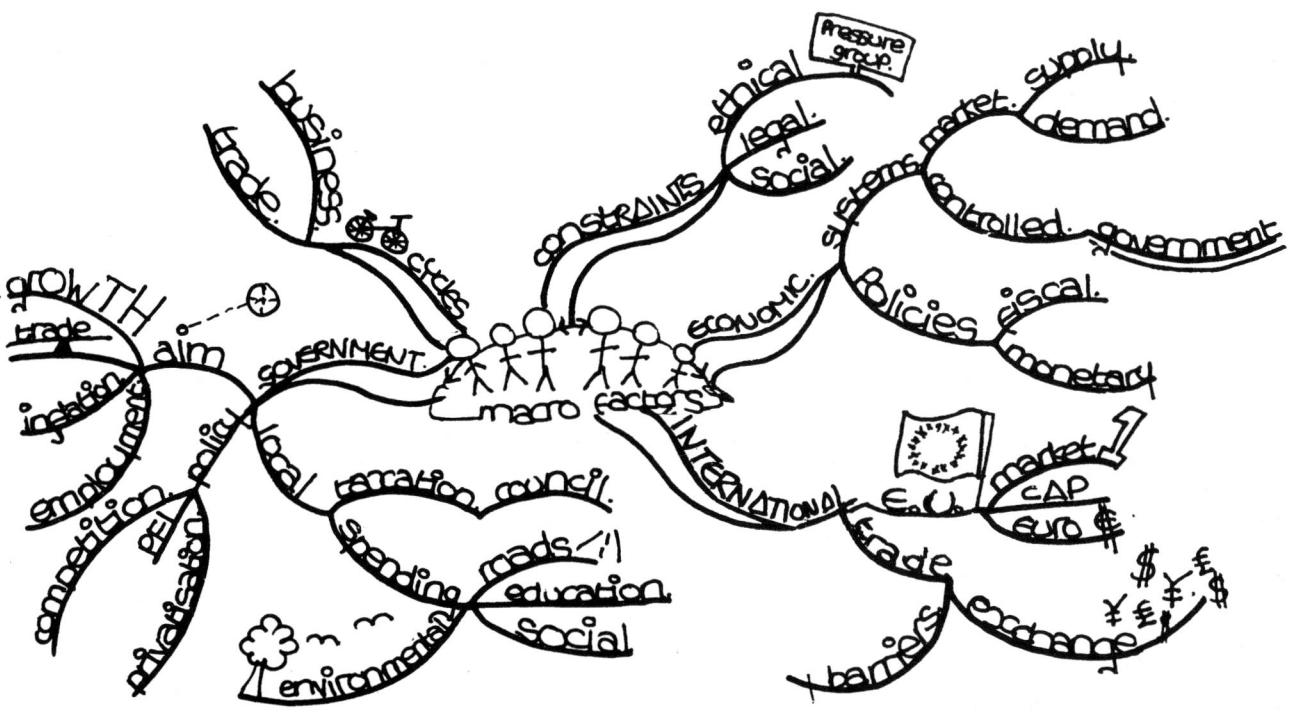

TEST YOURSELF

AS

1. Label this diagram of the trade cycle correctly.
2. List the possible barriers to trade that a country could erect.
3. Can you outline the UK's pattern of trade?

A2

1. Can you explain how the multiplier works – and how you would measure it?
2. Outline the pros and cons of Britain joining the Single Currency.
3. Explain what is meant by an 'ethical stance' in business.

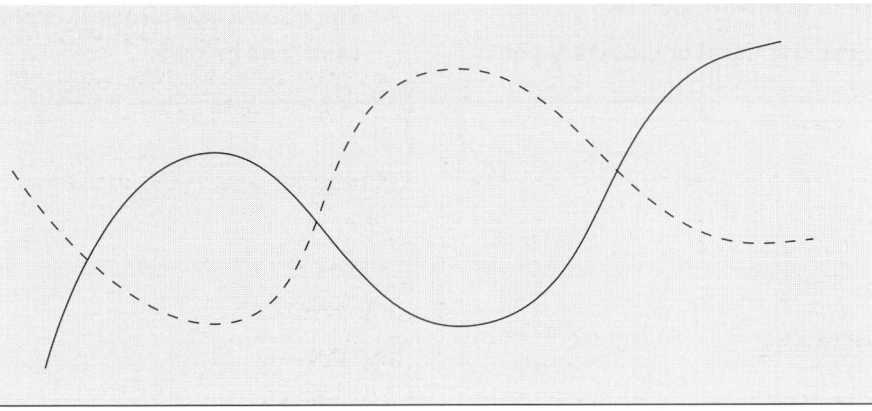

Study and Revise AS and A2 Level Business Studies

Objectives and the business environment

Sample question and answer

What is the Single European Market? Discuss whether its advantages have outweighed its disadvantages?

Tackle the question through a 'question and answer approach'. Organise your ideas with a mini Mind Map.

1. **What is it?**
   Single European Market (SEM) is a free trade area; a market of 350m people.

2. **What is its purpose?**
   Goods and factors of production within the market move freely and without tariffs. The factors of production which it has particularly freed up are labour and capital.

3. **Why free trade?**
   Specialisation (could bring in the theory of comparative advantage) means greater efficiency, more scale economies; better quality goods.

4. **Who benefits?**
   UK Business: through not having to change currency, pay tariffs, suffer delays crossing borders. Benefits from access to huge market. Further benefits come from investment from countries outside the EU, who need a market foothold inside it (e.g. Japanese companies).

   Consumers: should have greater choice and lower prices.
   Government: should have less bureaucracy (e.g. customs, tariffs).

5. **What are the disadvantages?**
   Business faces competition that it didn't previously have; EU regulations; new international companies can locate (and relocate) where labour is cheapest, damaging local economies.

   Consumers must buy goods regulated by European, not UK standards (give an example).

   Government fears loss of sovereignty; this is the first stage in monetary and maybe even political union.

6. **Conclusion.** 'It depends . . .' – make sure it is well argued!

Summary

- External factors will apply to every part of your course specification.
- Macro-factors which affect business are those at the level of national or international decision-making.
- Different economic systems affect business in different ways.
- Extreme systems are completely free market or totally planned. Most economies are a mixture – a mixed economy.
- The UK economy has, in recent years, moved more towards a free market system through privatisation and lower government expenditure.
- The four main aims of government are full employment, favourable balance of payments, stable prices and economic growth.
- Governments can use fiscal or monetary policy to reach their targets, but striking a balance is difficult.
- Businesses are affected by the business or trade cycle.
- The action of the multiplier and accelerator help to cause recession and recovery.
- Restrictions or freedom of international trade affect businesses.
- The EU is essentially a customs union which is moving more and more towards harmonisation of its members.
- The government provides protection and direction through the law.
- The social environment includes population and technological structure and changes.
- The ethical environment is how businesses think and behave.

Marketing — Section 2

Specification content

Advanced Supplementary (AS)

AQA
Module 1 is *'Marketing and Accounting and Finance'*. It includes:
- Market analysis
- Segmentation analysis
- Market research
- A qualitative understanding of the statistical significance of sample findings
- Marketing strategy
- Marketing objectives
- Niche vs. Mass marketing
- Product life cycle
- Marketing mix
- Product, price, promotion and place
- Application of elasticity

OCR
Module 2872 is *'Business Decisions'* and Module 2873 is *'Business Behaviour'*. They include:
- Marketing
- Market definitions and structures
- Market research and market analysis
- Marketing planning
- Marketing mix – price, product, promotion, place
- Calculation and interpretation of price elasticity of demand

Edexcel
Unit 2 is *'Marketing and Production'*. It includes:
- Nature and role of marketing
- Role, objectives and effect of competition
- Market research
- Marketing mix
- Product and product analysis techniques
- Pricing, place and promotion

Advanced Level (A2)

AQA
Module 1 is *'Marketing and Accounting and Finance'*. It includes:
- Market analysis
- Marketing strategy
- Asset vs. Market led strategies
- Extrapolation and correlation
- Marketing planning
- Marketing mix
- Marketing budget
- Sales forecasting

OCR
Module 2874 is *'Further Marketing'* (optional). It includes:
- The market
- The market plan and marketing objectives
- Market research
- Marketing planning, including segregation and aggregation, growth, the law
- Models of marketing including AIDA, SWOT and Ansoff
- The marketing mix – price, product, promotion, place

Edexcel
Unit 5 is *'Business Planning'*. It includes
- Developing marketing strategies in relation to the elements of the marketing mix
- Market audits
- Market research

Chapter 6: Marketing objectives and planning

PREVIEW

- In this chapter we look at the definition of marketing and at how and why businesses set marketing objectives.
- You will need to know about the importance of strategic planning and about the different reasons why a business may choose to market a particular product or service.
- You will be expected to be able to draw and analyse a chart to show marketing positioning, discuss the possibility of gaps in the market and suggest strategies for a business to fill those gaps.
- You will be expected to understand the difference between marketing objectives and marketing strategies and be able to suggest which strategies would be most appropriate with which objective.
- You will need to be able to show that firms will use different ways to reach their objectives.
- See if you can answer at least four of the following five questions before continuing with the chapter.

Questions

1. Can you define what is meant by marketing?
2. Fill in the missing spaces in the marketing cycle

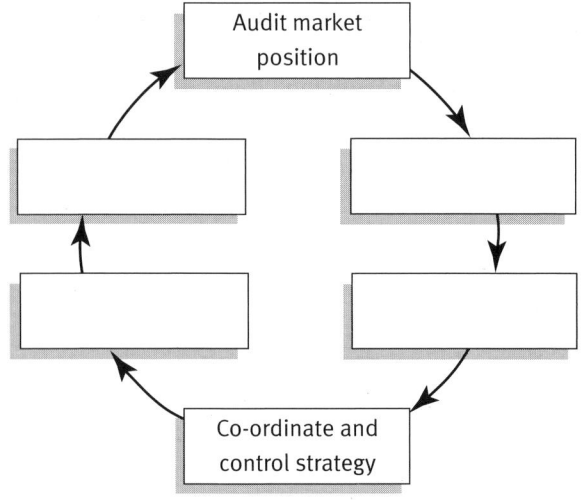

3. Can you explain why this cycle is important?
4. What is the difference between strategy, objectives and targets?
5. Why do you think it is important for a firm to plan?

Mind Map

Start a Mind Map similar to the one shown here. Put a central image of your own in the middle. This image reminds me that objectives are similar to targets. You need to draw an image that works for you! The first 'legs' of the Mind Map have been started for you. Add points to your map as you work through the chapter. At the end of the chapter is an example of what a finished Mind Map might look like. Don't forget, you can – and should – use several colours for your central image and a different colour for each 'leg' of your Mind Map.

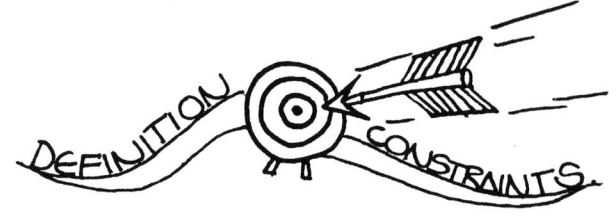

Check your answers before reading the rest of the chapter. Try answering the questions again when you've finished the chapter.

Definition

According to the British Institute of Marketing, marketing is the 'management process which identifies, anticipates and supplies customer requirements'. They could also have added that it discovers and even creates wants for the consumer.

Objectives

Marketing objectives face the same problems as any other business objectives in that they take place subject to a number of external factors. The planning cycle is similar to that for any other strategy except that it feeds off the organisation's corporate strategy or aim and will be linked to its corporate vision and mission statement.

The corporate objectives help define the type of marketing objectives for the business. The planning cycle is as follows:

Marketing objectives and planning

Why plan?

Planning allows a firm to set realistic targets which it can then try to achieve. It means that the firm will be in a position to use its resources in the most efficient way possible. When targets are reached, the firm can then review its position and set new targets. It means that progress is made within a framework or matrix, and is controllable and measurable. There is a continuous evaluation of the success of the firm.

Types of objective

Firms may have a number of different types of objective. It is important to realise that not all objectives are appropriate for all firms and nor are the methods of achieving objectives. Widening the range of products on sale in a corner store, for example, would count as diversification; it is much more easily achieved than if Boeing decide to diversify into the production of ocean liners!

Marketing strategy

You will need to recognise the difference between marketing strategy and marketing objectives. Strategy is the overall, long-term plan for the firm; objectives are major steps on the way to achieving that plan. For example, the strategy of a firm may be to 'offer the beverage of choice, replacing tea and coffee'; the objectives may be to increase sales in Asia, Russia and China by 5% in the next two years; intermediate targets will then be set to see if the objectives are being approached. (Can you guess which company this strategy might refer to?)

Questions

1 Write down a definition of marketing.
2 Draw and label a diagram to show the marketing cycle.
3 Explain the difference between a corporate objective and a marketing objective.

Add these points to your Mind Map

Growth

Firms may grow internally (organic growth) or externally through expanding markets or products, or through the acquisition of other firms. Organic growth is slower, but it is also cheaper and involves less risk. Objectives may be market orientated or product orientated.

Market orientated objectives are:

- increased market penetration: trying to take a greater share of an existing market with an existing product
- increased market development: finding or creating new markets

Safest			
Existing markets & products			New Products
	market penetration	product development	
	market development	product diversification	
New markets			
			Most risky

Ansoff's matrix

Marketing

> **FACTFILE**
>
> Product development is often in the nature of 'new', 'improved' or 'now with added . . .'. Look at a range of shampoo and hair products, for example, and see how many claim to contain magic chemicals or additional ingredients, or are merely flashed with the word 'new'!

Product orientated objectives include:

- product development: using the base of existing products to grow, e.g. a car manufacturer may decide to produce 'special editions', add features to models or create new models
- product diversification: seeking to create or develop new products or lines; for example, a car manufacturer deciding to produce boats

Ansoff's matrix shows how safe or risky each of these objectives is.

Product differentiation

This may be achieved through branding and the objective may be high levels of market recognition. The idea is to make a product or service distinctive from its competitors. A strong brand will achieve this. The strongest brands become generic terms – both Biro and Hoover started out as brand names.

Some manufacturers ensure that it is the company name that gives them their strong brand image. Examples include Adidas's three-stripe logo, and Cadbury's distinctive script and colour scheme. Others have strongly branded products (Whiskas, the cat food, is made by Pedigree Foods).

Brands can be strong enough to allow a firm to differentiate – Ben Sherman (shirts) and Wrangler (jeans) both produce branded watches and other goods as well as clothes.

Product differentiation allows firms to take a greater market share by providing different products for different parts of the market. There are only two major soap powder manufacturers in the UK (Lever Bros and Procter and Gamble) but see how many different products there are on the shelves!

Internal and external constraints

Objectives may not be achieved due to limitations or constraints placed on a firm either from within the company – internal constraints – or from outside the company – external constraints.

> **FACTFILE**
>
> Persil did not realise the strength of their brand when they decided to reposition the washing powder to take account of the strong environmental lobby. Sales of 'biological' and 'environment friendly' brands were strong, but Persil had to reintroduce its original powder (branded as Persil Original) due to the demand for it.

Internal constraints

- **Product diversification:** This can be dangerous and the risk of entering untried markets can be minimised through good research, but cannot be altogether eliminated. Specialisation can be safer in the short-term but may also lead to stagnation.
- **Personnel:** the type and calibre of staff will be important to a firm. They may not have staff with the requisite skills, training or expertise to cope with new products or markets. Taking on new staff may cause internal dissent.
- **Finance:** there may be a lack of finance or competing factions for the use of what finance there is.

External constraints

- **Competition:** competitors are unlikely to just sit by while a firm takes an extra 5% of a market. They will react and objectives need to take the likelihood and scale of such reactions into account.
- **Law:** some products are restricted by law. The law may also impose other constraints. For example, the manufacturers of alcoholic fizzy drinks ('alcopops') had to change their marketing when the government decided that these drinks were being aimed at underage drinkers.
- **Ethics:** with certain products there are moral objections to marketing.
- **Macro-factors:** the state of the economy, changes in population growth or structure, changes in fashion and taste may destroy or diminish markets.

> **FACTFILE**
>
> Coca-Cola successfully challenged Sainsbury's in the courts when Sainsbury's produced packaging for an own brand cola that closely mimicked the distinctive shape, style and colouring of the lettering which Coca-Cola uses. Not only the brand, but the brand image, was under threat.

Marketing objectives and planning

TEST YOURSELF

Use your Mind Map to see if you can answer the following questions.

AS

1. What is meant by organic growth?
2. Can you explain market orientated objectives?
3. Can you explain product orientated objectives?

A2

1. Can you complete this Ansoff matrix?
2. Explain the difference between diversification and differentiation.
3. Outline the internal and external constraints that may hinder a firm in achieving its marketing objectives.

Safest			
Existing markets & products →			New Products
↓			
New markets			
			Most risky

Sample question and answer

Discuss the statement that product differentiation confers benefits on both the business and the consumer.

With this sort of essay it is helpful to plan the advantages and disadvantages paragraph by paragraph. A mini Mind Map will do this.

1. Define your terms.
   Product differentiation is . . .
   It is used by firms to . . .

2. Advantages on product differentiation to firm:
   Means product competition rather than price competition.
   Price competition and possible price wars are damaging to profits.
   Cheaper than diversification or innovation.
   Firm is able to enter niche markets without extra cost.
   Strong brands confer other benefits – such as reputation.

3. Advantages on product differentiation to consumer:
   Means greater (apparent) choice.
   Consumers suffer from price wars in the long-term if choice is reduced.

4. Disadvantages of product differentiation to firm:
   Extra expenditure on advertising to establish product.
   If there is excess supply, price competition may lead to more efficient markets clearing at lower prices.
   Advertising is a waste of resources that could be better used elsewhere.

5. Disadvantages of product differentiation to consumer:
   Consumers benefit from price wars in the short-term.
   Consumer may not recognise products as differentiated. (Is there a point to branding salt or sugar?)
   Advertising costs are likely to result in higher prices.
   Differentiation means less innovation and improvement.

6. Conclusion
   'It depends . . . but must be well argued! Consider the sort of market that differentiation may be taking place in (usually a mature and fairly saturated market). You could mention the likely elasticity of products within the market and how differentiation, branding in particular, is meant to affect demand elasticity.

Marketing

Mind Map

Finish off your Mind Map by adding all the rest of the points mentioned. An example of a finished Mind Map is shown below. Don't forget to use word pictures where appropriate.

CHECKLIST

- ✓ Marketing identifies, anticipates and supplies customer requirements.
- ✓ Marketing objectives are part of overall strategy.
- ✓ Ansoff's matrix shows how risky certain objectives are.
- ✓ Marketing objectives will be constrained by:
  - internal considerations
  - competition
  - the economy
  - legal and ethical constraints.
- ✓ Businesses operate within a context which includes constraints and their own corporate culture.

Summary

- Marketing is the management process that identifies, anticipates and supplies customer requirements (Institute of Marketing).
- Firms set marketing objectives as part of a marketing strategy.
- Different objectives will be chosen by different firms according to their size, market position and circumstances.
- There may be different ways to achieve the same objective; a firm should choose the most suitable method.
- Planning to achieve objectives is essential.
- Intermediate targets let management know if a firm is going to reach its marketing objectives.
- Ansoff's matrix shows how safe or risky various objectives are.
- These objectives may be product orientated, seeking to develop products or diversify.
- They may be market orientated, seeking to take a greater share of an existing market or to find or create new ones.
- Product differentiation is making your product distinctive in some way – often through branding.
- Product differentiation can help a firm take a greater market share.
- Marketing objectives may be limited by internal and external constraints.
- Internal constraints include having the right product, personnel and finance.
- External constraints include competitors, government and the law, the economy and ethics.

Market analysis and research — CHAPTER 7

PREVIEW

- In this chapter we look at how a market may be analysed, that is, broken down into its component parts, and why a firm might wish to do this. Good market analysis and market research information is essential to successful decision-making. The better the information, the more likely management is to make the correct decisions.

- You need to know how and why a firm collects market information – you should be able to describe the methodology and argue as to which is the most accurate or appropriate in particular situations.

- You need to develop a cynical attitude towards figures and statistics presented to you. Remember that there are 'lies, damn lies and statistics'. You need to learn to ask who commissioned the research, what was its purpose, how was it presented – 'Kellogg's, all our cereals are 95% fat free' is different from 'Kellogg's, we add 5% fat to all our natural products' and yet the information is basically the same.

- You need to recognise that new firms in a market may struggle to gain a foothold in a market because they do not have the depth of knowledge of the market gained by established firms.

- See if you can answer at least four of the following five questions before reading the rest of the chapter.

Questions

1. Can you define what is meant by a market?
2. Can you describe how the size of a market may be measured?
3. Can you explain the difference between mass marketing and niche marketing?
4. What are the three main types of market? In what ways are they similar? In what ways are they different?
5. Can you outline what is meant by market segmentation?

Check your answers before reading the rest of the chapter. Try answering the questions again when you've finished the chapter.

Mind Map

Start a Mind Map similar to the one shown here. Put a central image of your own in the middle. This image reminds me that market analysis is really investigating the market. You need to draw an image that works for you! The first 'legs' of the Mind Map have been started for you. Add points to your map as you work through the chapter. At the end of the chapter is an example of what a finished Mind Map might look like. Don't forget, you can – and should – use several colours for your central image and a different colour for each 'leg' of your Mind Map.

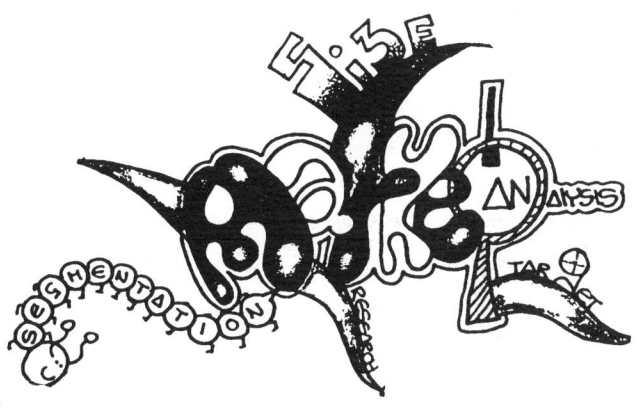

Definition

A market is anywhere where buyers and sellers come together to agree on an exchange. It does not have to have a physical existence (like a street market) but can exist by telephone, mail, Internet etc. To a firm, the market is defined as its potential customers. The analysis of that market will show them how large it is, what its structure is and the direction in which it is moving (growing or declining).

Market size

Firms need to know both the size and structure of their market. There is a difference between the *potential* market (which could be an entire population) and the *actual* market. The size of the actual market is measured by either the volume of sales or the value of those sales. For example, the market for cat food is worth £550 million per year by value, or an estimated 1,500 million cans per year by volume.

Firms need to decide whether they want a large or a small market.

- Mass markets are where goods or services are aimed at a large number of people – the whole

Study and Revise AS and A2 Level Business Studies

Marketing

market. The earliest example of mass marketing is probably the introduction of Henry Ford's Model T Ford, the car of which Ford famously said 'you can have any colour you like, as long as its black'. Mass marketing means mass production and goods that are identical. This quote serves to encapsulate this.

- Niche markets are small, specialised markets catering for a very small part, or niche, of the total market.

> **FACTFILE**
>
> Nokia, the mobile phone network company, made a conscious decision in the early 1990s to switch from a national market to a global market. They decided that the trend in telecommunications was towards global suppliers and a global service. They therefore marketed products globally and, by 1996, from their base in Finland, had a profile of sales as shown.
>
>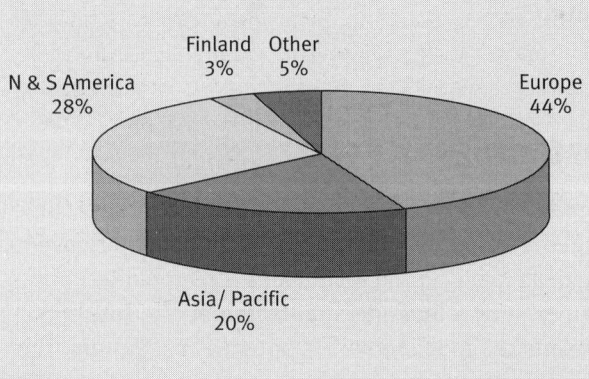
>
> Finland 3%
> Other 5%
> N & S America 28%
> Europe 44%
> Asia/Pacific 20%
>
> Nokia mobile telephones are used in a total of 130 countries where Nokia now has sales – a truly 'mass' market.

Market types

There are three main types of market:

Consumer goods

These can be divided into **consumer durables** (consumer goods that can be re-used many times, such as cars, cookers, freezers, electrical goods) and **consumer goods** (consumer non-durables that are 'used up', the biggest of these being food).

Services

These are **intangibles**, such as insurance, transport, banking and tourism (markets in financial services are sometimes treated separately).

Capital goods

Also called **industrial marketing**, these are goods that will be used to make other goods and services such as machinery, equipment and tools. Raw material marketing is also part of industrial marketing. Marketing in each type of market will be very different. Industrial marketing, for example, relies heavily on the personal approach and may be linked to the availability of finance.

Market segmentation

Although, obviously, cat owners are the people who buy cat food, there are many different types of cat owner. The market can be broken down into many different segments or parts – young, old, rich, poor, those wanting cheap cat food, those wanting expensive cat food, those wanting environmentally friendly cat food, and so on.

Markets are segmented by:

- **geography:** tastes and wants will differ in different parts or regions of a country, or internationally.
- **ethnography:** tastes and wants will differ amongst different racial and religious groups.
- **behavioural considerations:** why does someone buy a product (because it is functional, glamorous, colourful, cheap, expensive etc.)? Will they buy it again (repeat purchases)? Why?
- **demography:** the size, structure and trends in population will affect tastes and wants. In the 1960s Britain had a young population, and marketing was therefore aimed at young people's clothes, music, entertainment etc. Britain now has an ageing population. The structure of population may change in other ways, for example, there are many more divorcees and many more single parents than ever before.
- **socio-economic:** usually by household and based on the occupation of the head of the household.

Some of these characteristics can be linked – geo-demography, for example, links population characteristics with geographic areas. Often the marketing trick is to be able to identify or predict the trend in a particular market – the direction that a market is taking – before it actually happens.

Market analysis and research

Class	Group	Typically
1	A	professionals e.g. doctors, judges
2	B	managers, technical and executive e.g. directors, accountants
3	C1	supervisory and clerical (non manual) e.g. secretaries, salespeople
3	C2	skilled manual e.g. electrician, plumber
4	D	semi-skilled manual e.g. packers, assembly line workers
5	E	unskilled manual and low income groups – e.g. labourers, pensioners, students

Table of socio-economic groups. C1, C2 and D comprise almost three quarters of the population and so are the most heavily targeted sector.

Add these points to your Mind Map. Don't forget to use word pictures where they will help, for example:

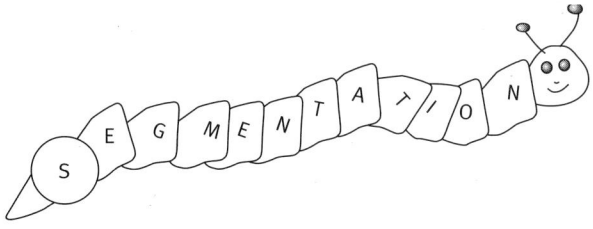

Target market

Having analysed the market, a firm should then decide which part or parts of the market it is going to target and ensure that the advertising, promotion and product features will appeal to that market. A firm may concentrate on one particular segment of the market – Mothercare is an obvious example of this – or decide to differentiate its products so that it reaches as many segments as possible. For example, look at the range of Cadbury's chocolate products – from Smarties to expensive boxed chocolates.

Market share

A firm's market share is usually measured as a percentage of sales value (Felix cat food has approximately 20% of the market, worth over £100 million). Having the largest market share may mean that your product is a brand leader. This is the product most likely to be stocked and therefore bought – think of the first brand that comes to mind in markets such as crisps, tomato sauce, ice cream, chocolate and satellite broadcasting.

Market domination

Market domination is measured by the size of the next biggest competitor to the leading player. Walmart, the American grocery chain had sales revenues of $139.2 billion in 1998; its next biggest rival in the world market (Metro AG of Germany) just $49.1 billion. The market can also be divided into international areas – leading grocery retailers in a much more closely contested market in the UK are Tesco ($27.2 billion), Safeway ($24.5 billion) and Sainsbury's ($24.1 billion).

Market research

This is the collection of information from existing and potential consumers. Its accuracy is of paramount importance and yet it can never be completely accurate as companies can't ask all their customers – and customers do not have to answer questions truthfully!

Research will be either:

- **Primary research:** collecting information that has not been collected before. This may also be called field research (speaking to consumers 'in the field', i.e. in their natural habitat, be it at home, work or out shopping.

- **Secondary research:** using information that is already published and available in one format or another. This is also termed desk research for the obvious reason that a great deal of it can be done whilst sitting at a desk.

Primary research

Researchers need to structure primary research carefully in an attempt to get the most accurate information possible. There are five main parts to their research:

Who do we ask?

A firm can target it's existing consumers through devices such as questionnaires in guarantees and competitions. It can target potential customers through a variety of sampling techniques.

How many people do we ask?

A firm will recognise that it cannot question the whole of its market and will therefore try to question a cross section that will accurately reflect the make-up of the market. Think of the ingredients that go into making a

Marketing

cake. If you take a slice of the cake then it is a fair bet that the slice contains equal proportions of the ingredients. Different types of slice can be taken, for example:

- **random sample:** each member of a population has an equal chance of being sampled. This is difficult, slow and expensive but can be accurate if the sample is large enough.
- **stratified sample:** asking only those in a particular stratum or level of a population. They may be identified by characteristics such as age, race, shared interests. For example, 'cat owners would be a stratified sample.
- **stratified random sample:** as long as everyone in the stratum fulfils the requirement (e.g. 'cat owner') then a random sample can be taken.
- **quota sample:** the population is defined by segments and the sample would reflect the size of each segment. If 52% of the population was female, then 52% of the quota sample should be female.
- **targeted sample:** sometimes called a cluster sample. This generally means that it is targeted at a particular geographical area; postcodes and commercial TV franchise areas may be used.

What do we ask them?

The types of question asked may often affect the answer given. Questions can be 'loaded' towards a particular answer. Questionnaire setters need to be careful that they do not build bias into a question. Questions may be

- **open:** used for qualitative answers
- **order of preference:** e.g. 'put the following into order of preference . . .'
- **closed:** multiple-choice type questions
- **Boolean:** a specialised form of closed question where if one answer is correct, the other must be incorrect ('yes/no' or 'male/female' are the most common).

How do we ask them?

The situation in which questions are asked will also affect the likelihood of accurate and honest answers. Questions may be asked:

- **Face-to-face:** either in a focus group, tasting and testing, or by being approached by an interviewer
- **Telephone:** increasingly popular but with low response rates

- **Fill in yourself:** delivering a form and either collecting it or encouraging the respondent to return it (perhaps with special offers or competition entries).

Response rates measure the number of people who actually respond, or complete, the questionnaire. Response rates to face-to-face 'street' surveys are highest. It is important to the researcher to achieve a high response rate as this makes the survey easier and cheaper to conduct.

Who is the information for?

The information may be required in a particular format; researchers need to ensure that, when designing a questionnaire, the answers can be delivered in that format.

> **FACTFILE**
>
> The Oxo advertisement featuring a family and Oxo gravy, which ran from 1983 onwards, did not lead to significant increases in sales of Oxo but did lead to increases in sales of pre-packed 'TV' dinners. Qualitative research could be used to find out where the appeal of the advertisement lay and why it should have this effect.

Quality or quantity?

Qualitative research seeks in-depth answers and is conducted through focus groups – a small cross-section of a firm's market divided into groups of five or six – or interviews with consumers. Qualitative research will not produce statistics but opinions. People who conduct qualitative research are often highly trained so that they can not only record the answers but also interpret them.

Quantitative research will produce statistics and percentages of the nature of '42% bought product X because . . .'. Quantitative research is easier to analyse and can reach a much larger proportion of a market than qualitative research. However, it has a tendency to be superficial and can be misleading if not carefully handled.

Secondary research

Secondary research has been previously published or made available. Published resources may be:

- **internal:** the firm's own records and internal reports

Market analysis and research

> **FACTFILE**
>
> **The cherry problem**
>
> If you have ever eaten cherry cake you will be aware of the cherry problem. One slice will have many cherries and another none at all! This serves to illustrate the fact that in some cases there may be an uneven distribution – there could be 'clusters' of consumers who will bias quantitative research. A firm should use qualitative research as well so that it gets a full picture of the market.

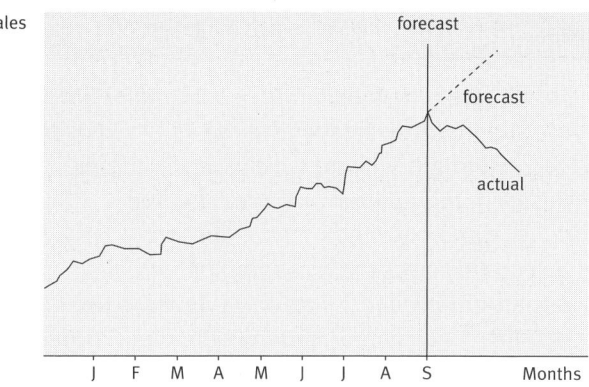

- **external:** information collected or collated by other organisations (such as the National Census information, information provided by the Office of National Statistics or information published in newspapers and magazines, especially trade publications).

Secondary data suffers from a number of problems. It may be:

- expensive
- not completely relevant by not addressing exactly the questions you want answering
- out-of-date, e.g. this year's company report is based on last years figures; the Census takes place every ten years
- inaccurate or incomplete
- in the wrong format for the firm's needs

Limitations

Market research can be wildly inaccurate. Often, large-scale polls, for instance predicting the win by one political party or another, will be inaccurate. You need to realise that people do not always want to give their right opinion or be honest.

Statistical techniques can also be misleading, for example, forecasting trends. The forecast from the graph on this page would be a continued rise. What actually happened was a fall. Further details on handling statistics are included in Chapter 9 on forecasting.

> **TEST YOURSELF**
>
> **AS**
>
> 1. Can you define what is meant by segmentation?
> 2. Can you describe how a market may be segmented?
> 3. Can you explain why it is important for a firm to know which segments it is targeting?
>
> **A2**
>
> 1. Why is accurate market research important to a firm?
> 2. Outline the different types of market research.
> 3. Can you recommend which type of market research might be appropriate for which type of firm or for collecting which type of information?

> **CHECKLIST**
>
> ✓ Markets analysis involves firms finding out about their market in terms of size, structure and position.
> ✓ Markets are divided into separate segments.
> ✓ Market research is used to find consumer opinion.
> ✓ Market research may be qualitative or quantitative.

Marketing

Sample questions and answers

Tate & Lyle is a global group whose major products are sugar and sweeteners. In the early 1990s they decided to expand into developing countries. Research information indicated that the consumption of sugar rises as income rises. What do you think was the reasoning behind this decision? How might Tate and Lyle make use of market research information in their new target markets?

1. The likely reasoning behind the decision is:
   - main markets in the developed world are maturing
   - little opportunity for growth in main markets
   - developing countries offer potential for developing markets
2. Market research information used will be:
   - primary – collecting original information
   - secondary – using published information and figures
   - quantitative – producing statistics and analysis
   - qualitative – will produce in-depth answers and opinions
3. Analysis of the market show sugar consumption rises as income rises. Draw the graph to show this. Explain what it means in terms of income elasticity.

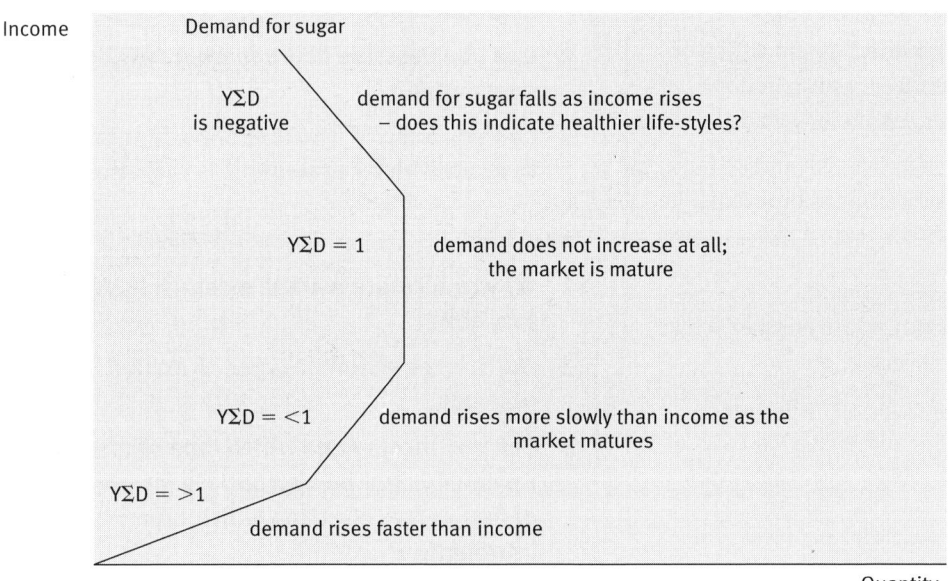

The reaction of demand for sugar as incomes rise

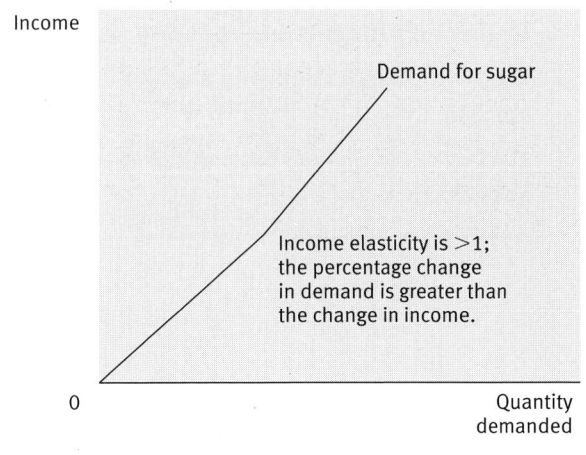

4. The developed world shows an income elasticity of 1 or negative. Demand in developing countries is at the first stage, when sugar may be considered a 'luxury' good.
5. Tate and Lyle will target their product according to the market research analysis. This probably means that sugar and sweeteners will be positioned as an attainable luxury to that segment of the market that has some excess income.

Market analysis and research

Mind Map

Finish off your Mind Map by adding all the rest of the points mentioned. Don't forget to use word pictures (like 'segmentation') where appropriate. An example of a completed Mind Map has been given below to help you.

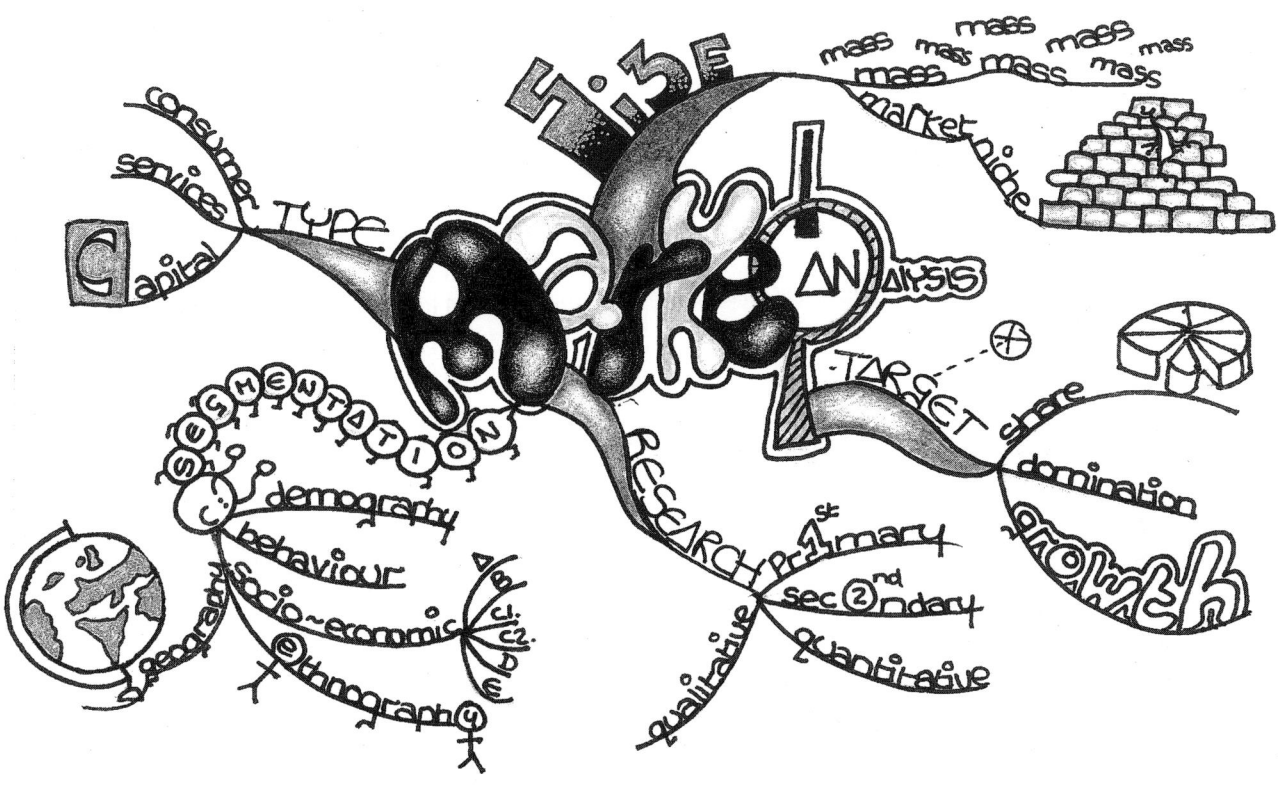

Summary

- Market analysis is essential for successful business decision-making.
- Firms need to know the size and structure of their market and their position in it.
- Firms tend to operate in one of three markets – consumer goods, services or capital goods.
- Markets are segmented so that firms can target particular segments.
- Market research is designed to let firms know what consumers and potential consumers think of their products.
- Market research may be primary or secondary, qualitative or quantitative.
- Market research is not always accurate; there is the possibility of bias, inaccurate information and inaccurate interpretation.

Chapter 8: Marketing planning

PREVIEW

- ✓ The marketing mix is the mixture of elements that make up a marketing 'package'. It is generally considered to have four major parts – the so-called Four Ps – price, product, promotion and place – see following chapters.
- ✓ You need to be able to put the elements of the marketing mix into context – different markets and different products require different mixes.
- ✓ You should be able to advise a given firm as to the structure of its marketing mix in a given situation.
- ✓ Marketing planning is how a firm decides on marketing objectives and on the best ways to achieve them.
- ✓ Planning will be based on various analyses and interpretations of the firm's products and of the market(s) within which it operates.
- ✓ You should be able to apply these analyses to given situations and make recommendations based on them.
- ✓ You need to know how to handle and interpret statistical data collected.
- ✓ See if you can answer at least four of the following five questions before reading the rest of the chapter.

Questions

1. Can you define what marketing planning is and outline what would be the contents of a marketing plan?
2. Can you outline how different types of objectives might be defined according to the time it takes to achieve them?
3. Can you explain how a firm might decide at what level to set its budget?
4. Can you explain what is meant by product portfolio analysis?
5. Can you complete this Boston matrix?

	High market share	Low market share
High market growth		
Low market growth		

Check your answers before reading the rest of the chapter. Try answering the questions again when you've finished the chapter.

Mind Map

Start a Mind Map similar to the one shown here. Put a central image of your own in the middle. This image works for me, as it reminds me that planning is a step-by-step process. You need to draw an image that works for you! The first 'legs' of the Mind Map have been started for you. Add points to your map as you work through the chapter. At the end of the chapter is an example of what a finished Mind Map might look like. Don't forget, you can – and should – use a different colour for each leg and at least three colours for your central image.

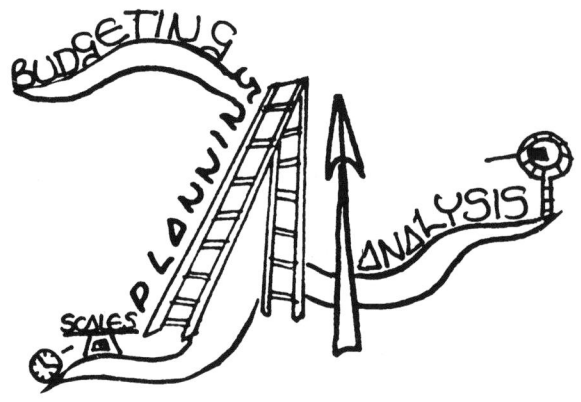

Definition

Marketing planning is when a firm produces an outline of marketing activities based on the decisions they have taken about the marketing mix. It is designed to show what sort of a mix of pricing, products, distribution and advertising and promotion will be the most successful for the business.

The marketing plan will be bound up with the company strategy, aims and objectives and will follow a similar planning cycle:

decide on objective → collect and analyse information → develop appropriate strategy → execute plans → measure and evaluate outcomes → set new objectives

Marketing plan

A marketing plan will contain the following elements: overview; corporate objectives, marketing objectives and their link to corporate objectives; strategies; budgets.

Marketing planning

These may be stated as:

where we are; where we would like to be as a company; how our marketing will get us there; what funding we are going to need (funding will be planned through a budget for marketing)

Time limitations

Part of the objective set will be a time limitation for its achievement. This will be linked to the type of management objective which is sought:

- **Strategic objectives** are long-term goals that involve major changes, e.g. whether or not to launch a new product on to the market.
- **Tactical objectives** are medium-term targets, e.g. promoting or advertising a particular product in order to increase sales to particular levels.
- **Operational objectives** are short-term, day-to-day objectives.

Budgeting

Analysis of product position will determine which brands or products will receive the heaviest budget. Budgets may also be set by looking at what competitors are spending. The most common ways of setting marketing budgets are:

Competitor parity

This means seeing what the competition is spending on marketing and match it. This is flawed in three major ways:

1. It is not always possible to accurately measure what competitors are spending.
2. It is unlikely that you are dealing in exactly the same product at exactly the same stage of life and in exactly the same market as your competitor. Matching their expenditure may thus be inappropriate.
3. Such expenditure can lead to 'war spending'. As your competitor sees his outlay matched, he increases expenditure. You follow suit.

Sales related

As sales increase, the amount of allowable expenditure – usually measured as a percentage of sales – increases in line with the sales increase.

Incremental

This means seeing what was spent in the previous time period and add an increment to it. The major flaw with this type of budgeting is that it does not take into account the dynamic nature of marketing and does not allow for switches in expenditure as circumstances dictate.

A small company may have little choice but to budget, not on the basis of what would be most effective, but on the basis of what they can actually afford. In a larger company there may be a number of departments or sectors, each of which has a budget – each needs to decide how to spend it effectively. This will depend on what the objective is and at what stage in the product life cycle the product is at.

- A new product in a competitive market, at the beginning of its life cycle, will require heavy marketing expenditure in order to launch it and establish a foothold in the market. Examples might include new models of cars.
- A new product in a 'blue sky' market – an area where there is little or no competition, may require very little marketing expenditure. A car that ran on water, for example, would require little marketing.
- Leading brands, particularly market leaders, require 'top up' advertising in order to keep the product in the consumers mind. Sponsorship, for example, will be used to confirm brand names and values. They may require extra marketing expenditure if a competitor threatens. These brands are often 'cash cows' (see the Boston matrix on page 52). An example might be Heinz tomato ketchup or Kraft cheese slices.
- Heavy marketing expenditure may be required when attempting to extend a product life cycle in order to introduce consumers to the new, improved or altered aspects of the product.
- In some markets heavy marketing expenditure is always required. Markets where there are a few dominant firms engage in non price competition, competing using promotion, competitions and public relations. A good example is the soap powder market in the UK.

FACTFILE

Polo (Nestlé's market leader countline mint) lost its market leadership position in 1992 to Trebor Extra Strong Mints. The response from Nestlé was to launch a diversified range of Polo products (extra strong, spearmint, sugar-free) and re-launch its core product as Original Polo. Within two years, Polo regained its market leadership with 19.6% of the market.

Marketing

Analysis

There are a variety of analyses, suggested by different analysts and business schools, to help a firm with its marketing planning. Basically they are all ways of collecting information on how well your product or range of products is doing in its chosen market. A product audit will show what contribution each product is making to costs and to profit, what market share each product has and whether it is growing or shrinking, the position of the product on the product life cycle and what action may need to be taken. The major ways of analysing markets and product positions are:

Product portfolio analysis

There a number of different ways in which a firm can analyse the range of products (its portfolio) that it offers and therefore make decisions about what sort of marketing mix is needed.

Perceptual map

A perceptual map of products shows where each is positioned in the market and indicates whether there are gaps in a firms portfolios which might be filled.

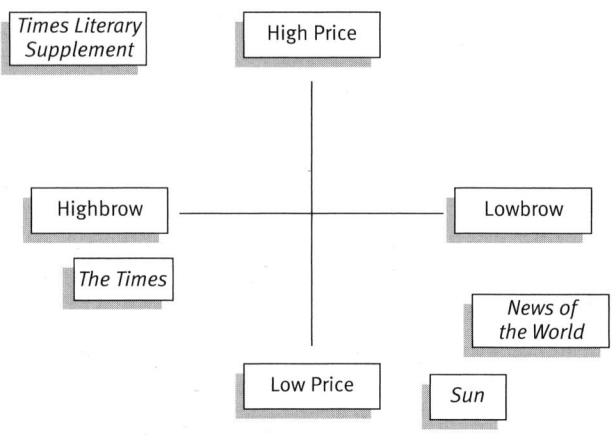

This diagram shows the way in which the news titles owned by News International might be perceived. There is a gap in this portfolio for a title which is expensive but has mass market appeal — perhaps a mass market 'glossy' might fill the bill.

Boston matrix

	High market share	Low market share
High market growth	stars	problem children
Low market growth	cash cows	dogs

The Boston matrix is used to plot the percentage of the market enjoyed by each product in a firm's portfolio against the type of market that it is in. It allows a firm to see which products are achieving their potential and which may need to be supported or divested. The four possibilities are:

- **stars:** have a high market share in a fast-growing market – they may have been first into a blue sky market and will need high marketing expenditure to keep them competitive as new entrants come into the market
- **problem children or question marks:** these products have a small market share of a fast-growing market; they could be the competitors that are trying to gain a foothold in a blue sky market
- **cash cows:** these have a large market share of a mature or slow-growing market; they are usually established product lines which need little marketing expenditure – often they are market leaders – and which produce cash that can be used to support other products
- **dogs:** these are products with a small share of a slow-growing market; they probably cost more than they are worth to maintain

Marketing managers can choose whether to keep or lose each product (hold or divest) and how to use the cash generated by successful products. The most usual tactics will be to:

- keep the cows, using the cash to support other products (also known as milking the cows)
- try to turn the stars into cows (holding the stars) by using cash cow money
- try to turn the problem children into stars by using cash cow money (building the problem children)
- lose the dogs – if you can think of a 'whatever happened to . . . ?' product, you have probably identified a dog (divesting the dogs)

FACTFILE

Cadbury Schweppes have a cash cow in Cadbury's Dairy Milk – the market leader in the mature market for chocolate. The confectionery market as a whole, however, has rapidly increased, growing by 20% between 1992 and 1997 so Cadbury's felt able to launch a star – the Yowie – to introduce children to Cadbury's chocolate. Had it failed, it could have been regarded as a problem child and re-launched – an expensive venture. Had it completely failed, it would have been regarded as a dog and divested.

Marketing planning

Ansoff matrix

lowest risk	Existing products	New products
Existing markets	market penetration	product development
New markets	market development	diversification
		highest risk

This matrix plots how safe or risky various marketing objectives are and can be used to judge the likelihood of success.

SWOT analysis

This looks at the factors that might affect the success or failure of a marketing strategy. The internal factors – strengths and weaknesses – of the firm and the external factors – opportunities and threats – which face it (see Chapter 1).

Consumer profiles

As well as market positioning and analysis, firms need an idea of the type of consumer that they are targeting. A consumer profile can be built from statistics collected on consumers. How many are female? How many are in a particular income bracket? Companies may build a picture of their 'ideal' consumer – e.g. a 28-year-old single professional female – and target marketing at them. Some groups are well enough recognised to have their own abbreviations – e.g. DINKYS are 'Double Income No Kids Yet' couples.

FACTFILE

Marketing expenditure isn't just advertising; it includes all expenditure on the marketing mix. Advertising and promotion may be a large part of this but research and development, market research, design, packaging, promotion and distribution are all included.

CHECKLIST

Marketing planning is . . .
- ✓ Collecting and interpreting market information.
- ✓ Deciding what marketing activities to undertake after analysing the market.
- ✓ Deciding on a particular marketing mix.
- ✓ Deciding on budgets and time scales.

The main tools used are . . .
- ✓ Market analysis such as the Boston Matrix.
- ✓ Consumer profiles.
- ✓ Internal and external market information.
- ✓ Statistical analysis.

TEST YOURSELF

Use your Mind Map to see if you can answer the following questions.

AS

1. List the main headings that you would find in a marketing plan.
2. Explain what is meant by price discrimination.
3. What tools could a firm use to analyse its market?

A2

1. What types of budgeting might a marketing manager use? Which is likely to be most effective?
2. How and why would a firm set prices that were not at market equilibrium?
3. Why would a firm use product portfolio analysis?

Mind Map

Finish off your Mind Map by adding all the rest of the points mentioned. Don't forget to use word pictures where appropriate. A completed Mind Map has been given on page 54 to help you.

Marketing

Sample question and answer

How useful is the Boston matrix in evaluating where marketing expenditure may be targeted?

1. Define your terms. What is the Boston matrix; why is it used?
   The Boston matrix is used to plot the percentage of the market each product in a firm's portfolio has against the type of market that it is in. It is used by firms to see which products are doing well and should be kept; which can be grown and which divested.

	High market share	Low market share
High market growth	stars	problem children
Low market growth	cash cows	dogs

   The four possibilities are:
   - stars: have a high market share in a fast-growing market
   - problem children or question marks: have a small market share of a fast-growing market
   - cash cows: have a large market share of a mature or slow-growing market
   - dogs: have a small share of a slow-growing market

2. The most usual tactics of a marketing manager will be to:
   - keep the cows, using the cash to support other products
   - hold the stars (try to turn them into cows by using cash cow money)
   - build the problem children try to turn them into stars by using cash cow money)
   - lose the dogs (divesting)

3. Decide how useful each of these sections is. Can products really be split down so simply? Can you think of an example for each type of product?

4. Conclusion. If the Boston matrix works – if these descriptions are fair – then it is a good tool for seeing where to target marketing expenditure.
   However – it may well be flawed in the simplicity of its approach and managers would be well advised to use other methods as well.

Summary

- Marketing planning is how a firm decides on marketing objectives and on the best ways to achieve them.
- Planning is based on various analyses and interpretations of the market.
- The marketing plan follows a similar planning cycle to that for corporate strategy and will be closely linked to the firm's corporate objectives.
- Accurate budgeting is a vital element of planning.
- Product portfolio analysis looks at the position of a product relative to its market and its competitors.
- The Boston Matrix is a common way of analysing portfolios.
- Marketing managers need to be able to understand and interpret statistical information.

Forecasting and predicting — CHAPTER 9

PREVIEW

- Business will use statistical and mathematical techniques in order to make sense of figures collected. These figures may be internal or external information but can all be useful in forecasting and predicting likely sales and sales patterns for the future.
- Accurate forecasting enables firms to gear production at the right level and in the right direction, thus increasing efficiency and lowering costs.
- Inaccurate prediction can mean disaster for a firm.
- You will need to know how a firm collects information, how it tries to eliminate errors in that information and how it tries to use that information to forecast.
- You will need to be able to use simple statistical techniques and explain how they are applied to help in forecasting.
- You need to be able to use mathematical techniques such as the measurement of elasticity.
- See if you can answer at least four of these five questions before continuing with the rest of the chapter.

Questions

1. Can you explain why a firm might want to forecast?
2. Can you outline what a firm might want to forecast?
3. Can you describe the methods that might be used by a firm to make forecasts?
4. What is meant by a measure of central tendency?
5. What is measured by statistical variance?

Check your answers before reading the rest of the chapter. Try answering the questions again when you've finished the chapter.

Mind Map

Start a Mind Map similar to the one shown here. Put a central image of your own in the middle. This image works for me – it reminds me that statistics are used to see into the future. You need to draw an image that works for you! The first 'legs' of the Mind Map have been started for you. Add points to your map as you work through the chapter. Don't forget, you can – and should – use colour!

Definition

Forecasting is an attempt by a business to estimate future levels, for example of sales, or to estimate changes in demand caused by changes in other factors.

Methods

- **Probability:** predicting future events on the basis of past ones
- **Extrapolation:** projecting a trend from existing information
- **Delphi technique:** named after the oracle at Delphi, where a priestess predicted the future; the Delphi technique uses panels of experts to forecast long-term trends

Sources of information

- **Internal:** sales, cost and production figures
- **External:** market research and sales research

Statistics

Marketing managers need to be able to understand and interpret statistical information before coming to decisions. The following analysis is based on one example question.

Example question: How many of Brand X do you buy in a week?

Twelve respondents said:

1 2 9 4 1 2 3 1 2 1 4 0

Marketing

Much of the information that is collected and used by a firm for forecasting will be in the form of statistics. You need to have a reasonable understanding of how such statistics are interpreted. The most commonly used method is to see what the 'average' response was, also called the measure of 'central tendency'. There are a number of ways to take this:

Mean

This is an arithmetical average – in the example above it is the total number bought (30) divided by the number of responses (12): 30 ÷ 12 = 2.5 Knowing that he is selling an average of two to three per customer per week allows the shopkeeper to forecast what stock he needs.

Median

This is the value which divides the distribution into a 'top half' and a 'bottom half'. If the responses are put in order, it is the value which falls in the middle. In this case, with an even number of responses, the sixth unit. Thus:

0 1 1 1 1 2 2 2 3 4 4 9

Mode

This is the most commonly occurring value, in this example '1'. This is a value which is important for anyone selling goods that need to be different for different people, e.g. how many size 12 dresses; how many red cars?

Range of distribution

The range shows the extremes of responses, in this case a range from 0 to 9. The most ever demanded will be 9, the least 0. A normal range of distribution will produce a graphed curve as shown below.

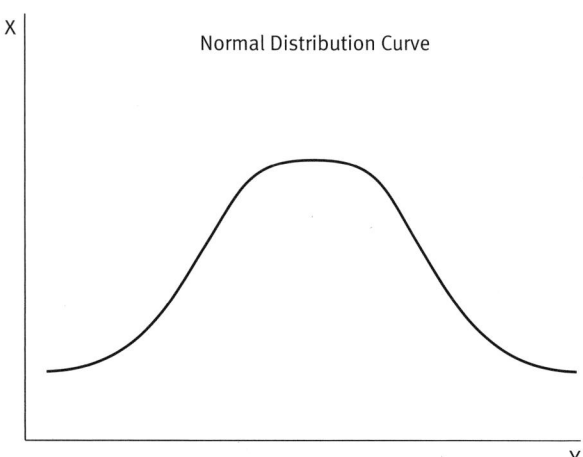

Normal Distribution Curve

As half the results are above the mean and half below, predictions can be made that responses are as likely to fall in one half as in the other. This curve is used to predict the probability of events.

Standard deviation

The standard deviation is a standardised measure of the distribution of data around the mean value; the higher the standard deviation, the more dispersed the results were, the lower the standard deviation, the more concentrated is the spread of results.

Inter-quartile range

Often there are extremes at either end of a range which are not statistically significant. These are discounted by taking the inter-quartile range – the values 25% from the top and the bottom of the range are used to describe this, in this case 1 and 4. Even more concentrated areas may also be used, half or semi-quartiles and deciles (tenths). Ranges can be further analysed by using variances and standard deviation.

Statistical variance

To remove the anomalies caused by there being minus and plus figures, variance is calculated by squaring the difference between the actual response and the mean. Thus in this example the recorded responses (a) are:

0 1 1 1 1 2 2 2 3 4 4 9

The mean is 2.5

a	a – mean (2.5)	(a – mean)^2
0	−2.5	6.25
1	−1.5	2.25
1	−1.5	2.25
1	−1.5	2.25
1	−1.5	2.25
2	−0.5	0.25
2	−0.5	0.25
2	−0.5	0.25
3	0.5	0.25
4	1.5	2.25
4	1.5	2.25
9	6.5	42.25
(must be) **0**		**63.00**

Variance is measured as the total of the squared differences over the number of responses: 63/12 = 5.25

The variance measures the dispersion of responses around the mean.

Standard deviation is the square root of the variance. In this example $\sqrt{5.25} = 2.29$.

Probability

In cases where there is a choice of only two alternatives, known as a Boolean case (see page 46) where one alternative must preclude the other (e.g. in 'yes/no' questions) then probabilities can be accurately worked out. The chances of a tossed coin landing either heads or tails is $50/50 = 0.5$. The odds are even. The odds on throwing a double six with two dice are much longer, giving a 1 in 21 possibility = a probability of 0.0047.

Correlation

Correlation is used to analyse the effect of one variable on another. It might, for instance, be used to plot advertising expenditure against sales. There are three possibilities

- **positive correlation:** as advertising expenditure increases, so do sales

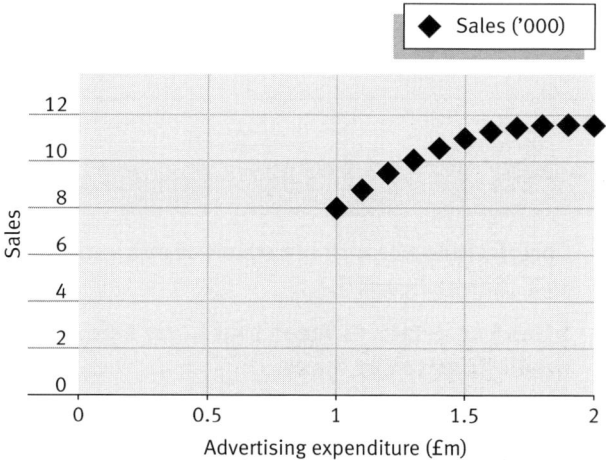

- **negative correlation:** as advertising expenditure increases, sales fall. This might be the desired effect on a competitor product.

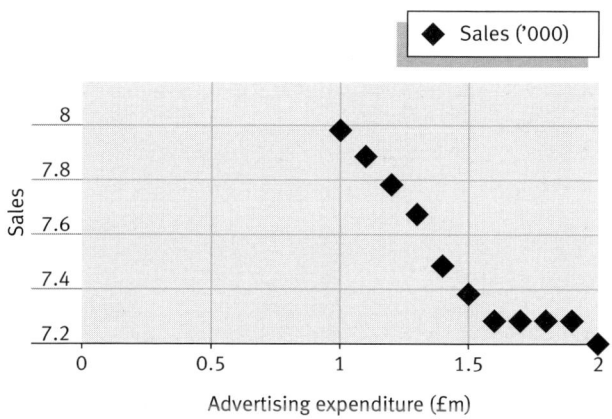

- **zero correlation:** there is no discernible relationship

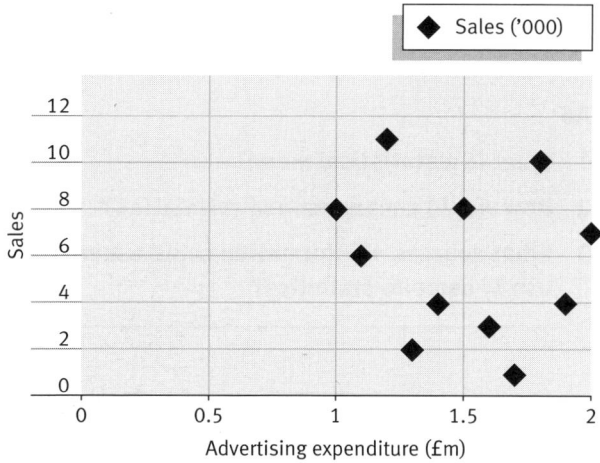

The line of best fit shows the relationship and can be extended or extrapolated in order to forecast future sales.

Confidence levels can be estimated from the closeness of the correlation and the line of best fit (or regression line). For example, a very high correlation, with the regression line extremely close to the points, might lead to a 95% level of confidence that further expenditure of £x would lead to further sales of £y.

Variance interpretation

The difference between forecast levels of sales, expenditure and profits and actual levels is called variance. This is not the same as statistical variance (showing dispersion) but is a term used by managers to see whether a particular factor is above or below forecast levels. It is covered in detail in Chapter 14 (management accounting).

- **Positive variances** show that a factor is doing better than predicted (more sales are being made than were forecast).
- **Negative variance** shows a failure (more expenditure is needed than was forecast).

Remember that a positive figure may show positive variance (actual profits are higher than predicted profits) or negative variance (actual costs are higher than predicted costs) depending on whether the difference is a good or bad thing for the business. Variances are only of use if analysed along with the other elements of the market – a fall in sales may be due to other external factors, for example.

Mind Map

Finish off your Mind Map by adding all the rest of the points mentioned. Don't forget to use word pictures where appropriate.

Marketing

TEST YOURSELF

Use your Mind Map to see if you can answer the following questions.

AS

1. What is a statistical mean?
2. How would a manager use correlation?
3. What sources of information could a manager use to compile statistics?

A2

1. How would a manager discount extremes at either end of a range?
2. Can you say what is the main problem with statistical analysis?
3. How could a scatter graph be used to forecast a trend?

Sample question and answer

State the methods a manager could use to forecast future sales levels. What problems might occur with such forecasts?

State the methods with associated problems:

1. Probability – predicting future events on the basis of past ones.
   If a particular sales drive or price variation caused a particular reaction in sales before; how probable is it that it will do so again?
   Could look at present correlations. Are they positive or negative? How strong is the correlation? What does the regression line look like?
   Problem: too many variables involved to be able to say exactly what causes what. Correlations may be weak.

2. Extrapolation – projecting a trend from existing information. Look at existing levels of sales and the factors which are contributing to them. Can the manager identify a trend? How likely is it to continue?
   Problem. The trend may not continue as forecast.

3. Delphi technique – buying in expertise. A group of experts all report separately to a central facilitator, who produces a report based on their predictions. They can then produce further forecasts using the report.
   Problem. Relying on opinion; only really useful for long-term predictions.

Summary

- Firms collect both internal and external information in the form of figures.
- Statistical analysis of these figures can be used to inform future planning.
- Probabilities can be used to make accurate forecasts based on past events.
- Extrapolation can be used to predict future levels from trends on current graphs.
- Correlations show the reaction of one variable to a change in another.
- Strong correlations mean that fairly safe predictions can be made.
- Experts can be used to make their own interpretation.
- All statistical analysis depends on the initial accuracy of the figures.

The marketing mix – price — CHAPTER 10

PREVIEW

- In this chapter we look at how price is decided in a market in theory and then at how sellers actually set their prices in order to achieve certain effects.
- You need to know the theory of price determination but to realise that theory is not always applicable and that there are different motives for setting prices.
- You need to be able to describe the different pricing methods and explain when they will be used.
- You should be able to recommend, in particular situations, which particular strategies are most appropriate and be able to give reasons for your choices.
- You need to be able to describe how responsive particular demands are to changes in price (price elasticity of demand) and why different goods and services respond in different ways.
- See if you can answer at least four of the following five questions before reading the rest of the chapter.

Questions

1. Give a definition of price.
2. Explain why the theoretical determination of price is of limited use to a business.
3. Explain what is meant by cost plus pricing.
4. Explain what is meant by marginal pricing.
5. Outline the difference between a price-taker and a price-maker.

Check your answers before reading the rest of the chapter. Try answering the questions again when you've finished the chapter.

Mind Map

Start a Mind Map similar to the one shown here. Put a central image of your own in the middle. This image works for me – it reminds me that there are many different types of prices. You need to draw an image that works for you! The first 'legs' of the Mind Map have been started for you. Add points to your map as you work through the chapter. Don't forget, you can – and should – use a different colour for each leg and at least three colours for your central image.

Definition

In any market there are buyers and sellers. When they agree on a transaction, price is the amount that the consumer decides they are willing to pay for a good or service and the amount that the seller decides that they are willing to accept.

Pricing in theory

Theoretically, all prices are determined by the interaction of supply and demand. Each consumer decides how much use or 'utility' they will gain from purchasing a product and equates that with price. The supplier decides what price they are willing to accept for a quantity supplied. In some countries, buyer and seller will haggle and bargain until both are satisfied at the price at which the good or service is to change hands. However, for many products, this system is untenable. Try walking into your corner shop on your way to school or college and haggling with the shopkeeper over the price of a bag of crisps!

Consumers and suppliers thus accept the 'market price'. However, many businesses will find it advantageous to set prices at a different level.

Most prices are 'consumer led' to some degree. This means that a good or service will only be considered for purchase if it falls within a particular price range. Consumers have an idea of what they think things should cost and of what they are worth to them. A diamond engagement ring priced at £2.50 would find few takers – consumers would be convinced that it was not worth much more. One priced at £25,000, however, will be out of the price range of most consumers. Opportunity cost is an important facet in determining whether consumers will or won't buy.

Marketing

> **FACTFILE**
>
> Jewellers who have tried to clear stock by lowering prices can sometimes have more success by raising them as people equate price with value!
>
> A detailed treatment of the interaction of supply and demand to set market prices is given in Chapter 4.

Pricing in practice

In practice, prices are set by firms according to cost, competition or the current marketing needs of the business.

Cost-based prices are:

- **cost-plus pricing:** the business adds up the various costs of making the product and then adds on a percentage of 'mark-up' for profit. The price is the cost of making the product plus the profit. This not as easy as it sounds when many products are involved or, as is usual, many different costs.
- **marginal pricing:** marginal or contribution pricing is where a firm calculates price so that it will cover the variable costs of production and make a contribution to fixed costs. Once fixed costs (overheads) are covered, the product then makes a contribution to profits. Using marginal pricing, firms can see how well each product that it produces is doing and alter strategy accordingly.

> **FACTFILE**
>
> Price-takers are those firms in a market where there is a lot of competition so that no one firm can affect the market price. Such firms can only compete effectively by using non-price competition. Price-makers are those firms which are large enough to set the price in their market. The price of coffee, for example, is 'made' or set by the price of Brazilian coffee due to their market dominating position.

Competition-based prices are:

- **market price:** the firm cannot affect price so must accept that set by the market; this may be the same for all firms in the market – competitive price-takers – or due to price being set by a dominant firm – price leadership.
- **competitive price:** in a market where products are very similar and there is a lot of competition, firms will not be able to charge significantly more or significantly less than market rivals. The price they charge will therefore be very close to that charged by their rivals and competition will tend to be 'non-price' competition (see below).
- **loss leaders:** a business may be prepared to make a loss on an item in order to attract buyers into its market; it can only do this if it has the resources – the financial muscle – to be able to stand the losses for the period of time necessary for it to achieve its objectives. Loss leaders are also used by firms who expect customers to return for other purchases. For example, a cable TV broadcaster might give set top boxes knowing that further purchases of entertainment channels will recoup their losses. Often it is better to give such goods away than to sell them extremely cheaply to avoid people equating price with value.

Prices based on the marketing needs of the business are:

- **creaming or skimming:** a new product that is seen as a luxury item may be introduced to the market at an initial high price in order to take advantage of that segment of the market that is willing to pay to be 'the first' with the product. Innovations such as camcorders, mobile telephones and computers were all initially launched at a high price which later fell as the market expanded.
- **penetration price:** this is a price that is set lower than that of competitors so that a firm can gain a foothold in the market. A telephone company, for example, may offer discounts and low prices to new customers. Even though these may be short-term, and price advantages may be eroded, customers may stay loyal to the company. There is a certain amount of inertia in markets such as those for banking, building societies, gas, water, electricity and telecommunications with people reluctant to move from one service provider to another. Thus, once a business has established a market share through penetration pricing, they are likely to keep it.
- **psychological point pricing:** this is a price tactic whereby firms try to make goods and services sound like they are cheaper than they are, e.g. £99.99 sounds like a lot less than £100. You will notice that many prices finish in .99.
- **promotional pricing:** usually short-term pricing strategies to increase sales in the short-term. Special offers, sales, discounts etc. are all promotional prices. Often they are used in order to clear space for new stock.

The marketing mix – price

- **undercutting:** also called predatory or destroyer pricing. A firm deliberately undercuts a rival's price with the intention of driving that rival out of business. The success or failure of the strategy depends on which firm can best carry the losses.

Price elasticity of demand:

- This measures the responsiveness of demand to a change in price and is extremely important to a business contemplating a price change. If a small change in price causes a large change in demand then the good is price elastic; if a large change in price causes a small change in demand then the good is price inelastic.
- One way for a firm to judge whether demand is elastic or inelastic over a particular price range is to see what happens to total revenue if price is reduced. If a reduction in price leads to an increase in total revenue, the good is price elastic – consumers have switched to it from alternatives.

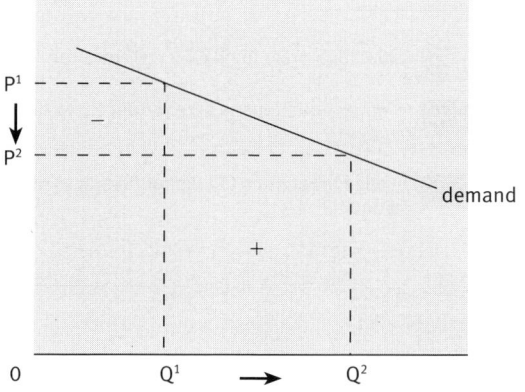

- If a reduction in price leads to a decrease in total revenue, the good is price inelastic (to increase revenue, this producer needs to increase price).

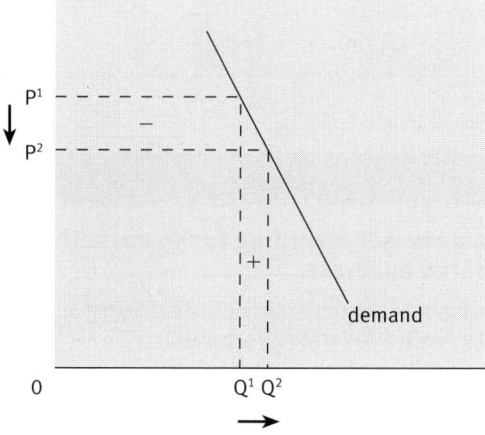

Other elasticities

Income elasticity of demand is the responsiveness of demand to a change in income. Cross elasticity of demand is the responsiveness of demand to a change in the price of another good – a substitute or complement.

FACTFILE

Price discrimination is where a firm can charge two different prices for the same good or service. This is only possible if there are two different markets – separated in some way – and if the cheaper priced market is not able to resell to the more expensively priced one. Separation may be by time ('off peak' and 'peak' charges); by geography (Birmingham is charged less for water than Cardiff) or by targeting specific markets (student railcards, pensioners bus travel etc.).

New or existing?

Some of these pricing strategies are more useful for existing products, some for the introduction of new products.

Existing products	New products
psychological point	loss leaders
promotional	creaming
undercutting	penetration
competitive	psychological point
market	

FACTFILE

Markets where a few firms dominate are called oligopolies. In extreme cases where there are only two firms, they are called duopolies. One duopoly in the UK is that for soap powder and related products where the two firms that dominate the market are Lever Brothers and Procter and Gamble.

These firms cannot compete using price so therefore use non-price competition – a range of differentiated products, promotions and competitions, discounts and joint marketing all feature in their competition. If two or more firms in the same market agree to keep prices high, this is called a cartel: in most countries such price agreements are illegal. (OPEC, the Organisation of Petroleum Exporting Companies ran a cartel to fix the price of crude oil in the late seventies and eighties).

Marketing

CHECKLIST

✓ Market price is determined by supply and demand.
✓ Some firms can influence price.
✓ Prices can be set on the basis of costs, competition and marketing needs.
✓ Different prices can be charged in different markets.
✓ Make sure that these points have been added to your Mind Map.

Mind Map

Finish off your Mind Map by adding all the rest of the points mentioned. Don't forget to use word pictures where appropriate.

TEST YOURSELF

Use your Mind Map to see if you can answer the following questions.

AS

1. Explain how demand and supply determine price.
2. Can you define marginal pricing?
3. What sort of market structure is likely to have price-takers in it?

A2

1. What is the importance of price elasticity of demand to a firm when setting prices?
2. What is price leadership? Who benefits from it?
3. Why might a firm use a loss leader?

Sample question and answer

FonesFirst has developed a mobile phone that can be worn on the wrist. It is technologically more advanced than any other mobile on the market. Suggest and explain the pricing strategies that they might use. What benefits could they gain from price discrimination?

1. This is a new and technologically innovative product. The most probable strategy will be creaming i.e. charging an initial high price in order to take that part of the market that is willing to pay this price. The diagram below shows what might happen if they adopt this strategy. As competition enters the market, prices fall, but the firm has already gained a large slice of revenue at a high price.
2. An alternative would be penetration pricing – a price set below the level of rival products if they feel that they would like to take an immediate market share.
3. Another alternative would be to use a promotion pricing. This would mean charging a lower price to gain sales. This might be a better policy to use once the product is established,
4. Price discrimination is where a firm can charge two different prices for the same good or service. This is only possible if there are two different markets which are separated in some way. If this firm could sell the phone to its London customers at a higher price than its Leeds customers by artificially keeping the markets apart and preventing the London customers buying from Leeds, then it could benefit. It is unlikely that this firm could discriminate in sales. They could, however, discriminate in tariffs by charging a cheap rate and a premium rate.

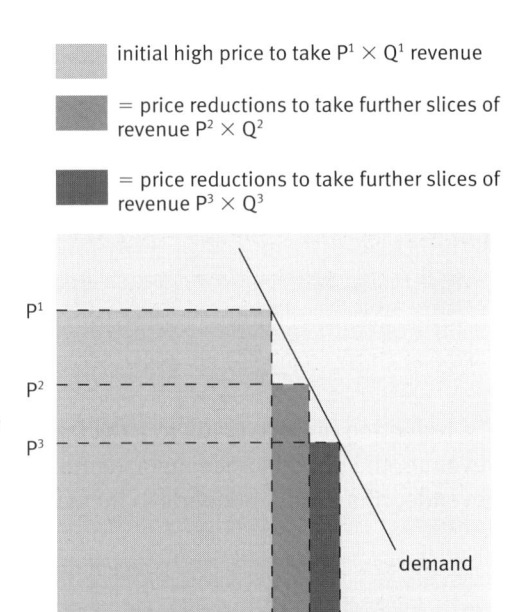

initial high price to take $P^1 \times Q^1$ revenue

= price reductions to take further slices of revenue $P^2 \times Q^2$

= price reductions to take further slices of revenue $P^3 \times Q^3$

Summary

- Market price is determined by the operation of supply and demand.
- Some businesses can control market price (price-makers); others cannot (price-takers).
- Many businesses operate pricing strategies which mean that they do not set price at the market price.
- Prices may be based on cost considerations.
- Prices may be set in order to take account of competition.
- Prices may be set according to the marketing needs of the business.
- Some prices are more useful for existing products, some for new products.
- Price discrimination is where firms can separate markets and charge different prices for the same good or service.
- Price elasticity of demand – the responsiveness of demand to a change in price – is an important factor when businesses are considering changing prices.

The marketing mix – product CHAPTER 11

> **PREVIEW**
>
> - In this chapter you will learn about another element of the marketing mix – the good or service produced by a firm.
> - You need to know how a firm analyses the range and variety of products that it produces, how it develops new products and how it might expect a product to be introduced, grow and decline. You will need to know the product life cycle and be able to relate this to other models such as the Boston matrix and Ansoff's matrix.
> - You need to realise that the information is of little use in itself, but is part of a range of information and tools.
> - Remember the skill of synthesis. The product is part of the 'Four Ps' and therefore part of overall strategy. You will need to draw from several areas of the specification in order to answer questions fully.
> - See if you can answer at least four of these five questions before continuing with the rest of the chapter.

> **Questions**
>
> 1 Outline the different forms that a product might take.
> 2 Explain the difference between core, actual and augmented product values.
> 3 Describe a normal product life cycle.
> 4 Discuss different types of life cycle and say why they might be important.
> 5 Show how cashflow is related to the product life cycle using a diagram.

Check your answers before reading the rest of the chapter. Try answering the questions again when you've finished the chapter.

Mind Map

Start a Mind Map similar to the one shown here. Put a central image of your own in the middle. This image works for me – it reminds me that there are a range of different things that can be considered as products and that not all of them are tangible. You need to draw an image that works for you! The first 'legs' of the Mind Map have been started for you. Add points to your map as you work through the chapter. Don't forget, you can – and should – use colour!

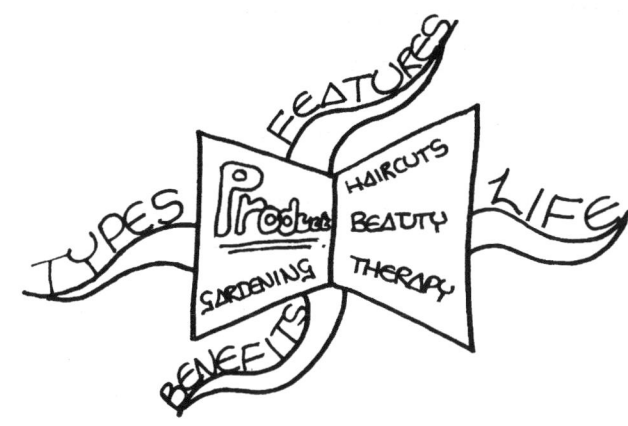

Definition

The product is what is produced by the firm and what the consumer actually buys; it provides the consumer with utility (use or enjoyment) in return for payment. It is part of the marketing mix.

What is it?

A product can be one of a number of things:

Goods

These can be touched or seen usually divided into three categories:

- **consumer durables:** goods that last and can be reused, e.g. cars, white goods, electrical goods
- **consumer non-durables:** goods that cannot be reused, e.g. food, washing powder, petrol
- **industrial goods:** e.g. factories and equipment; tools and accessories; plant and office furniture and supplies

Services

These include entertainment and tourism, e.g.:

- **places:** products such as Alton Towers or Euro Disney
- **people:** products such as Madonna or Frank Skinner

Product levels

Products may provide tangible and intangible benefits at a number of levels. The tangible benefit from wearing Adidas trainers may be to keep your feet dry; the intangible benefit may be to impress your friends.

Marketing

FACTFILE

Sometimes it is difficult to distinguish exactly where the product falls. The comedian Frank Skinner, for example, recently asked £20m for his talents to front two entertainment slots on the television. Is this a person or a service as product?

Buy a bar of chocolate and eat it. Then consider why you bought that particular product:

- Your core reason might be to satisfy a hunger; this can be seen as the core value of the chocolate bar – the 'core product'.
- Your secondary reason for buying that particular product will be a combination of packaging, brand and other product features such as ingredients and quality – the 'actual product' or 'tangible benefits'.
- Your tertiary (third level) reason might be linked to the products availability, guarantees of quality; special offers and so forth – the 'augmented product' or 'intangible benefits'.

Reasons will differ in importance depending on the product that is being purchased. For example, the core product may be more important when buying a holiday; the actual product may be more important with a chocolate bar; the augmented product more important with a car (servicing, after-sales service, warranties). Firms will concentrate on the values which research shows to be most important to their consumers. You would not expect an extended warranty on a bar of chocolate or fancy packaging on a car!

Product life cycle

The product life cycle is the stages through which a product passes from its initial introduction to its final withdrawal. Product life cycles can be extremely brief or very lengthy, depending on the type of product and on the marketing strategy used to sell it.

The standard phases of the product life cycle are:

1. **Introduction or launch:** high marketing expenditure and high risk levels. The firm is not benefiting from economies of scale and distribution channels need to be established.
2. **Growth:** sales volume grows; the successful navigation of this stage will be watched by competitors, who will use it as a signal to enter the market.

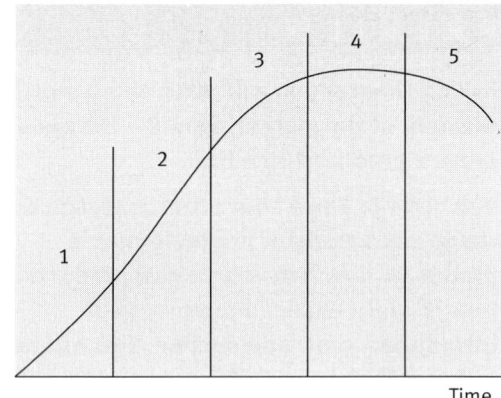

3. **Maturity:** growth of sales slows down. Competition has entered the market. The firm needs to develop product loyalty and encourage repeat purchases.
4. **Saturation:** there are so many competing products on the market that it is saturated, i.e. there is no room for any new product. This does not mean that the market is finished, just that there is no room for growth.
5. **Decline:** the product is no longer seen as necessary or useful and sales therefore go into decline. The product is likely to be withdrawn from sale.

You should be able to find examples of products from your own experience to fit into each category. Examples have not been given here as they may well not be relevant by the time you read this chapter.

Different cycles

Products do not always follow all stages of the life cycle:

Explosive life cycle

Some products are launched and quickly reach market saturation, then decline just as rapidly. These tend to be items with instant 'fad' appeal – 'Tamagotchi' electronic pets and 'Furbies' are examples.

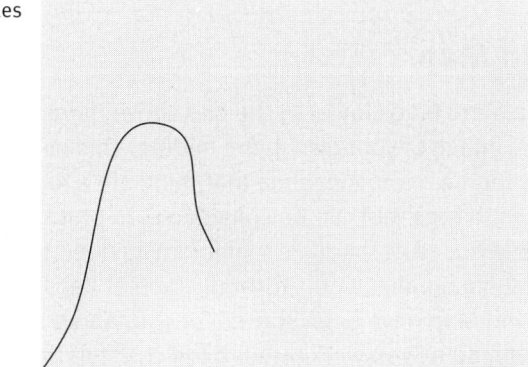

The marketing mix – product

Aborted life cycle

Some products fail to reach a growth stage and are withdrawn at a fairly early stage, perhaps because demand does not materialise (e.g. the Sinclair C5 electric vehicle) or because competition is too strong (e.g. Betamax video cassette recorders).

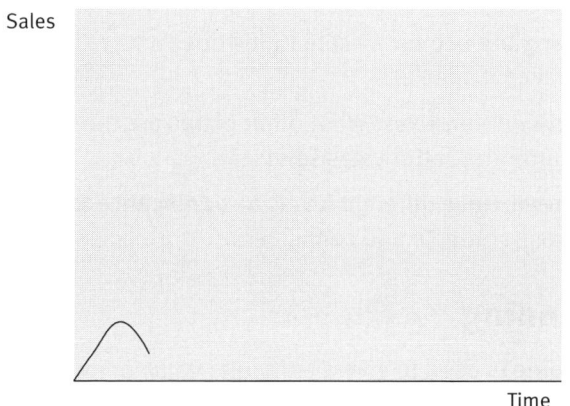

Extended life cycle

Some products will benefit from additions, alterations or modifications that extend their 'natural' life cycle. Look at the life cycle for Ariel products below, produced by Procter and Gamble.

As each product is perceived to be reaching maturity, an extension strategy is used – a modification of the original product. The brand thus continues to grow. The washing powder industry is a good one to study to see how products can be differentiated and product life cycles extended. It has developed new ways of packaging, presenting and delivering what is essentially a basic household necessity (would you like powder or liquid? in a box, bag or bottle? to add before the wash, with the wash, or during the wash?).

Other extension strategies include:

- developing new uses for a product, e.g. technology developed for space exploration has been adapted for use in kitchens and clothing
- encouraging more consumption by changing habits or perceptions, e.g. wine is no longer seen as a luxury item
- more promotion and advertising; some products need to be re-launched, e.g. Marathon bar was re-launched under its global brand name of 'Snickers'
- extending the product range, e.g. Procter and Gamble also produce softeners, whiteners and similar products for tumble driers which complement the basic product

Revived life cycle

These are products that appear to be in terminal decline but can be revived through being relaunched or repositioned in the market. No.7, Boots' brand of cosmetics was declining in sales although it still held a strong position in the middle market sector. It was successfully repositioned in 1995 in the premium market sector through a combination of research, repackaging and promotion.

FACTFILE

There is a tale told in marketing circles of how a certain ailing product was turned round by the simple expedient of changing the instructions on the container from 'use sparingly' to 'use liberally'. If true, it was an inspired piece of modification!

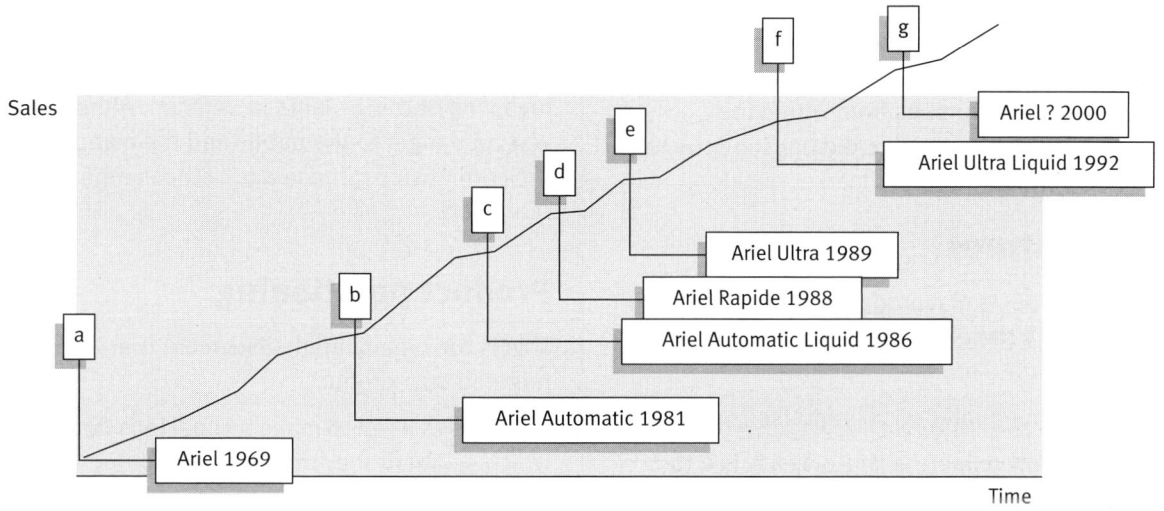

Marketing

Cashflow and the life cycle

Cashflow from the sales of a product will start off as negative during the phase where the product is being researched and developed. It will increase as the firm sells more of the product and is able to benefit from economies of scale. As the life cycle is extended, there will be dips as extra cash is used to support the extension strategy.

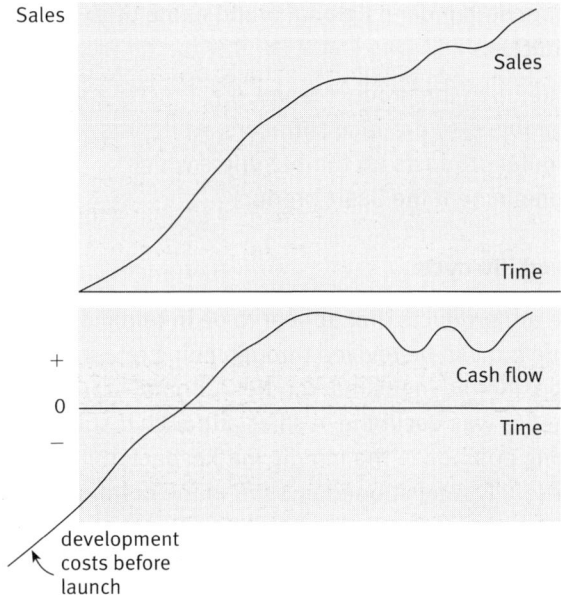

The life cycle of a product

Using the product life cycle

The main use for the product life cycle is as *one* of the tools that a firm uses for marketing planning. If a firm knows where its product is sitting on the life cycle then it can alter marketing expenditure accordingly. Businesses need to remember that the product life cycle is a continuous one and should avoid becoming complacent. Often, the point at which a firm is most vulnerable is the point at which they appear to have conquered the market. Charles Handy is an exponent of organic growth – i.e. firms should be always seeking growth opportunities from within the business. If Procter and Gamble did not continue to innovate, they would lose their market position.

Product features

These are the aspects of a product that are important to consumers and therefore those which the business needs to concentrate on:

- **Identity:** often equated with brand (see opposite).
- **Reliability:** how reliable is it? How easy is it to mend if it goes wrong?
- **Durability:** how long will it last? Will it stand up to heavy use?
- **Performance:** how well does it work? How efficient is it?
- **Aesthetic appeal:** what does it look like? Is it pleasing to the eye?
- **Affordability:** does it come within my price range?
- **Tangible extras:** what features does it have? What makes it special?
- **Intangible extras:** What other extras are there e.g. warranties, after sales service?

These will have different levels of significance for different products and consumers.

Branding

Branding is used to give a particular value or image to a product. Successful branding means that new products can be launched bearing the brand name and consumers will assume that they have the same brand values. Most brands cultivate a particular image, closely linked to the range of products that they produce. Some examples are:

- **Virgin:** value for money, quality, adventurous, innovative
- **Nike:** exclusive, original, success
- **Heinz:** family values, value for money, quality ingredients
- **The Body Shop:** environmentally friendly

In some cases a firm will segment their own market according to the brands that they produce. This is called product segmentation. For example, Procter and Gamble do not just produce Ariel, but also Daz, Tide and Bold.

A strong brand image can promote sales throughout a product range – the 'halo effect' – and make it easier to launch new products. Damage to a brand image can have far-reaching consequences. Coca-Cola's European operation was damaged in 1999 by a scare involving bottling plants in Belgium. Although there was no danger to the public and the company took the correct steps, the image of the company was tarnished.

Product positioning

This is the type of market segment that is being targeted by a product.

Businesses need to make a conscious decision as to which segment they intend to aim at and then ensure that the product features and promotion appeal to

The marketing mix – product

Segment	Age group	Examples
Teenage/budget	17–20	L'Oreal, Outdoor Girl
Mid market	21–30	Max Factor, Revlon
Premium	31–45	Estee Lauder, Givenchy

that segment. A product positioning or perceptual map can be used to show where a firms range of products lies.

Product range

The product range is the different lines that a company markets. Sometimes they will be in the same market, such as a range of chocolate or confectionery products; sometimes they will be in different markets – Young's seafood, Lea & Perrin's Worcestershire sauce and Ogden's tobacco were all produced by the same company at one time, Nestlé produce both chocolate products and breakfast cereal. Most firms tend to concentrate on that part of the market where they have the most knowledge. Companies may concentrate on the whole market or on particular segments of a market (e.g. Thomsons cater for most holidaymakers; Kuoni, however, concentrate on long haul and exotic destinations).

The product mix is the variety of products which a firm has in its range. A narrow mix means that the firm is heavily dependent on one particular market segment. Narrow product mixes also run the risk of cannibalising each other. For example, Pizza Hut have a range of products in their outlets but all based on pizza. If there were a slump in the pizza market, the company has nothing to fall back on. If they introduce a new pizza, it runs the risk of eating into the sales of existing lines.

Product development

New products will be brought to the market either as a result of product-led development or of consumer-led development.

Product-led development is where a manufacturer develops a new product and then introduces it to the market. Sometimes this is blue sky development, i.e. there are no competitors. Sometimes the product is a competitor to existing products.

New products go through a process that begins with ideas and ends with the product launch. There may be a few months or many years between the idea and the actuality. A typical process is:

innovatory idea → product analysis → market analysis → prototype → test → alter/adapt → test market → analysis → alter/adapt → launch

However thorough this process is, it does not guarantee the success of the product.

Market-led development is where a producer sees a gap in the market and then fills it. For example, Dixons realised that there was a market for a free Internet access service and introduced Freeserve. This took an initial high share of this new market but then attracted competition, e.g. BTclick and currantbun.com. This market moves so fast that innovation is the only way to stay in front – the latest services are beginning to offer amounts of free call-time as well as free access. Profits are made by carrying advertising and by taking a tiny increment of the call fee charged by the telecommunications provider.

FACTFILE

Cannibalism
When introducing a new product to the market, firms need to take care that they are not 'cannibalising' their own market share. Virgin has a train business in the southwest; to gain increased market share of travellers, they might decide to operate a bus service. However, this might have the effect of taking passengers away from their trains. Effectively, they could end up with the same market share of travellers but twice the costs. The bus service could cannibalise the train operation.

CHECKLIST

✓ **Products are:**
  - goods or services, consumer or industrial
  - bought for a variety of reasons

✓ **They can be studied using:**
  - product life cycles
  - product positioning and perceptual maps
  - devices such as the Boston matrix

✓ **Firms may produce:**
  - a range of products
  - a mixture of products
  - a range of brands

New products are:
  - market-led (a gap in the market is found)
  - product-led (a new product is developed)

Study and Revise AS and A2 Level Business Studies

Marketing

Mind Map

Finish off your Mind Map by adding all the rest of the points mentioned. Don't forget to use word pictures and colour where appropriate.

Sample question and answer

Explain what is meant by product life cycle and of what use it would be to a manager. How does the life cycle affect cashflow?

1. Define terms – product life cycle is the cycle of: launch; growth; maturity; saturation; decline. (Give details for each and draw the life cycle diagram)
2. The main importance of the life cycle to a manager is to be able to see where his product is and adopt an appropriate strategy. (Use examples of products at various stages of the life cycle drawn from your own experience.) If, for example, it looks like the market is becoming saturated then he may try product differentiation. If the market is declining, the manager may decide to concentrate effort on other products in growing markets.
3. In the initial stages there is no revenue but there are costs as money is spent on development. Once the product is launched, revenues begin to come in; initially, there will still be an excess of costs over revenues.
4. At market saturation revenues may begin to fall as pricing or promotional strategies are used to keep sales up. If extension strategies are used, these will increase costs and reduce cash flow. If successful, cash flow will recover again.

TEST YOURSELF

Use your Mind Map to see if you can answer the following questions.

AS

1. Which product features do you think would be most important for:
   a. a washing machine?
   b. a chocolate bar?
   c. a range of cosmetics?
2. Outline the main features that are important to the success of a product.
3. How might a manager use a product life cycle?

A2

1. Explain what other tools or information a businessman could use to study his product apart from the product life cycle.
2. Explain the importance of maintaining a positive brand image.
3. What is the difference between product-led and market-led development?

Summary

- Products are the goods or services produced by a firm; they are a part of the marketing mix.
- Products give tangible and intangible benefits; each is important.
- The product life cycle is the stages through which a product passes from its initial introduction to its final withdrawal.
- Product life cycles can be extremely brief or very lengthy depending on the type of product and on the marketing strategy used to sell it.
- Cycles can be shortened or extended using various strategies; cashflow is linked to the life cycle.
- Businesses can strengthen their market position by producing a range of products or a range of brands.
- Brand image and brand values are extremely important to firms.
- New products are constantly being brought to the market. Some succeed, others fail. They are either market-led or product-led developments.

The marketing mix – promotion — CHAPTER 12

PREVIEW

- Promotion is part of the marketing mix. You need to use the skill of synthesis to draw on other parts of your specification in order to study it.
- In this chapter we look at the way in which a firm communicates its range of products to the consumer. Promotion is about communication.
- See if you can answer at least four of these five questions before continuing with the rest of the chapter.

Questions

1. Define what is meant by promotion.
2. List the major functions of promotion.
3. Say what the acronym AIDA stands for? Why is it important.
4. List the different kinds of advertising media and rank them in order of effectiveness.
5. Outline what the main controls on advertising are.

Check your answers before reading the rest of the chapter. Try answering the questions again when you've finished the chapter.

Mind Map

Start a Mind Map similar to the one shown here. Put a central image of your own in the middle. This image works for me – it reminds me that promotion is all about passing on information. You need to draw an image that works for you! The first 'legs' of the Mind Map have been started for you. Add points to your map as you work through the chapter. At the end of the chapter is an example of what a finished Mind Map might look like. Don't forget, you can – and should – use three colours at least for your central image and a different colour for each 'leg' of your Mind Map.

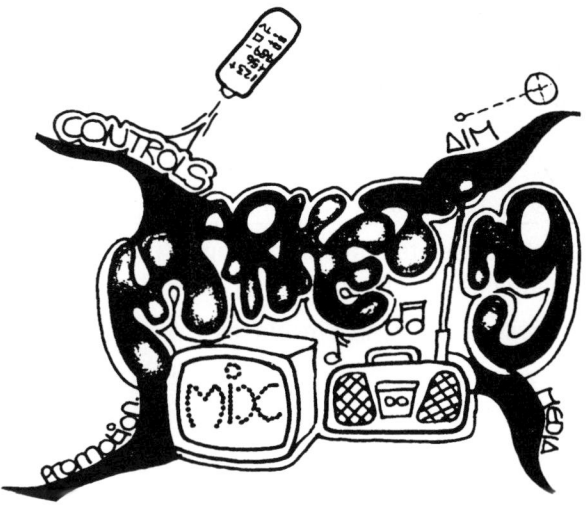

Definition

Promotion involves communicating the existence, features and benefits of a product to a consumer or potential consumer.

Aim

The intention of promotion is to do one of three things:

- make consumers **aware** of new products and lines that come to the market
- encourage consumers to **remember** that a product is on the market
- **persuade** consumers to buy the product

Methods

The main method of achieving these aims is through advertising. Advertising is paid-for publicity for a product. Because it is paid for directly it is called 'above-the-line' promotional expenditure. Other methods of promotion are called 'below-the-line' expenditure.

AIDA

The AIDA acronym is used to remind us of the qualities that advertising should possess. It should:

Attract	**A**ttention
Create	**I**nterest
Develop	**D**esire
Lead to	**A**ction.

Media

Advertising is a way of getting a message from the vendor to the buyer. The message needs, as with all communication, a medium to carry it. The plural of medium is media. Advertising media are more expensive the more wide-ranging they are and the more effective they are. Businesses need to choose media as a part of their marketing strategy to ensure that the message is being delivered to the right market segment. Some advertising can be targeted (using particular broadcast times, programmes, magazines and journals). Other advertising, such as posters, will aim to reach as many people as possible.

Study and Revise AS and A2 Level Business Studies

Marketing

The main advertising media are:

- **broadcast media**, e.g. television, radio, cinema advertisements. These are expensive to make, expensive to show, but highly effective.
- **published media**, e.g. newspapers, magazines and, increasingly, the Internet. Many publications are specialist ones such as the trade press and magazines covering particular interests. Advertising costs will depend on the circulation of the magazine. Figures and costs are published each year in BRAD (British Rate and Data). This heading also includes leaflets and catalogues (trade or consumer).
- **posters and billboards:** the largest of these are '64 sheet' billboards. Posters can be placed almost anywhere, an effective spot being on vehicles, where many different people will see the message. A national poster campaign can be highly effective, but is also quite expensive.

Controls

Advertising is a powerful tool and it can, of course, mislead. To police this there are a number of controls, both statutory and voluntary.

Statutory controls include:

- **Trades Descriptions Act 1968** (and many updates and amendments) – sellers must be honest about products or face court action
- **Broadcasting Act (1990)** set up a Radio Authority and the Independent Television Commission – both issue licenses to broadcast franchisees and operate a Code of Practice which includes advertising.
- **Other Acts** can be brought into play if advertising is seen to be offensive or indecent.

Voluntary controls include:

- **Advertising Standards Authority:** This operates the British Code of Advertising Practice which states that all advertisements should be 'legal, decent, honest and truthful'.
- **Broadcast Complaints Commission:** investigates complaints made by viewers.

FACTFILE

Remember that a whole section of advertising, on which much printed media relies, is that for job vacancies. This is purely informative advertising.

Measuring effectiveness

Advertising is only partially effective if there is an increase in sales. If that increase in sales produces sufficient revenue to offset the advertising expenditure then it is totally effective.

Planning an advertising campaign follows the same steps as other marketing planning. Objectives must be set and the success of the campaign measured against those objectives. Some objectives, such as brand recognition, may be easy to check and quantify. However, these tend to be objectives that do not necessarily have a direct bearing on sales.

Market research techniques can be used to see whether particular advertisements were effective but, in general, it is difficult to draw a direct correlation between advertising activity and sales. This is because there are so many other factors involved.

In judging whether a campaign was a success, a firm will look at all the objectives and all the factors involved over a period of time. Statistical techniques will be used to observe whether a positive correlation exists.

FACTFILE

Some newspaper and magazine adverts inviting a direct response are coded or keyed so that an advertiser can see exactly how effective they are.

Advertising – good or bad?

Arguments for advertising include:

- it is necessary for information purposes, essential in some cases
- the advertising industry is a job creator and foreign income earner
- it acts as the 'research and development' department for other creative industries such as cinema

Arguments against advertising include:

- it can be used to reinforce monopoly power by creating barriers to market entry
- it is wasteful of scarce resources
- it is an unnecessary cost which is passed on to the consumer
- it encourages a culture of acquisition, possibly adding to the crime rate

The marketing mix – promotion

Promotion types

Below-the-line expenditure is promotional expenditure that is not directly spent on advertising. It may be spent on promotion:

- to the trade – selling products into the distribution system
- to the consumer – selling products out of the distribution system i.e. directly to the consumer

Different types of promotion will be effective depending on the circumstances. Selling to the trade tends to involve face-to-face selling, using representatives. Almost all industrial and capital products are sold in this way, called personal selling. Sales representatives will be armed with specialist publications, samples and catalogues. Firms may provide information/education seminars and training, and may mount and attend exhibitions and trade fairs. Businesses will also run trade promotions to encourage distributors to stock their products. Businesses also provide point-of-sale material such as display stands, cards and posters.

Promotion to the consumer comprises devices such as coupons, competitions, free offers, samples, loyalty cards, money-off etc.

Public relations

This is designed to project a positive image of the firm, brand or product to the public.

Endorsement

This involves persuading a public figure to recommend the product (e.g. one ex-Chief Constable endorses tyres).

Sponsorship

This is where a product can be seen to be associated with a sport or event that is popular, e.g. the FA Carling Premiership. This also gains the product extra publicity in places where it would otherwise not be possible, such as the BBC.

Product placement

This is where the product is seen, worn or used on film, television or in photographs. Aston Martin were happy to supply the cars for the early James Bond films because of the enormous publicity they gained as a result.

Customer relations

If customers are kept happy a good company image will be maintained.

Social marketing

This is a new form of marketing where a firm goes into partnership with another organisation in order to show its social credentials. Cause-related marketing is one part of it, where a product or service is jointly marketed for the benefit of the commercial operator and the cause. Cadbury's Yowie chocolate snack, launched in Australia in 1997, successfully linked the product with a raising of environmental awareness and an educational programme for schools. Other examples are Tesco's 'Computers for Schools' promotion, and the airline British Caledonian and the children's hospital appeal (the airline collects unwanted foreign currency from passengers returning to the UK).

Direct selling

This is the delivery of promotional material, offers or sales 'pitches', directly to a potential consumer. It includes direct mail by post and fax, advertising e-mails (known as spam) and 'cold calling' telephone sales. An entire industry has grown up around direct selling due to its effectiveness in targeting consumers.

FACTFILE

Corporate hospitality, where a firm buys tickets for a sporting or other event and gives them away to clients, is seen by firms as an effective means of public relations. Such hospitality may, however, have a negative effect if genuine fans cannot obtain tickets.

CHECKLIST

- ✓ Promotion is how a firm communicates to consumers.
- ✓ It is split into advertising (above-the-line) and promotional (below-the-line) expenditure.
- ✓ The AIDA acronym is used to remind us that advertising should Attract Attention; Create Interest; Develop Desire and lead to Action.
- ✓ The media are the way of getting the message to the receiver.
- ✓ Advertising has proponents and opponents; it is regulated both voluntarily and by law.
- ✓ Sales promotion, public relations and personal selling are the other main operations of promotion.

Marketing

Mind Map

Finish off your Mind Map by adding all the rest of the points mentioned. An example of a finished Mind Map is shown below. Don't forget to use word pictures where appropriate.

TEST YOURSELF

Use your Mind Map to see if you can answer the following questions.

AS

1. Explain what is meant by the promotional mix.
2. State three ways in which advertisers may try to see if advertising is effective.
3. Outline the different methods of 'below-the-line' promotion.

A2

1. Explain how the promotional mix is linked to marketing planning.
2. Explain how an advertiser might use statistical tools to measure advertising effectiveness.
3. Evaluate the different methods of 'below-the-line' promotion. What factors govern their relative effectiveness?

The marketing mix – promotion

Sample question and answer

'Above-the-line promotional expenditure is unnecessary and may even be harmful'. Discuss this statement with regard to advertising and promotion.

1. Define your terms – make the distinction between advertising and promotion; 'above-the-line' and 'below-the-line' expenditure. Then discuss the advantages and disadvantages of advertising.
2. Advantages
   - Advertising is informative – without it people would not be aware of new products.
   - Advertising creates jobs.
   - The advertising industry is not just the 'front end' of advertising but also includes all the design and development work that goes into creating effective advertisements.
   - There are further positive effects as advertising uses technologies and effects which are then applied to things like movie making.
   - In effect, advertising can be seen as a research and development body which can afford the R & D that other producers cannot.
3. Disadvantages
   - Advertising creates unnecessary costs which are inevitably passed on to the consumer thus making prices higher than they need to be.
   - There is a moral argument against advertising – it encourages acquisition. There is evidence that it adds to the incidence of crime as the portrayal of possessions – and the message that 'everyone should have one' – encourages the 'have-nots' to steal from the 'haves'.
   - Advertising persuades people to spend money unwisely by buying goods which they don't want or need and from which they are going to get little utility.
   - Advertising encourages the maintenance of monopoly power. It can effectively be used as a barrier to market entry.
4. Discuss 'below-the-line expenditure'.
   - Promotion methods other than advertising should add little cost to a good and still have the effect of getting the message across.
   - Public relations can be more effective than advertising in getting a message across and at the same time also be cheaper. However, it is difficult to control public relations output and people may say the wrong things.
   - Point-of-sale material is essential and reasonably inexpensive.
   - Branding: the establishment of a strong brand name and image will allow a firm to cut back on or even cut out advertising.
5. Synthesis. Come to a conclusion that brings in the effectiveness of each form of expenditure, their relative costs and their relative merits and demerits. It does not matter what conclusion you come to – whether or not you agree with the statement – as long as it is well argued.

Summary

- **Promotion is a part of the marketing mix; it needs to be studied along with the other three 'Ps'.**
- **It is designed to communicate to consumers so that they are aware of products, remember them and buy them.**
- **Advertising is a major part of promotion. Expenditure on advertising is 'above-the-line'.**
- **Media are priced according to their coverage and effectiveness.**
- **There are both statutory and voluntary controls on advertising.**
- **The effectiveness of advertising may be difficult to measure; a positive correlation between advertising expenditure and sales is needed for success.**
- **There are arguments for and against advertising.**
- **Other forms of promotion are called 'below-the-line expenditure'. These include public relations, personal selling, point-of-sale and sales promotion.**
- **Remember, you need to use the skill of synthesis when dealing with any element of the marketing mix. Choosing the right promotional mix depends on the size and structure of the targeted market segment, the budget and the objectives or desired effect of the promotion. Promotional mix is inextricably linked to marketing strategy.**

Chapter 13: The marketing mix – place

PREVIEW

- In this chapter we look at the final element of the marketing mix – place or distribution. This is how the products get from the manufacturer or producer to the final consumer.
- There are different channels of distribution, stemming from the traditional long channel which can then be adapted and shortened in a number of different ways.
- You need to be able to look at a case or situation and advise a firm as to which would be the most suitable distribution channel and why.
- You should understand how the concept of opportunity cost can be applied to decisions taken by outlets on whether or not to stock items.
- You should be aware of how channels of distribution have changed over recent years and be able to evaluate such changes.
- You must remember that place or distribution is only a part of the marketing mix. You need to use the skill of synthesis to draw on other parts of your specification in order to study it.
- See if you can answer at least four of these five questions before continuing with the rest of the chapter.

Questions

1. Define what is meant by 'place' in the marketing mix.
2. Outline the stages in the traditional long distribution channel.
3. Suggest three different ways in which the long channel might be shortened.
4. Describe three different types of intermediary.
5. Outline what functions intermediaries carry out.

Check your answers before reading the rest of the chapter. Try answering the questions again when you've finished the chapter.

Mind Map

Start a Mind Map similar to the one shown here. Put a central image of your own in the middle. This image works for me – it makes me think of transport systems and the physical distribution of products. You need to draw an image that works for you! The first 'legs' of the Mind Map have been started for you. Add points to your map as you work through the chapter. Don't forget, you can – and should – use colour!

Definition

Place is about getting the product to the right place, at the right time and in the right condition to be bought by the consumer. It is about the distribution of the product.

Distribution

Distribution is the way in which the product travels from the producer to the consumer. The traditional distribution channel was:

manufacturer/producer → wholesaler → retailer → consumer

This is called long channel distribution. Short channel distribution means cutting out a part of the long channel. It may be that the manufacturer distributes to the retailer, or the wholesaler to the consumer. The shortest channel is direct supply.

Direct supply is when the producer sells directly to the consumer, for example through mail order or home delivery. It is only truly direct supply if no intermediary (e.g. an agent) is involved.

Many contemporary firms no longer use the traditional long chain, preferring to have their own stock and distribution systems. Major retailers, such as Tesco and Asda stores are able to act as their own 'wholesaler' for many goods. For some distribution channels, major retailers have taken over the channel completely, increasing their market power and dominance.

The marketing mix – place

Intermediaries

Intermediaries are the 'middle' men or women who provide a service to the people before and after them in the chain. The major intermediaries are wholesalers, merchants and agents.

Wholesalers

Wholesalers break bulk, i.e. buy in bulk and then sell to retailers in smaller amounts. They carry stock, providing storage space for producers and giving retailers a choice. They reduce the number of transactions – many retailers and producers can deal with a single wholesaler thus reducing both the number of transactions and the costs involved.

Merchants or agents

A merchant buys goods with the intention of selling them on; an agent (e.g. estate agent) never owns the goods that he is selling. Merchants or agents may provide a link in the distribution chain between producer and retailer or between producer and consumer. They will have specialist knowledge about the products and be able to answer questions. Their knowledge, advice and availability may make them a more efficient way of distributing products than using a wholesaler.

> **FACTFILE**
>
> Factors, brokers, merchants, agents and wholesalers are all 'middlemen'. They all act as intermediaries.

Strategies

The overarching objective of the producer is to get their products to the consumer. They can either push them out to intermediaries, hoping they will push them on, or rely on consumer demand pulling the products from the distribution chain.

- **Push strategy** involves intermediaries receiving benefits and incentives to persuade them to take the items from the producer; effectively pushing the product down the chain of distribution; intermediaries such as wholesalers may also used push strategies to get products into retailers
- **Pull strategy** involves special offers, promotions and similar devices to affect consumer demand. The focus of marketing activity is on the consumer to persuade them to demand the product.

Which channel?

Channels are chosen by firms according to the nature of the product and the nature of the market. Product size, fragility and perishability are factors, as are market size, concentration or diversification. Producers may want the widest possible distribution or only to selected outlets, for example, a producer of luxury goods would not wish to see them on sale in a discount store.

Choices are made about the type of distribution needed by consumers, producers and the sales outlets – retailers – themselves.

Consumer

The consumer wants the product to be available:

- when it is needed
- where it is most easily obtained from
- in their preferred format (size, shape, colour, variety)

Producer

The producer will consider:

- at which outlets he would like the product to be available
- which channels are appropriate bearing in mind the nature of the product
- how easy it is to reach a particular outlet through a particular channel
- what is the likelihood of repeat orders
- what opportunities there are for cross-selling (selling a range of products into an outlet rather than just a single one)

Outlet

The various outlets will need to consider

- which products are likely to have high sales/turnover
- which products offer the highest margins
- which products they actually have room for
- the market position of the product – if you only have room to sell two brands of a particular product you are much more likely to stock the market leader, supported as it is by a strong brand image and extensive advertising and promotion, than any other brand.
- what incentives are being offered
- the range and strength of competition – to stock one particular item when there is only limited space means that something else cannot be stocked. This is the opportunity cost of carrying a particular line or brand.

Marketing

> **FACTFILE**
>
> Some types of distribution need to be carefully planned so that products arrive with the consumer in their best condition. Bananas, for example, are in an unripe green condition when they are shipped from Africa.

Types of retail outlet

Retailers are the final link in the chain of distribution. Anyone who sells a product to a final consumer has 'retailed' it. Retailing takes place through:

- **direct sales:** using a representative or agent. Most industrial products are sold in this way. This method also covers door-to-door and party sales, e.g. Avon, Tupperware and Ann Summers.
- **postal sales:** e.g. catalogues, mail order and responses to direct mail shots
- **vending machines**
- **department stores**, e.g. Selfridges and Harrods
- **multiples:** stores with many very similar branches, e.g. Boots, Marks and Spencer. Many specialise in particular ranges of goods, e.g. Barratts, Dewhurst, Dixons.
- **franchises:** stores selling the same goods but operated as franchises under the aegis of the parent company, e.g. Body Shop, Pizza Hut, MacDonalds
- **service outlets:** providing services rather than products, e.g. BSM, Kwik-fit
- **independents:** small independently owned outlets
- **co-operatives:** some co-operatives have their own wholesale operations, others have formed together into voluntary groups
- **supermarkets and hypermarkets:** the growth sector in retailing. Such outlets house many different types of product at a single location, generally out-of-town, and provide variety and low prices.

Where it used to be possible to distinguish one type of outlet from another, the distinguishing characteristics are becoming increasingly blurred.

Why do small retailers survive?

With the advent of giant shopping malls and hypermarkets the death of the small retailer has long been forecast. As early as the 1950s, newspapers carried reports of how the new self-service stores would 'encourage shoplifting' and 'wipe out small retailers'. However, many small retailers continue to survive because they:

- offer a specialised product or service, perhaps rooted in the local community
- are local – consumers will pay higher prices for convenience
- offer personal service and other benefits, such as informal credit and local advertising
- offer local delivery services

> **FACTFILE**
>
> **Internet shopping**
> Some major supermarkets are trying to take the pain out of shopping completely. With a visit to the Asda on-line shopping site, you can pick from the entire range of stock, order and pay for – electronically – your shopping. It will be delivered free (providing you've bought up to a certain amount) to your door.

> **FACTFILE**
>
> Stockless distribution is an adaptation of the 'just-in-time' production strategy. It means that stock is designed to arrive at a store when it is needed and should be rapidly moved on to the shelves. Products are therefore fresher and costs are saved by the need for warehouse space being reduced. A continuous cycle of stocking and selling is needed for this to be effective.

> **CHECKLIST**
>
> ✓ Channels of distribution may be long or short.
> ✓ Channels are effective if they satisfy
>   - consumers
>   - producers
>   - outlets.
> ✓ Intermediaries are middlemen between two or more stages of a chain.
> ✓ Good distribution is vital to producers, to achieve it they can use:
>   - push strategy – focusing attention on intermediaries to take products.
>   - pull strategy – focusing on consumers to buy products.
> ✓ Established distribution networks can choke off competition.
> ✓ Retail outlets vary according to their different functions.

The marketing mix – place

Sample question and answer

Trends in distribution mean that place is no longer a vital element of the marketing mix. Evaluate this statement with regard to changes in distribution over the past few years.

1. Define your terms:
   - Early trends – shortening of the chain of distribution so that long channel distribution becomes short channel.
   - Large retailers taking over or forming their own distribution channels; the effect that this has on the rest of the distribution network.
   - Stockless distribution and the effect this has on the distribution network.
   - Growth of direct sales.
   - Erosion of traditional role of the intermediary, which in many cases included advice and market knowledge.
   - Disputes arising between producers and outlets over the suitability of the outlet for a particular product e.g. Levi jeans in Tesco, Adidas products in Asda. This is important because brands use restricted availability to keep prices high – not good for the consumer, however lower prices are not good for the brand image.
   - Internet sales and Internet shopping – could this be the future?
2. You must mention the other elements of the marketing mix – price, promotion and product – and relate marketing planning as a whole to distribution. Emphasise that distribution is only a part of the marketing mix, and that the marketing mix is only a part of marketing strategy. Changes in distribution thus need to be considered in the light of changes to the other elements of the mix.
3. Conclusion. My conclusion would be that traditional long channel distribution is no longer as important in a domestic context, but may be increasingly important in an international context. Changes in distribution have allowed companies to pass on benefits to other parts of the marketing mix by, for example, lowering prices. It is still just as important to consumers to be able to know where to obtain a product conveniently and inexpensively. This may not be your conclusion. As long as it is well argued and supported, this doesn't matter.

Mind Map

Finish off your Mind Map by adding all the rest of the points mentioned. Don't forget to use word pictures where appropriate as well as sketches and colour.

TEST YOURSELF

Use your Mind Map to see if you can answer the following questions.

AS

1. Explain the difference between the traditional distribution chain and two other methods of distribution.
2. Explain what advantages can be gained by shortening the distribution chain.
3. Discuss why small retailers survive.

A2

1. Explain how large businesses with high stock turnover can take advantage of shorter distribution changes.
2. Explain the importance of 'place' in the marketing mix for services.
3. Explain how product differentiation might help a firm to gain distribution economies.

Summary

- Place is the fourth of the 'Four Ps' that make up the marketing mix.
- Place is concerned with distribution and availability.
- Distribution may be by traditional long channels – the chain of distribution – but, increasingly, it is being shortened.
- The shortest channel of distribution is manufacturer selling direct to consumer; this can lower prices to the consumer.
- Intermediaries traditionally provide a service to both the person above and the person below them in the chain.
- Effective channels must satisfy producer, consumer and outlets.
- There are many different types of retailer. Small retailers survive because of the services that they offer.

Section 3: Finance and accounts

Specification content

Advanced Supplementary (AS)

AQA

Module 1 is *'Marketing and Accounting and Finance'*. It includes:

- Classification of costs
- Profit, contribution and break even analysis
- Cash flow management
- Distinction between cash flow and profit
- Sources of finance
- Budgeting and variance interpretation
- Cost centres and profit centres
- Management accounting

OCR

Module 2872 is *'Business Decisions'* and Module 2873 is *'Business Behaviour'*. They include:

- Accounting and finance
- Budgets
- Cash flow
- Costs
- Investment decisions
- Final accounts

Edexcel

Unit 3 is *'Financial Management'* and Unit 4 is *'Analysis and Decision Making'*. They include:

- Financial accounting including company accounts, profitability and liquidity ratios
- Budgeting, cash flow forecasting and variance calculations
- Classification of costs and cost analysis and decision making
- Cost and profit centres
- Costing and pricing, methods of pricing
- Ratio analysis

Advanced Level (A2)

AQA

Module 1 is *'Marketing and Accounting and Finance'*. It includes:

- Financial accounting: company accounts; understanding, interpreting, using
- Ration analysis, including liquidity, financial efficiency, gearing and profitability
- Contribution and break even analysis
- Investment decision making and appraisal

OCR

Module 2875 is *'Further Accounting and Finance'* (optional). It includes:

- The role of accounting: accounting perspectives
- Accounting concepts: consistency, materiality, prudence, objectivity
- Sources of finance – factors that influence choice
- Costs and benefits of finance
- Budgets and budgeting
- Costs and costing
- Final accounts
- Accounting's role in decision making
- Investment appraisal understanding

Edexcel

Unit 3 is *'Financial Management'*. It includes:

- Financial accounting including company accounts, profitability and liquidity ratios
- Budgeting, cash flow forecasting and variance calculations
- Classification of costs and cost analysis
- Data presentation and interpretation

Management accounting — Chapter 14

PREVIEW

- In this chapter you will revise management accounting – the financial and accounting information which a firm generates other than that which it must publish. Managers use this information for forecasting, planning and analysis.

- The emphasis for AS level students is on the use of accounting information to aid decision-making and financial control. For an A2 student, the emphasis is on being able to apply measures yourself and to be able to evaluate the appropriateness of different techniques.

- The main tools used are budgeting and forecasting and variances from those predicted budgets. You need to understand what variance is and be able to analyse variances.

- You should understand the significance of cost and profit centres and how costs are allocated to them.

- You should remember that finance is only one part of the business 'mix' and needs to be studied in the context of the strategic objectives of the business. This is where you will use the skill of synthesis.

- See if you can answer at least four of these five questions before continuing with the rest of the chapter.

Questions

1. Describe the distinction between management accounting and financial accounting.
2. Describe the different kinds of costs.
3. Outline the difference between revenue and profit.
4. Explain what is meant by zero budgeting.
5. What is the main advantage and the main disadvantage of zero budgeting?

Mind Map

Start a Mind Map similar to the one shown here. Put a central image of your own in the middle. This image works for me – it reminds me that management accounting deals with the internal financial information available to managers. You need to draw an image that works for you! The first 'legs' of the Mind Map have been started for you. Add points to your map as you work through the chapter. Don't forget, you can – and should – use colour!

Definition

Management accounting involves the internal financial information available to managers, as opposed to that information which must be published by law. This information is used for forward planning, reviewing and analysing the performance of the firm.

Classifying costs

Costs are:

- **Fixed:** those costs which do not vary with output, e.g. rent
- **Variable:** those costs that do vary with output, e.g. raw materials
- **Semi variable:** those costs that vary with output, but not directly
- **Direct costs:** vary directly with the output of a particular product, or with a particular process. These can be allocated to cost centres.
- **Indirect costs:** cannot easily be allocated to a particular activity or cost centre
- **Average costs:** the total cost divided by total output. Average costs must be covered in the long run before the firm makes a profit.
- **Marginal costs:** the cost of producing one extra item; it is used to calculate the contribution of a product or centre.

Finance and accounts

Revenues

Revenue is the amount of money coming into a firm. The main source of revenue will be from sales turnover. It is calculated as the number of items sold x price. Other revenue streams may be from the sale of expertise or from investments.

Don't confuse revenue with profit. If a firm has more costs than revenues it is making a loss, however high its revenues might be!

Cash flow forecasting

Cash flow tables show the cash leaving (flowing out of) a business and cash coming in (flowing into) a business. They are used by a firm to predict the amount of money they will need to borrow.

Look at the simple example below. Some figures will be estimates, others will be linked to costs such as wages and raw materials, others calculated because a firm knows that, for example, a particular account falls due for payment in that quarter. They are, however, still predictions – if levels of sales are overestimated and do not come up to expectations, for instance, this will cause problems.

Budgeting

A budget is a statement of intended expenditure over a particular period of time. It is part of the planning process for a business. Budgets may be set within different departments and there may be competition between departments for levels of budgeting. Budgets are set within an overall budget which reflects what the firm can afford. They are set in the context of expected revenues and expected costs.

The master budget is a summary of individual budgets and part of the firm's strategic planning. It will contain the budgets and targets for individual departments.

Zero budgeting means that a further budget for an activity or department is not assured, but must be won. The assumption made is that zero budget will be allocated unless the department can show how successfully it used its previous budget. The main advantage of this is that managers have to justify their departmental allocation each year; the main disadvantage is that such justification wastes valuable management time which could be better used elsewhere.

Variance interpretation

The variance (not the same as a statistical variance) is the difference between budgeted or forecast levels and actual levels. It is used by managers to see whether a particular factor is above or below forecast levels. Positive or favourable variances show that a factor is doing better than predicted (more sales are being made than were forecast). Negative or adverse variance shows a failure (more expenditure is needed than was forecast). A positive figure may show negative variance (actual output is lower than budgeted output) or positive variance (actual sales are higher than budgeted sales) depending on whether the difference is a good or bad thing for the business. Many businesses use spreadsheets to analyse variances and bracket negative variances rather than using plus or minus signs.

Cumulative figures are also shown on a firm's variance analysis so that managers can identify trends.

Variances have the problem that they can only be worked out if standard costs are allocated to factors such as raw materials or labour. These may be different, however, in different regions or production centres or may be estimated inaccurately.

Variances should be contextualised with the other variables in the market. A variance may be caused by a number of different factors, some of which are outside the control of the company.

Variance analysis

The main variances used by a business occur in the costs of materials and labour. All will use standard costs and prices.

	Q1	Q2	Q3	Q4	Q5	Q6	Q7	Q8	Q9
BALANCE B/F	20	10	−10	−15	5	10	15	10	10
IN	10	20	20	20	10	10	20	20	20
OUT	20	40	5	0	5	15	25	20	20
BALANCE	10	−10	−15	5	10	5	10	10	10

The maximum which this firm needs to borrow is 15 (in the third quarter). They could also use the figures to decide to invest the cash surplus which runs from quarter 4 to quarter 9.

Management accounting

Material variances

Materials are **bought** in by a firm and then **used** meaning that material variances are either caused by differences in price or differences in usage.

Price variance

The difference between the actual quantity produced at the **standard** price and the actual quantity produced at the **real** price. Variances may be due to:

- buying/not buying the best materials
- using/not using the lowest cost suppliers
- obtaining/not obtaining volume discounts

Usage variance is the difference between standard quantity produced at the standard price and actual quantity produced at the standard price. Variances may be due to:

- more/less wastage
- better/worse quality of materials
- better/worse labour efficiency

Labour variances

Labour variances concern either the productivity or efficiency of labour or its price.

Price or wage rate variance

The difference between the standard rate for the job and the actual rate. Variances may be due to:

- pay awards
- minimum wages
- using better/worse qualified labour than is needed

Productivity or efficiency variance is the difference between actual levels of production and standard levels expected from that time worked. Variances may be due to:

- more/less motivated workers
- better/worse trained workers
- good/poor working methods

Many other variances can be calculated. A variance can be found for any factor to which a standard price, cost or other level can be allocated.

The value of using variance

This lies in managers being able to identify problems and, in many cases, allocate them to particular plants, processes and departments. Once a variance (positive or negative) is identified, managers can begin to analyse why it has happened and how the lessons could be applied elsewhere.

The problems with variances lie in that, while a variance might be identified, the cause of that variance is not. It is therefore down to individual managers to interpret the figures.

FACTFILE

Variances are favourable or adverse. Favourable variances are good (lower costs, higher productivity); adverse variances are bad (higher costs, lower productivity).

Cost centres and profit centres

These are the business or parts of a business to which particular costs are allocated. To a multi-national a country or region might represent a cost centre; to a national firm it might represent a region, factory or division; to a smaller firm it may be a particular plant or product. The company decides on how it is going to divide itself up, e.g. in the example below the cost centres are based on plants and processes. The divisions allow managers:

- to retain a closer control over parts
- to compare the performance of one part with another
- to discover what 'best practice' is and apply it to other parts, if appropriate
- to set targets relevant to individual parts
- to engender competition between parts to improve efficiency

Profit centres take the cost idea one step further by also allocating profits to particular sections of a business. A cost and profit centre can be treated as a 'business within a business'.

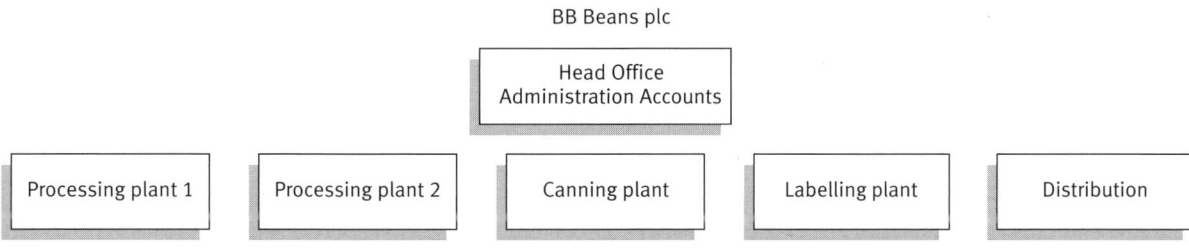

Finance and accounts

Direct costs are those which can be allocated to a cost centre, for example, the amount of metal used for canning will increase if more beans are canned.

Indirect costs are those which cannot be directly allocated to a cost centre. If this company advertised its beans nationally, this would be an indirect cost. It could be allocated to cost centres in proportion – for example the same proportion as direct costs. This is called full costing.

Full costing and absorption costing

These are the two ways of allocating indirect costs to cost centres. In full costing, the fixed costs are allocated to the cost centre in a proportion, e.g. the same proportion as direct costs.

Absorption costing allocates indirect costs as far as possible to the cost centre where they actually occur. In the figure on page 81, distribution would bear greater transport costs than the other cost centres, rent for Processing Plant 1 would be higher then for Processing Plant 2 if it was bigger; rent for Head Office will be higher than that for the Processing Plants due, perhaps, to its position.

The problem with full and absorption costing is that each cost centre can be made to look better or worse than others depending on how the costs are allocated.

Contribution/marginal costing

In both full and absorption costing, fixed costs are allocated to cost centres. In contribution or marginal costing, fixed costs are not arbitrarily allocated to cost centres, they are calculated. The contribution made by each cost centre is calculated as its revenue minus its variable costs. This can also be stated as price minus marginal cost. In this way, the contribution of each cost centre can clearly be seen. It may be that one cost centre is actually making a loss, however, as long as variable costs are covered, they could still be contributing to overall fixed costs and therefore, in the short-term, should be kept in production.

Mind Map

Finish off your Mind Map by adding the rest of the points mentioned. Don't forget to use word pictures where appropriate.

CHECKLIST

- ✓ Management accounting is the use of internal financial information for planning, reviewing and analysing.
- ✓ It is one of the tools used in strategic planning.
- ✓ It involves:
  – the classification of costs and revenues
  – the setting of budgets.
- ✓ Variance is the difference between budgeted levels and actual levels.
- ✓ It may be favourable or unfavourable.
- ✓ It can only be worked out using standard measures.
- ✓ It needs to be studied in the context of other factors.
- ✓ Cost centres and profit centres are parts of a business to which particular costs/profits are allocated.
- ✓ Direct costs may be allocated to a cost centre.
- ✓ Indirect costs are allocated by:
  – full costing
  – absorption costing
  – contribution costing.

TEST YOURSELF

Use your Mind Map to see if you can answer the following questions.

AS

1. Define fixed, variable and semi-variable costs. Give an example of each.
2. What is a cost centre and what is its purpose?
3. What is a variance, why is it used?

A2

1. What are direct and indirect costs? How could you allocate them to cost centres?
2. How would a manager identify the contribution of a product to indirect costs?
3. What are the main variances used by managers?

Management accounting

Sample questions and answers

Azed plc sell maps across the Internet. The business has several divisions including one that is responsible for surveying and printing the maps. The printers is a cost centre within the business. The business sets budgets and uses standard costing to interpret variance. Look at the information below available for a single month in 2000.

	Budget	Actual	Variance
Production	50,000 maps	50,000 maps	
Materials cost	£10,000	£9,500	
Materials usage	100 reams	102 reams	
Labour hours	4000	4020	
Labour pay rate	£8 per hour	£8 per hour	
Overheads	?	?	

1. Explain what is meant by standard costing and variance.
2. Calculate the variances for the month and complete the table.
3. Analyse the possible reasons for the variances.
4. Critically assess the various methods of allocating indirect costs

---

1. Standard costing is where a business decides the amount which a unit of labour, materials or production should cost. Variance measures the difference between budgeted and actual factors.
2. Variances shown in bold. You *must* show favourable or adverse, either by stating it or using brackets for adverse variances.
3. Reasons for the variances include cheaper materials (perhaps a discount for a large order or a new supplier), more wastage of materials or poorer quality materials, higher labour productivity, better qualified or more experienced labour, higher wage rates.
4. Indirect costs can be allocated by:
   - full costing – this is arbitrary and may lead to inequalities – for example a cost centre employing four people could be allocated the same indirect labour costs as one employing 400
   - absorption costing – this is better than full costing as it allocates indirect costs as far as possible where they occur. It still has a tendency to be inaccurate as cost allocation is still subjective
   - contribution costing – the contribution of each cost centre to indirect costs is calculated, rather than allocated. It is calculated as revenue minus its variable cost or price minus marginal cost. This is a fairer way to look at how indirect costs are covered.

	Budget	Actual	Variance
Production	50,000 maps	50,000 maps	0
Materials	£10,000	£9,800	(£10k × 100) − (£9.8k × 102) cost
Materials usage	100 reams	102 reams	**= £400**
Labour	4000	3990	(4000 × £8) − (3990 × £8.10) hours
Labour pay rate	£8 per hour	£8.10 per hour	**= (£319)**
Overheads	?	?	

Summary

- Management accounting uses financial tools to help plan strategy.
- Managers need to define different costs and revenues.
- The main tool used is budgeting.
- Variance is the difference between a budgeted and an actual figure.
- An analysis of variance should reveal where a firm is doing well, where it is doing badly.
- In larger businesses this analysis is helped by dividing the business up into segments.
- These segments are called cost/profit centres.
- It is easy to allocate direct costs to these centres.
- There are various ways of allocating indirect costs.
- Variances are open to interpretation.

Chapter 15 — Break-even analysis

PREVIEW

- Break-even analysis is a further tool used in management accounting. It is a way of predicting when a firm is going to move from making a loss into making a profit.
- The analysis in this chapter is used as a vehicle to show that financial information can be given and interpreted in different formats, either as words, graphs or figures.
- You should be able to deal with financial information in whatever format it is presented to you. However, when writing essay answers, you should use the format with which you are most comfortable unless specifically asked for information in one format or another.
- Remember, break-even analysis is just one financial tool of management accounting. Decisions would be made using it and other techniques, not it alone. You therefore need to use the skill of synthesis to draw on other areas of your specification.
- See if you can answer at least four of these five questions before continuing with the rest of the chapter.

Questions

1. Define the break-even point.
2. What measures do you need to calculate a break-even point?
3. Why would a manager use break-even analysis?
4. Can you draw and label a simple break-even chart?
5. What are the limitations to break-even analysis?

Check your answers before reading the rest of the chapter. Try answering the questions again when you've finished the chapter.

Mind Map

Start a Mind Map similar to the one shown here. Put a central image of your own in the middle. This image works for me — it reminds me that break-even is reached when costs are equal to revenues. You need to draw an image that works for you! The first 'legs' of the Mind Map have been started for you. Add points to your map as you work through the chapter. Don't forget, you can — and should — use at least three colours for your central image and different colours for each 'leg' of your map.

Definition

The break-even point is the point at which sales revenue equals cost. Below this point, costs are greater than revenue — a loss is being made. Above this point, costs are greater than revenue — a profit is being made.

Terms

To be able to calculate or graph fixed costs you need to know the following:

Fixed costs

These are calculated as those costs which do not vary directly with output. They are costs such as rent and rates. If you consider what costs have to be paid before the firm can even start production, then you have defined fixed costs.

Variable costs

These are those costs that do vary with production. Some of these vary directly, such as the amount of raw materials used, some only vary indirectly. A furnace, for example, may use a lot of fuel to get to a certain temperature but then only need small additions of fuel to maintain that temperature. The amount of fuel used varies, but not directly with production.

Output

This is the amount of the product or service produced in a given time period. Break-even looks at how much of the output is sold.

Revenue

This is calculated as the price of the product or service multiplied by the number sold.

Break-even analysis

FACTFILE

Some costs may contain elements of both fixed and variable costs. A telephone bill, for example, will contain the monthly rental for the line (fixed) and the amount charged for calls (variable).

Working out break-even

Information can be presented as:

a a table
b a chart
c words and numbers

Which is best? The three below all show the same information but use different formats.

Building the graph

There are seven stages to building the break-even graph or chart:

1. Draw the axes: output sold on the horizontal axis, costs and revenues on the vertical axis.
2. Find the point that corresponds to 0 output and £54 fixed cost.
3. Draw the fixed cost line from this point, it does not vary with output so is drawn as a horizontal line.
4. Draw the variable cost line – this starts at 0 and increases at £6 per unit.
5. Move this line upwards to start at £54 – this is now the total cost line.
6. Draw the revenue line, this starts from 0 and increases at £15 per unit.
7. Read break-even output sold from the point where total cost crosses total revenue. In this case it is an output of 6 units.

You could have discovered the same position from the table by adding a row which subtracted revenue from total cost. Where the difference is 0, break-even is reached.

a

Output	1	2	3	4	5	6	7	8	9
FC	54	54	54	54	54	54	54	54	54
VC	6	12	18	24	30	36	42	48	54
TC	60	66	72	78	84	90	96	102	108
Revenue	15	30	45	60	75	90	105	120	135

b

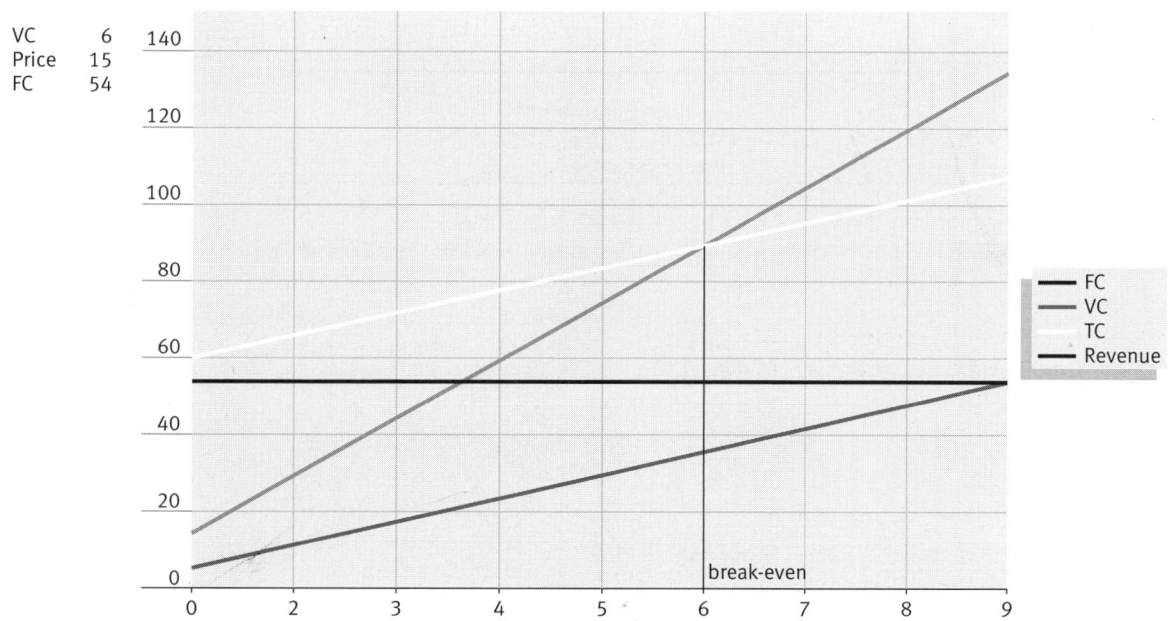

c

The company calculated its fixed cost at £54; the variable cost of producing each unit at £6 and it sells each unit for a price of £15.

Finance and accounts

Calculating break-even

The calculation for break-even is expressed as FC/P-VC where FC is fixed cost, P is price per unit and VC is variable cost per unit.

In this example £54/£15-£6 = 6 units

What happens if variables change?

You can use a break-even chart to demonstrate what happens if any of the variables change for any reason. Changes in fixed or variable costs or in revenue. For example, events such as the imposition of a tax on the product, a wage rise or an increase in the cost of raw materials could be plotted. Effects to the break-even point are as follows:

Increased price

Output	1	2	3	4	5	6	7	8	9
FC	54	54	54	54	54	54	54	54	54
VC	6	12	18	24	30	36	42	48	54
TC	60	66	72	78	84	90	96	102	108
Revenue	20	40	60	80	100	120	140	160	180

VC   6
Price   20
FC   54

Increased price leads to a lower break-even

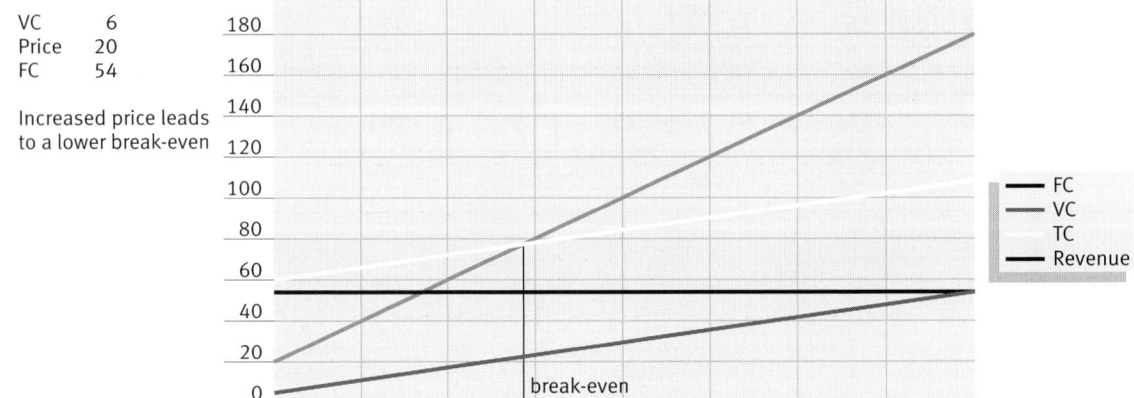

86   Study and Revise AS and A2 Level Business Studies

Break-even analysis

Higher fixed costs

Output	1	2	3	4	5	6	7	8	9
FC	65	65	65	65	65	65	65	65	65
VC	6	12	18	24	30	36	42	48	54
TC	71	77	83	89	95	101	107	113	119
Revenue	15	30	45	60	75	90	105	120	135

VC 6
Price 15
FC 65

Higher fixed costs lead to a higher break-even

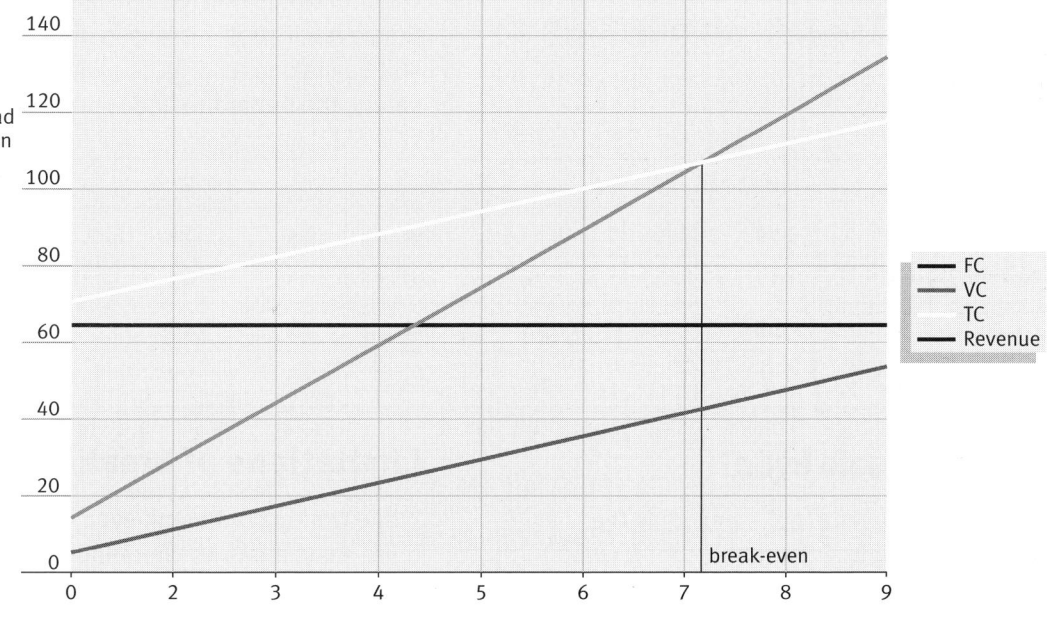

Higher variable costs

Output	1	2	3	4	5	6	7	8	9
FC	54	54	54	54	54	54	54	54	54
VC	9	18	27	36	45	54	63	72	81
TC	63	72	81	90	99	108	117	126	135
Revenue	15	30	45	60	75	90	105	120	135

VC 9
Price 15
FC 54

Higher variable costs lead to a higher break-even

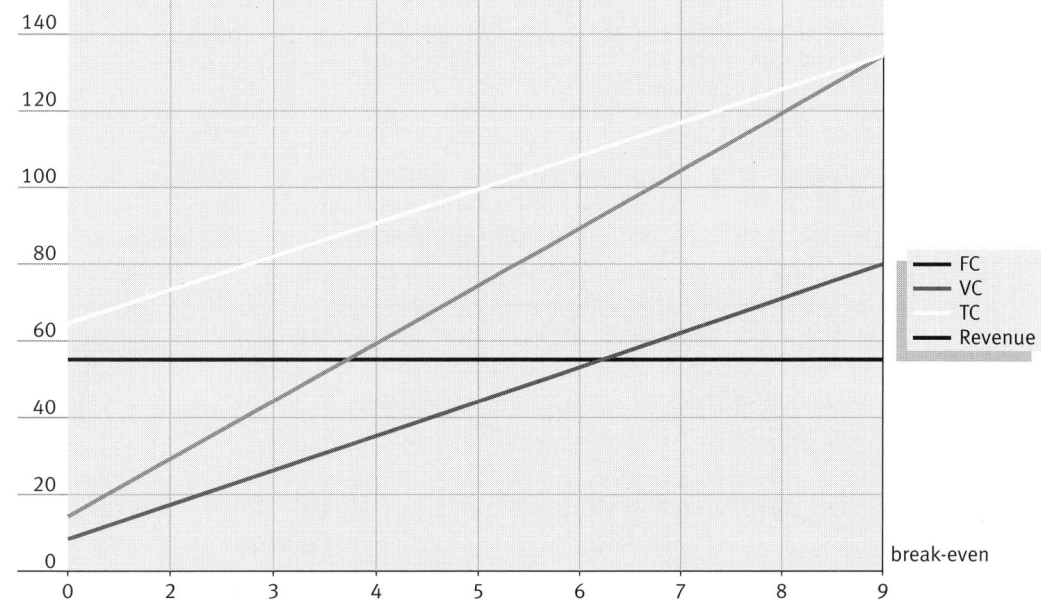

Study and Revise AS and A2 Level Business Studies

Finance and accounts

Contribution

The contribution methods looks at how much each unit of output sold is contributing to the fixed costs of the business. It is calculated as:

- P-VC = contribution
- FC/contribution = break-even

In our example £15 − £6 = £9. Each unit sold contributes £9 towards fixed costs.

£54/9 = 6 units are needed to cover fixed cost completely.

Other information

The chart also has the advantage of showing the firm the amount of profit earned or losses made at each possible level of output. The business can use this information to establish a 'margin of safety' – a position to the right of the break-even point which shows how much demand a business could afford to lose before beginning to make losses.

The firm would aim for a position above break-even so that, even if costs increased or demand fell, it would still be making a profit. The wider the margin of safety, the better the firm is doing.

Output	1	2	3	4	5	6	7	8	9
FC	54	54	54	54	54	54	54	54	54
VC	6	12	17	24	30	35	42	45	45
TC	60	66	71	78	84	89	96	99	99
Revenue	15	30	45	60	75	88	99	106	111

Who uses break-even?

This is thus a very useful tool – providing the business has the right information – for forward planning and predicting. It is used by owners, particularly of small- to medium-sized businesses, where costs and revenues are less complex.

Managers use break-even to predict what happens if any of the variables change.

Lenders use break-even to see the potential of a proposed business.

Limitations of break-even analysis

While working out break-even is quick and usually quite easy, it has its limitations. The figure below shows that the neat straight lines of the break-even chart may also not be correct. A firm may experience economies of scale, meaning that the variable cost line begins to flatten out, or it may have to lower price in order to sell greater amounts (this could also be the result of discounting for bulk purchases).

It is usually calculated as an amount of output, making the assumption that all output is sold. You

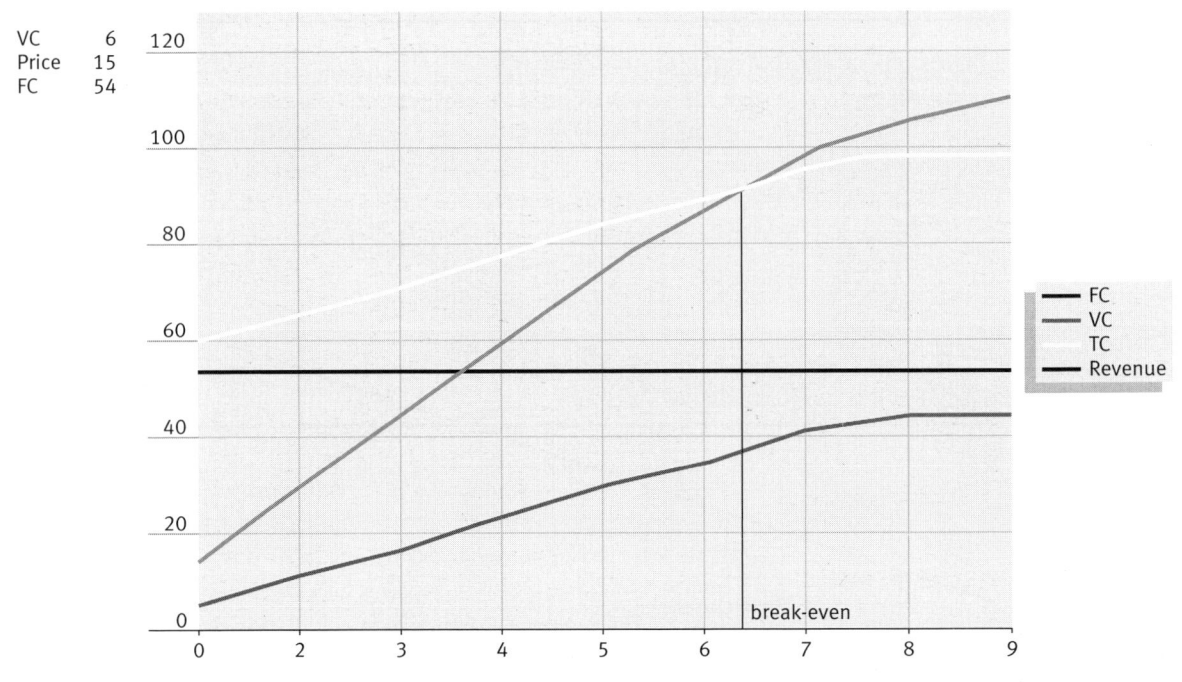

Break-even analysis

need to remember that it is sales revenue from actual sales that is important.

In our example, if the firm produced an output of 9 but only sold 6, would it have reached break-even? The costs of the 3 unsold units would have to be taken into account. A firm may thus be apparently at break-even because it is selling enough, but other costs may have been incurred.

The other main problem with break-even is that there are so many variables which it tries to keep track of. Prices, tastes, raw material costs, taxes, wage rates, etc. are all volatile variables. A plethora of changes could quickly make predictions inaccurate.

CHECKLIST

✓ Calculating break-even involves:
  – classification of costs
  – calculation of revenue.

✓ Break-even analysis is used to show:
  – when a loss/profit making position is reached
  – the effects of changes in variables
  – the margin of safety.

✓ It can be calculated by:
  – drawing a chart or graph
  – calculating FC/P−VC
  – using contribution (c) – P−VC = c; FC/c = break-even.

TEST YOURSELF

Use your Mind Map to see if you can answer the following questions.

AS

1 Describe what is meant by the break-even point.
2 What is the difference between break-even output and break-even sales?
3 What information does a business need to be able to draw a break-even chart?

A2

1 What are the benefits of break-even analysis?
2 What are the limitations of break-even analysis?
3 Why is contribution a good method of calculating break-even?

Mind Map

Finish off your Mind Map by adding all the rest of the points mentioned. Don't forget to use word pictures where appropriate.

Sample question and answer

Discuss the statement that break-even analysis is of only limited use to a large firm.

1 What is break-even analysis?
  - Explain the elements involved – fixed costs, variable costs and revenues.
  - Draw a diagram to demonstrate break-even.
2 What are its drawbacks?
  - Variable costs may begin to fall if economies of scale are reached, altering break-even point.
  - Not all output is necessarily sold; this is an assumption which weakens the analysis.
  - Other variables may affect calculations.
3 Are these drawbacks more likely to affect large or small firms?
  - Give example of single product firm (e.g. hairdressers).
  - Break-even could be useful to a single product firm with one set of overheads, They can calculate quite easily how many units they need to sell to break-even.
  - Give example of multiple product firm. A multiple product firm may have different break-even levels of output for each product. If this is the case, then no one break-even figure will be accurate. A multiple product firm will also be more affected by changes in other variables.
  - Draw from other parts of the specification, for example Boston matrix to show how cash from one product can be used to support another.
4 Conclusion.
  - A useful tool for a small or single product business but fraught with problems for larger firms. (Argue your own case based on the evidence you have quoted.)

Summary

- Break-even point is where total costs are covered by total revenue.
- To calculate break-even you need to know fixed costs, variable costs, revenue and output.
- Information can be presented and used as a graph, a table or in words and figures.
- Break-even can be read from the chart or calculated.
- The chart also shows possible profit and loss and the margin of safety.
- The contribution method of calculating break-even shows how much each additional unit sold contributes to fixed cost.
- Beware when using break-even: it has its limitations.

Chapter 16: Investment appraisal

PREVIEW

- In this chapter you will revise how firms assess the likely returns on large-scale capital projects. Investment appraisal is a further tool of management accounting; it will not be used in isolation but in conjunction with other tools such as variance analysis.
- Such appraisal is part of the planning process so you should look at investment appraisal in the context of the overall objectives of the business.
- Investment appraisal relies mainly on quantitative factors; don't forget that qualitative factors must also be considered.
- This chapter is used to give a practical example of how spreadsheets are used in business. Many calculations would be extremely difficult without them.
- Don't forget to use your skill of synthesis – you will need to draw on information from other parts of your specification in order to answer questions on investment appraisal well.
- See if you can answer at least four of these five questions before reading the rest of the chapter.

Questions

1. Define investment appraisal.
2. Explain why opportunity cost is important in investment appraisal.
3. What are the similarities and differences between cost benefit analysis and investment appraisal?
4. What are the main problems associated with investment appraisal?
5. Can you use the main tools in a spreadsheet?

Check your answers before reading the rest of the chapter. Try answering the questions again when you've finished the chapter.

Mind Map

Start a Mind Map similar to the one shown here. Put a central image of your own in the middle. This image works for me – it makes me think of large-scale capital projects, such as factories. You need to draw an image that works for you! The first 'legs' of the Mind Map have been started for you. Add points to your map as you work through the chapter. Don't forget, you can – and should – use colour!

Definition

Investment appraisal is appraising or assessing different large-scale capital projects to see what is affordable and what is possible. Firms will consider both risk factors and benefits involved. Investment appraisal also involves looking at different projects and choosing the one that offers the best chance of success.

FACTFILE

Laing, the building conglomerate, lost money on their building of the Millennium Stadium, which replaced Cardiff Arms Park, because they accepted a maximum price for the job. Their appraisal led them to believe that they could make a profit within that price; in fact, various problems meant that they made a loss. They could not, however, pull out of the project.

Minimising risk

If a firm wishes to expand, or move, or increase its productive capacity, then it needs to make capital investment decisions. You should remember that such decisions are made in a context of market uncertainty – what the market is about to do can only

Investment appraisal

be predicted – and of cost uncertainty. Firms try to minimise risk by accurately predicting costs from a known base. The known base must include the initial cost of the investment at current prices. Predictions involve the estimated amounts of cash that will flow for the project once it is on stream and the estimated life span of the project. Four main techniques are used:

Average rate of return

This is measured as **average annual return/initial cost** and is expressed as a percentage. It shows average return per year as a percentage of initial cost. To calculate it a firm needs to:

- estimate the life span of the project
- work out the total profit over that life span by taking net cash inflows from the initial cost (this is also called net return)
- divide this by the life span to give average annual return
- divide this by initial cost
- multiply by 100

A firm will have already established a criterion for implementation (say, 5% above current interest rates) and can use this information to help make a decision.

The major problem with ARR is that it assumes the returns will be spread evenly over the life span of the project when this may not actually be the case.

Payback

The length of time it takes for a business to recoup its original outlay. An average rate of return of 10% a year would mean that the initial cost would be covered in a ten year period.

The longer the period of payback, the higher the level of risk involved with the project and the less likely figures are to be accurate. (It is much easier to predict one or two years ahead than ten or twelve.)

Net Present Value (NPV)

This measures how the value of money decreases over time. If a firm earns £100 today, that is worth less than £100 in a year's time, even less in five year's time. Future returns are therefore discounted according to the firm's estimate of the future value of money. This is called discounting the cash flow. The discount rate is based on current rates of interest and on inflation estimates. If the project is a high risk investment, then this will also affect discount rates as will international currency fluctuations if the firm is, for example, buying materials from abroad. The firm will be asking the question 'What will £100 be worth in one year's/three years'/five years' time?'. The calculation is important as it can be measured against risk-free investment such as banking the money. Remember, the opportunity cost (cost of the next best alternative) of any decision must always be taken into account.

Internal rate of return

This method also uses discounted cash flows and is really a subset of NPV. Instead of using interest rates to work out NPV it involves a calculation whereby the rate of interest is the unknown factor. The firm looks for the point where NPV is zero and reads off the interest rate where this occurs. This can then be compared with current or future predicted rates. The main advantage of this method is that it can be used to compare two capital projects with different initial outlays. This is a technique where a firm will use a cell reference in a spreadsheet. See the example using spreadsheets on page 92.

Investment appraisal calculations

Consider this example for a firm that is thinking about building a new processing plant. It will cost £100m to build and the firm has already decided, having studied interest rates and inflation predictions, that it expects £1 to be worth 90p in 2002. It has calculated the initial inflows from the plant at £30m a year for the first year, rising as the whole plant comes on-stream and becomes more efficient.

The current discount factor is set at 5%.

Year	£m (a)	discount factor (b)	present value (a x b)
2000	−100	1	−100
2001	30	0.95	28.5
2002	30	0.90	27.08
2003	40	0.86	34.30
2004	40	0.81	32.58
2005	50	0.77	38.69

- Payback is in 2003, when total inflows match the £100m initial outflow

Finance and accounts

- Average Annual Return is net return (−100 + 190 = 90) divided by years (5) = £18m
- Average Rate of Return is Average Annual Return divided by initial outlay (18/100) × 100 = 18%
- Net present value (NPV) is the total discounted inflows minus the initial outlay (161.14 -100 =£61.14m)
- Opportunity cost will involve other investment projects or safer investments. £100m at 5% interest earns around £27.5m in five years, at 10% it would outstrip this particular project, earning around £62m with no risk attached.

Using spreadsheets for investment appraisal

The table on page 91 could be entered on a spreadsheet as follows:

	A	B	C	D
1	0.05			
2	Year	£m (a)	discount factor (b)	presentvalue (a x b)
3	2000	−100	1	= B3*C3
4	2001	30	= C3-(C3*A1)	= B4*C4
5	2002	30	= C4-(C4*A1)	= B5*C5
6	2003	40	= C5-(C5*A1)	= B6*C6
7	2004	40	= C6-(C6*A1)	= B7*C7
8	2005	50	= C7-(C7*A1)	= B8*C8
9				= sum (D3:D8)

- The discount rate is entered as a cell reference. If it is changed at A1, all calculations are updated.
- The $ is used in most spreadsheet programs to indicate an absolute reference.
- The sum of column D gives the NPV.

To work out the internal rate of return (IRR) in this example, a figure needs to be entered at A1 which returns a net present value of zero. In this case a discount factor of just under 19%.

	A	B	C	D
1	0.1897			
2	Year	£m (a)	discount factor (b)	present value (a x b)
3	2000	−100	1	−100
4	2001	30	0.81	24.30
5	2002	30	0.66	19.70
6	2003	40	0.53	21.28
7	2004	40	0.43	17.24
8	2005	50	0.35	17.47
9				0.00

The firm would consider whether a 19% discounted cash flow would make the product viable by comparing this with predicted rates of interest and inflation and with their own pre-set criteria.

Investment appraisal

Cost benefit analysis

Cost benefit analysis is used to measure the social costs of a project against its social benefits. Social costs are the internal costs to the firm (labour, materials etc.) plus the external costs (such as pollution and congestion) borne by the community. Social benefits are internal benefits plus external benefits. These are sometimes referred to as private and public costs and benefits.

Private costs and benefits are easy to quantify; public costs are extremely difficult.

FACTFILE

When analysing the costs and benefits of a proposed link road between the M1 and the M62 motorways, the government estimated the journey time that would be saved as ten minutes a journey, gave that a monetary value and multiplied it by the number of journeys. The number of deaths and injuries that would be avoided by channelling traffic onto the new road was estimated – a money value is given to death and various gradations of injury. Even costs such as noise pollution and the loss of a view were given money values. The link road was not built.

Sources and quality of data

Investment appraisal sounds extremely scientific and, with complex calculations such as those involved in discounting, looks foolproof. However, there are a number of independent factors which (as in the case of Laing) can make the appraisal incorrect or inaccurate. Look at the calculations above and underline all those statements or figures that involve speculation or prediction. Apart from the problems with predictions of quantitative data, there are also qualitative factors to take into account such as external costs and the firm's image. Changing to a cheaper but less environmentally friendly supplier, for example, may cause more damage to reputation than any positive benefits. Factors affecting investment appraisal include:

- rates of interest and rates of inflation change
- as predictions move further away in time, they will be less and less accurate
- as predictions move further away in time, small early errors become exponential – multiplied with each year

- only quantitative factors are used – figures don't tell the whole story
- it can't take into account the unexpected – Laing's problems were caused by the weather

CHECKLIST

✓ **Investment appraisal is a tool of management accounting.**

✓ **It is used to make decisions on capital projects.**

✓ **It is measured by:**
 – Average rate of return
 – Payback
 – Net Present Value
 – Internal Rate of Return.

✓ **It can be calculated using spreadsheets.**

✓ **It needs to use qualitative data as well as cost and revenue predictions.**

Mind Map

Finish off your Mind Map by adding all the rest of the points mentioned. Don't forget to use word pictures where appropriate.

TEST YOURSELF

Use your Mind Map to see if you can answer the following questions.

AS

1 **Explain why managers should treat predictions with caution.**

2 **Why are discounted cash flows used?**

3 **Explain the factors that will determine at what level a firm will set discounted cash flows.**

A2

1 **What is the difference between quantitative and qualitative data?**

2 **What are the benefits and drawbacks of using IRR as a measure?**

3 **What other techniques would you recommend that a firm uses before making investment decisions?**

Finance and accounts

Sample questions and answers (data response)

Oasis plc is considering building a new water processing plant or expanding their existing facilities. Their existing facilities are on an industrial estate. They see one of the benefits of their new plant being that it would be built on a greenfield site near to a housing estate. It will cost £80m to build and the firm has already decided, having studied interest rates and inflation predictions, what it expects £1 to be worth in the future. For example, it thinks that £1 now will be worth 90p in 2001. Oasis has calculated the inflows from the plant at £20m a year for the first year, rising as the plant becomes more efficient. They have decided that the effective life-span of the project is 7 years.

The current discount factor is set at 7%

a When does Oasis predict it will reach payback?

b What is the average annual return?

c What is the average rate of return?

d What is the NPV?

e What use could Oasis plc make of these figures? What problems might they encounter?

a 2003

b Average Annual Return is net return ($-80 + 215 = 135$) divided by years (7) = £19.28m

c Average Rate of Return is Average Annual Return divided by initial outlay $(19.28/80) \times 100 = 24.1\%$

d Net present value (NPV) is the total discounted inflows minus the initial outlay ($161.95 - 80 = £81.95$m)

e Oasis is trying to assess the risks attached to a capital investment decision. It should try to minimise risk by accurately predicting costs. By doing so it should be able to compare the project with other possibilities for investment, such as the expansion project. Oasis will establish their criterion for implementing the project and can use this information to help make a decision.

The problems associated with investment appraisal are that it involves speculation or prediction. The figures are only as accurate as the predictions that went into making them. The process also does not take into account qualitative factors, like the firm's reputation, which could be harmed by building a new plant on a greenfield site.

The table you draw should look like this:

Year	£m (a)	discount factor (b)	present value (a × b)
2000	−80	1	−80
2001	20	0.93	18.60
2002	25	0.86	21.62
2003	35	0.80	28.15
2004	40	0.75	29.92
2005	45	0.70	31.31
2006	50	0.65	32.35

Summary

- Investment appraisal is just one of the tools of management accounting.
- It is used to make decisions regarding large-scale capital projects.
- Full appraisal requires both quantitative and qualitative data.
- Four main measures are used to appraise investment:
  - Average rate of return – used to compare projects.
  - Payback – used to see how long before the project 'pays for itself'.
  - Net Present Value – used to see what the project is worth in today's terms.
  - Internal Rate of Return – used to determine levels of interest at which projects are viable and to compare projects with different initial outlays.
- Cost benefit analysis is another way to appraise investment.

Financial accounting — Chapter 17

PREVIEW

- This chapter looks at what financial information must be made public according to the terms of the Companies Act. Remember, only companies are obliged to publish such information; sole traders, and partnerships for example can keep their financial affairs private.
- If you are an AS student, the emphasis is on the use of accounting and financial decision-making in order to aid financial control and decision-making.
- If you are an A2 student, the emphasis is on your ability to use performance measures critically and to evaluate the appropriateness of different financial techniques.
- Whether AS or A2, you will need the skill of synthesis in order to relate the financial accounting information to both management accounting and to the wider strategic aims of the firm.
- See if you can answer at least four of these five questions before reading the rest of the chapter.

Questions

1. Describe the distinction between financial accounting and management accounting.
2. Outline the conventions used in financial accounting.
3. What is the purpose of these conventions? Why are they important?
4. Outline the main sources of finance.
5. What is the difference between long-, medium- and short-term finance?

Check your answers before reading the rest of the chapter. Try answering the questions again when you've finished the chapter.

Mind Map

Start a Mind Map similar to the one shown here. Put a central image of your own in the middle. This image works for me – it makes me think of reports and finances that are in the public domain. You need to draw an image that works for you! The first 'legs' of the Mind Map have been started for you. Add points to your map as you work through the chapter. At the end of the chapter is an example of what a finished Mind Map might look like. Don't forget, you can – and should – use colour!

Definition

Financial accounting involves the calculation, use and publication of those figures regarding a firm's performance, profitability etc. that must be made available to the public under the provisions of the Companies Act.

Conventions of accounting

These five conventions are designed to ensure that managers can measure one set of accounts against another knowing that figures have been entered according to the same criteria.

Consistency

Whatever methodology is adopted, this should always be used so that the accounts from one accounting period can be directly compared with those from another.

Matching

Revenues and expenses are allocated when a benefit or cost is felt by the organisation. An example of this is depreciation, where the cost of a machine is allocated over the life time of the machine.

Materiality

Only costs and revenues material (i.e. important) to the accounts are included; for example, expenditure on coffee and mints for directors meetings would not feature in the accounts.

Finance and accounts

Prudence

Accounts should be compiled as cautiously as possible. Where two values or revenues are possible, the accountant should always use the least favourable one. In this way, any discrepancies will be in the company's favour.

Realisation

Profit is realised when a sale or delivery is made, not when it is actually paid for.

Companies Acts 1985 and 1989

The 1985 Act updated existing legislation. It sets out the legal procedures for forming and winding up a company.

1. A Memorandum of Association and the Articles of Association must be lodged at Companies House. The Memorandum outlines the external nature of the company. It includes the name and address of the company, at least one director and the company secretary; the purpose of the company; details of capital and details of liability. The Articles are the internal rules of the company such as voting rights, rights of shareholders and dates of meetings.

2. Companies House issues a Certificate of Incorporation. This is the legal document which gives the company a separate legal existence from its owners.

3. The company's accounts, in a format acceptable to the Act, must be lodged at Companies House. They are available to the public on payment of a nominal fee.

The 1989 Act brought requirements more into line with EU law.

Sources of finance

Finance is categorised as to whether it is internal or external, short-, medium- or long-term.

Internal finance may come from:

- owner's funds – the owner using their own personal money
- profits which are 'ploughed back' into the firm
- the sale of the firm's assets
- working capital = current assets minus current liabilities

External finance may come from:

- grants – both local and national government provide various grant and loan assistance
- loans – mortgages, fixed term or overdraft facilities. These have the advantage of being immediate and certain, but the disadvantages of lenders having a say in the control of the firm, and thus able to force managers into decisions which may be to the benefit of the lender, but not the company. There is also a certainty that loans are going to cost; interest must be paid whether or not the firm is profitable.
- the sale of equity in the company – this could lead to the 'divorce of ownership from control'; again, shareholders may want to move the company in a direction that benefits them rather than the company. Dividends can, however, be reduced or delayed.

> **FACTFILE**
>
> Don't forget your skill of synthesis – look at the overdraft facility in the context of cash flow.

Short-term finance

Short-term finance is used for the day-to-day requirements of the firm. The most common and flexible form of short-term finance is an overdraft facility, where a company is allowed to draw more from its current account than it has deposited, up to an agreed limit.

Medium-term finance

Medium-term finance will be raised through:

Loans

A bank loan is a fixed sum, borrowed for a fixed amount of time, repayable – with interest – in regular instalments. It is therefore not a flexible way to borrow money.

Trade credit

This involves buying items and paying for them later.

Leasing

This means renting equipment rather than buying it. Sometimes, particularly with fast moving technology, this is the best way to ensure that you are using current technology. Many firms, for example, lease computers. In order to raise money firms may sell equipment and then lease it back in a 'sale and lease-back' agreement.

Factoring

This is essentially the sale of debts. Instead of collecting a debt owed, say in 90 days time, the company sells the debt to a factor at a discount, governed by current rates of interest. The factor then collects the debt when it becomes due. The company gets its money now, the factor takes on the risk and makes a profit for so doing, the debtor is not pressured for early repayment.

Long-term finance

Long-term finance is raised through:

Mortgages

Borrowing money against the value of property.

Venture capital

Borrowing money from an entrepreneur or entrepreneurial institution that specialises in supporting new and risky business ventures. They will expect a return, but will be prepared to wait.

Equity

The issuing of shares in a company.

Debentures

Specialised forms of borrowing which give the owner a stake in the company but protect their investment, which will eventually be paid pack. These are sometimes used to fund sporting venues, with the return that the owner receives being a guaranteed seat for events.

> **FACTFILE**
>
> **It was reported in late 1999 that small business failures have fallen by over 15%, according to one firm of City accountants. Lower interest rates are the main reason for this upturn. Small businesses are still, however, the worst sufferers from late payers. Many big businesses deliberately delay paying small businesses for supplies etc. in order to maintain their own cash flows.**

Balance sheet

The balance sheet is a 'snapshot' of the financial position of a firm. It shows what assets the business has and its liabilities. Your personal balance sheet would show what you owned (assets) and what you owed (liabilities – how the 'ownings' were financed).

A balance sheet would be presented as total assets – fixed assets plus current assets and total liabilities:

Assets

Fixed assets

These include buildings, plant and machinery, financial assets such as the ownership of shares in other firms and intangible assets such as a brand image or a firm's 'goodwill'.

Current assets

These include:

- **material assets:** any stock held by the company either of finished or part-finished goods or inputs such as parts, components and raw materials.
- **financial assets:** cash-in-hand and money owed to the firm (debtors)

Liabilities

- **Current liabilities:** amounts that must be paid within 12 months, which could include tax liabilities and dividends
- **Long-term liabilities:** do not have to be paid for at least 12 months, e.g. mortgages and loans
- Shareholders funds comprise issued shares and reserves

A balance sheet would show **net assets** as total assets minus current liabilities and long-term liabilities plus shareholders funds as **capital employed**.

Working capital

The working capital of a business is considered to be its current assets minus its current liabilities. It represents the finance available for the day-to-day operations of the business. Levels of working capital have to be managed, too little and the firm runs the risk of not having enough to meet immediate needs; too much and the firm is losing out on interest payments.

> **FACTFILE**
>
> **Goodwill includes the reputation and other intangible values of a business. In a small business it may be reliability, courteous service or a valuable location. In a large company it might include the management structure and teamwork skills of the organisation. Fixed assets provide long-term benefits.**

Finance and accounts

Depreciation

Fixed assets depreciate in value, i.e. lose value over time. Straight-line depreciation is the easiest way to show this diminishing value on a balance sheet (called net book value). It is called 'writing down' the value. When the asset is considered worthless, it is 'written off'.

Accountants use different terms for each stage of its life. For example, a piece of machinery may have a useful life estimated at ten years and cost £1000 (historic value). Its value will therefore be written down at £100 a year (depreciation) and at any point the machine will be considered to be worth the original cost minus accumulated depreciation (net book value). The asset may not be totally worthless at the end of ten years and the firm may be able to sell it, even if it is only for scrap (residual value).

Year 1	2	3	4	5	6	7	8	9	10
1000	900	800	700	600	500	400	300	200	100

Straight-line depreciation

Profit and loss account

This shows the profit generated or losses made over a period of time.

A simple profit and loss account shows the following:

1. Turnover minus cost of sales = gross profit.
2. Gross profit minus expenses = operating profit.
3. Operating profit plus other revenue minus interest payable = net profit
4. Net profit minus tax = profit to shareholders
- Turnover is the number of sales times price. It is also called total revenue.
- Cost of sales is the expenditure that had to be made to produce the goods or services sold (raw materials, parts, ingredients etc.).
- Expenses are the fixed and variable costs that the business must pay such as wages, power, marketing and publicity.
- Other revenue is revenue from other sources e.g. dividends from shareholdings in other businesses.

Item	Cost	Revenue	Totals
Trading Account			
Turnover		100	
Cost of sales	80		
Gross profit			20
Profit & Loss Account			
Gross profit			20
Expenses	10		
Operating profit			10
Other revenue		10	
Interest on borrowings	2		
Net profit			18
Tax	3		
Profit for distribution (earnings)			15
Dividends paid (distributed profit)			12
Profit kept (retained profit)			3

A simple example of a profit and loss account

Window dressing

This is the term used to refer to the presentation of accounts in a favourable light. When a firm wishes to raise money in some way – usually through a share issue or by borrowing – or needs to be seen in a favourable light for other reasons, such as during a take-over battle or public relations crisis, then the firm's financial position may be made to appear stronger. Tactics include:

- giving intangibles, such as goodwill, a money value
- slowing down the rate of asset depreciation by writing assets down over a longer period
- deciding whether stocks are considered to be used 'from the back' or 'from the front'; using from the back assumes FIFO (first in first out), from the front, LIFO (last in, first out)

This simple example shows how figures could be stated differently for the same operation.

Month	J	F	M	A	M	J	J	A	S	O	N	D
Cost (£)	100	101	102	103	104	105	106	107	108	109	110	111
Stock in	10	10	10	10	10	10	10	10	10	10	10	10

Stock used = 50
If taken from the back (FIFO) stock used = £510 left in stock = £560
If taken from the front (LIFO) stock used = £545 left in stock = £521

This can affect various balances and ratios:

- entering costs and revenues at times that are more favourable; for example, a firm might delay a large payment until after the accounts are published
- the use of different accounting conventions

Window dressing is a legal way to show a company in a better light.

Limitations of accounts

Accounts need to be looked at in the context of the aims and current position of the business. Sky TV, for example, made huge losses in its first few years of operation whilst building up a formidable market base. The losses were quickly recouped once they went into profit but, in the early years, the accounts would have told a story of failure.

- Accounts only show quantitative data – qualitative data should also be used
- The balance sheet is a snapshot – taken at a particular moment in time – and may not accurately reflect the firm's position
- Figures may not be accurate, up-to-date or presented in accessible language
- Inter-firm comparisons can be made difficult by the use of different accounting conventions and methods of presenting figures.

CHECKLIST

✓ Financial accounting figures are available to the public.
✓ Finance is raised internally or externally.
✓ It is considered to be short-, medium- or long-term.
✓ The main tools of financial accounting are the
  – balance sheet: a snapshot showing what the firm owns against what it owes
  – profit and loss account: profits made or losses suffered in a time period.
✓ Accounts can be 'massaged' to make them look more favourable to a company. This is not illegal. It is called window dressing.

Mind Map

Finish off your Mind Map by adding all the rest of the points mentioned. Don't forget to use word pictures where appropriate. A completed Mind Map has been given at the end of the chapter to help you.

Sample question and answer

You may be required to interpret sets of company accounts like the ones shown on page 98 and to work out various ratios. You may be asked to complete a set of accounts which are partially written from information provided. The question below is of the third type, where you are asked to demonstrate your knowledge of the use of financial accounts.

'Financial accounts are vital to a firm.' Discuss this statement with regards to business accounts.

1 Explain the difference between financial accounts and management accounts.
   - Financial accounts are as required by law to keep a true record of all financial dealings.
   - Management accounting is the use of internal information for predicting and forecasting (for example, variance analysis, budgeting).

2 Why is it important for businesses to keep financial accounts?
   - to keep a record of financial transactions
   - because they are required by law
   - to provide information to help mangers plan, respond and control
   - to provide information for the owners/shareholders of a firm
   - to allow the firm's performance to be measured against other businesses.

3 Explain the difference between the accounts that are kept by a small business, such as a sole trader – whose accounts are not in the public domain – and those of a plc.

4 Explain how financial accounts are used to give a picture of the financial strengths and financial weaknesses of a company.

5 Conclude by explaining the drawbacks to financial accounts, such as window dressing, the lack of qualitative data, the importance of the context of the accounts and the fact that all accounts are only a snapshot – they do not really help to indicate flows.

Finance and accounts

TEST YOURSELF

Use your Mind Map to see if you can answer the following questions.

AS

1. What is the difference between financial accounting and management accounting?
2. How would managers use financial accounts to help them make decisions about a company?
3. What information other than financial accounts might a manager need in order to make more informed decisions?

A2

1. How would you use the accounts of a company to measure its performance?
2. What problems would you encounter if you were only using published accounts?
3. What is the difference between management accounting and financial accounting? Which is more effective in evaluating the performance of a company?

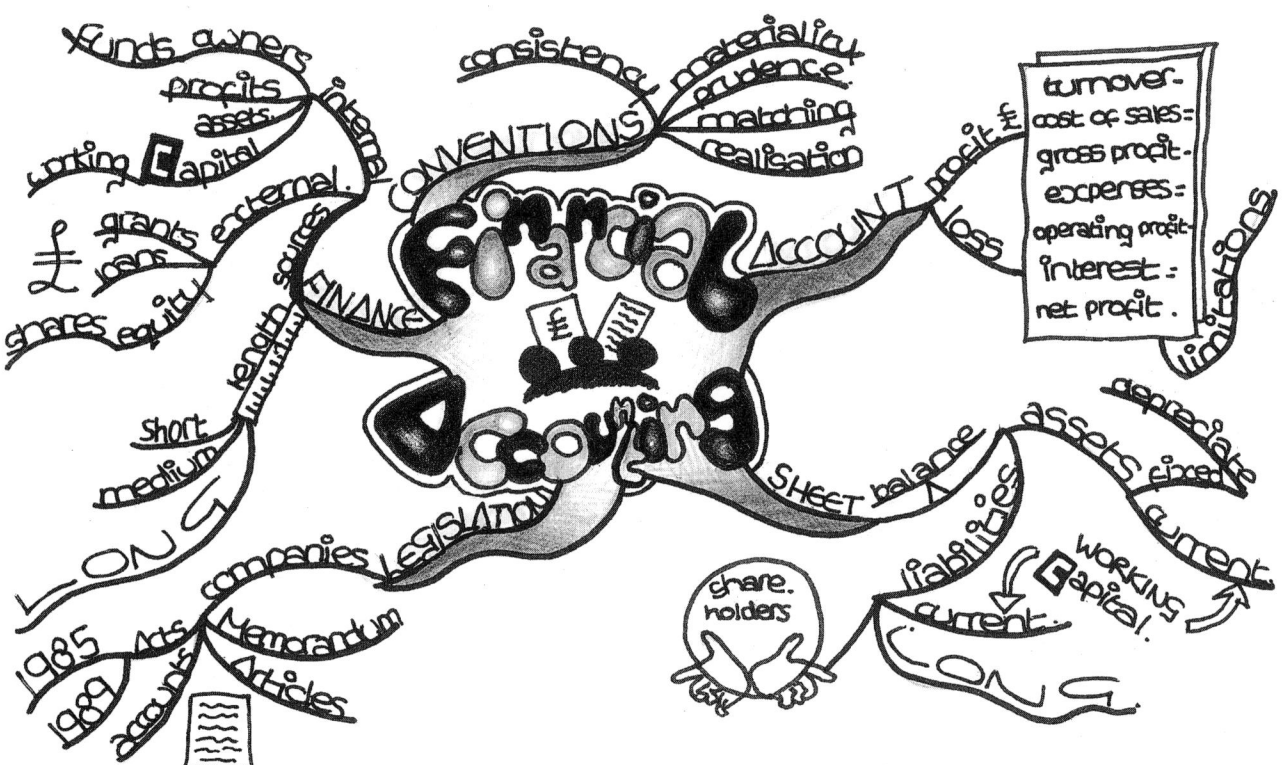

Summary

- Financial accounting involves the figures that must be made public under the Companies Act.
- They are a record of a company's dealings rather than the predictions involved in management accounting.
- Accounting conventions are used to ensure that like is compared with like when comparing accounts.
- Financial Accounting is governed by the Companies Acts of 1985 and 1989.
- The balance sheet balances what a company owns (assets) against what it owes (liabilities).
- The profit and loss account uses the company's revenues and expenditures to show what profit or loss has been made.
- Window dressing means presenting accounts in a favourable light.

Ratio analysis — CHAPTER 18

PREVIEW

- In this chapter you will revise the various ratios which can be generated from a firm's financial accounts. Ratios are one variable measured in terms of another – for example the ratio of number of girls to number of boys, or of wins to losses.
- You need to remember that business ratios are of limited use in isolation but must be used in conjunction with each other to gain an overall picture of the firm's financial position.
- Ratios are used so that comparisons of like with like can be made.
- Remember that ratio analysis is just one part of the strategic decision-making process; when answering questions you need to use your skill of synthesis to draw on other elements of your specification.
- See if you can answer at least four of these five questions before continuing with the rest of the chapter.

Questions

1. Explain what is meant by a ratio.
2. Give three examples of simple ratios.
3. List the main types of ratio to be found in a company's accounts.
4. Which ratio is likely to be of most importance to a potential supplier? Why?
5. Which ratio is likely to be of most importance to a potential shareholder? Why?

Check your answers before reading the rest of the chapter. Try answering the questions again when you've finished the chapter.

Mind Map

Start a Mind Map similar to the one shown here. Put a central image of your own in the middle. This image works for me – it makes me think of measuring one variable in terms of another. You need to draw an image that works for you! The first 'legs' of the Mind Map have been started for you. Add points to your map as you work through the chapter. Don't forget, you can – and should – use colour!

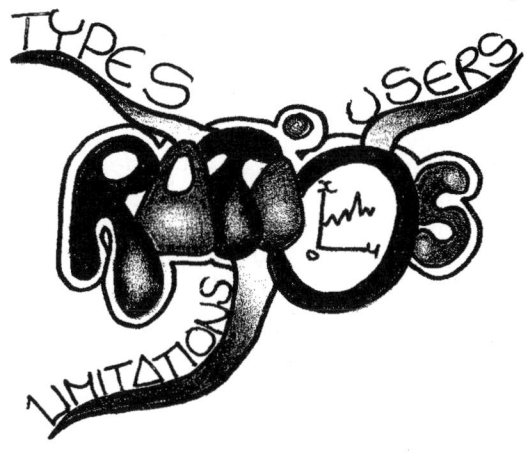

Definition

Ratio analysis is another part of the decision-making process. Financial data is analysed and each ratio compared with the other in order to give a picture of the firm's performance, liquidity, profitability, efficiency and vulnerability.

Who uses ratio analysis?

- Managers who will be particularly interested in relating their performance to that of other managers either in their own company or in similar positions in other companies. They may also want to measure their performance in the current time period to previous periods of time.
- Investors and potential investors – these will be interested in the return on capital employed and gearing plus of course the earnings per share and dividends they might expect.
- Creditors will be interested in ratios such as liquidity and the acid test ratio in order to assess the position of the firm before lending it money or allowing it credit.
- Suppliers will be interested to know how likely the company is to be able to pay its debt if allowed credit.
- Competitors will want to know how vulnerable or solid a company may be before, for example, launching a new line or a take-over bid.

Ratios

The main ratios used are as follows:

- efficiency or activity ratios measure how efficiently a firm is using its resources
- gearing measures how dependent a company is on long-term finance

Finance and accounts

- liquidity ratios are a special subset of activity ratios – they measure the short-term financial health of a company by looking at how capable it is of paying short-term liabilities
- profitability or performance ratios – measure the relationship between profit and other factors
- shareholders ratios are a special subset of these. They are ratios used by shareholders to assess the return they are getting or expect to get on their investment.

Activity ratios

Stock turnover is calculated as **cost of sales/stock** and measures the speed at which stock is being turned over; the higher the figure, the faster the stock turnover.

Asset turnover is calculated as **sales turnover/assets** employed and measure how hard the assets of the company are working. A higher figure for the asset turnover ratio means that the company is generating greater amounts of turnover from the same assets. Changes in the asset ratio will affect a company's ROCE (see below). Making assets work harder or selling off underutilised assets would both improve ROCE.

Interest cover is how many times the operating profit can pay interest payments. If it is less than 1, the firm cannot afford to pay its interest; if it is 1 then all profits must go to pay interest and there will be none for distribution to shareholders. In general a firm would be looking for a ratio of between 3 and 4.

Gearing

Gearing measures long-term borrowing as a percentage of the firm's long-term capital employed. It is measured as **long-term borrowing/capital employed** expressed as a percentage. A high level of gearing means that a firm has a high percentage of borrowings and is therefore more vulnerable to adverse changes in the economy than a company with low gearing. High gearing means that the company has a long-term commitment to paying interest. A high level of gearing may mean that there is no money left to pay shareholder dividends. High gearing, therefore, can mean low levels of interest cover.

Liquidity

Liquidity ratios measure how capable a business is of paying its short-term liabilities i.e. the financial wellbeing of the company in the short-term. The figures would be taken from the balance sheet of a company.

Current ratio or working capital ratio is measured as **current assets/current liabilities.** A healthy ratio would be in the region of 1.5:1 to 2:1. It measures how many times over the company could pay its current liabilities from its current assets. A figure too low means that the company is over-stretched. A figure too high means that assets are being underused.

Acid test ratio is measured as **current assets – stock/current liabilities**. A healthy ratio is in the region of 0.8:1 to 1:1. This is the same measure as the current ratio except that the company's stock is not included as part of its assets. Consider a company which produces blue chewing gum going through a period of difficulty because the demand for blue chewing gum has fallen. It will have stocks of blue chewing gum that will be included when working out its current ratio. However, the reason it is in difficulty is because the chewing gum is no longer wanted. Stock may not be as valuable as a company says so this measure is a much more genuine measure of a company's ability to pay short-term debt.

Profitability ratios

These ratios measure how profitable a company is in terms of the assets it has employed and the capital it has invested. There are various measures of profit and therefore various profitability ratios.

Gross profit margin

The gross profit margin, is measured as **gross profit/turnover** expressed as a percentage. Gross profit margins need to be interpreted in the light of the type of business that the company is in. Are overheads likely to be high or low? Whether or not a firm's gross profit margins are improving can be decided by considering past gross profit margin figures and establishing trends.

Net profit margin

The net profit margin is measured as **net profit/turnover** expressed as a percentage. The higher the percentage, the better the company is performing. This is a more accurate measure than gross profit ratio as it takes overheads into account.

ROCE

The most important profitability ratio is ROCE or Return On Capital Employed. It is calculated as **operating profit/capital employed** as a percentage. Its importance is such that it is sometimes referred to as the primary efficiency ratio. It shows the return that

Ratio analysis

the firm is getting on the long-term capital it is using. ROCE needs to be higher than returns that could be earned from safer investments, such as banking the money. An average firm generates between 15% and 25% ROCE.

> **FACTFILE**
>
> You must always judge ratios in the light of the business that the company is in. A railway company, for example, will have a lot of assets but a poor asset turnover ratio; a firm of City analysts may have virtually no tangible assets.

Shareholder ratios

These are used by shareholders to assess the value of their investment against other companies and against other possible uses for their money. They will usually wish to maximise their returns. The main ratios used are:

- return on equity: **earnings/shareholders funds** expressed as a percentage. This shows how much profit a shareholder might expect compared to their investment – the higher the percentage, the better.
- earnings per share: **earnings/number of shares issued** expressed in money terms. This can be compared to previous levels of earnings.
- p/e ratio: the price to earnings ratio measured **as share price/profit available for distribution** – this measures the value of the share against the dividends earned by the share. The higher the figure, the more an investor will be willing to pay to buy the share, reflecting confidence in the business.
- dividend yield: the **dividend per share/price of share** expressed as a percentage. The higher the figure, the better the return on the share. This return needs to be above that which could be obtained by no-risk activities such as banking the money.

Add these points to your Mind Map

Limitations to ratio analysis

These are similar to those stated for accounts in general:

- Ratios are of limited use if looked at in isolation; they need to be studied in the context of the firm's strategic objectives and long-term goals.
- Figures may not be accurate or up-to-date. In many cases the information being used is merely 'the best available' meaning that it is as current as can be managed. Sometimes figures from previous years, twelve months out of date, have to be used as they are the 'best available'.
- Figures are often not absolutes and are therefore open to interpretation.
- It is in the interests of the business to window dress its public accounts to provide competitors with misleading information.

Analysing financial accounts

If you are analysing financial accounts in order to answer an examination question, use the 'Who? Why? Which? How 3?' method.

- **Who** wants to know the information? Is it a prospective lender, investor, supplier, competitor?
- **Why** do they want to know? Are they thinking of buying shares, investing, lending money, accepting an order (can they pay), taking the firm over?
- **Which** figures are they interested in? Are they interested in profitability, liquidity, efficiency, gearing, shareholder ratios?
- **How** can the figures be analysed? 'How 1' is to find the figures in the accounts. 'How 2' is to work out the relevant ratios. 'How 3' is to compare these figures with previous periods (analyse trends) or with competitors.

> **CHECKLIST**
>
> ✓ Ratio analysis is just part of financial accounting.
>
> ✓ Ratio analysis will be used by managers, investors, creditors, suppliers and competitors.
>
> ✓ The main ratios used measure
>   - efficiency or activity
>   - the ability of a company to pay debt (liquidity and gearing)
>   - profitability.
>
> ✓ Ratios need to be used to make comparisons; without other information they are fairly meaningless.

Mind Map

Finish off your Mind Map by adding all the rest of the points mentioned. Don't forget to use word pictures where appropriate.

Study and Revise AS and A2 Level Business Studies

Finance and accounts

TEST YOURSELF

Use your Mind Map to see if you can answer the following questions.

AS

1. Which ratio would you recommend as being most important to:
   a a supplier?
   b a shareholder?
   c a manager?
2. Explain why ROCE is considered to be the primary efficiency ratio.
3. How would you analyse financial accounts?

A2

1. What are the main 'families' of ratios?
2. Outline which group of people would be particularly interested in which ratio.
3. How would you analyse financial accounts?

Sample question and answer

What are the main ratios used in business? Explain how these would be used by a manager.

1. The main ratios used are:
   - activity ratios which measure how efficiently a firm is using its resources
   - liquidity ratios which measure how easily the firm can pay its debts
   - gearing which measures how dependent a company is on long-term finance
   - performance ratios – measure the amount of profit being made compared to the inputs being used
   - shareholders ratios which allow shareholders to judge how well their investments are doing
2. For each state which ratio you think is most important, how it is measured, and what it is used for. For example, for performance ratios ROCE is probably the most important, it is measured by net profit/capital employed x 100 and it is used to show how good a return investors are getting on their money.
3. Managers' use of ratios will be to:
   - measure their performance against that of other managers either in their own company or a rivals
   - measure their performance in the current time period to previous periods of time
   - make predictions of future levels of return
4. The main problem with the use of such figures is that they are all studied with 'hindsight' – they are what has happened, up to twelve months ago in some cases. They should also be viewed with some caution as they may not be accurate, may be presented in a misleading way and are open to interpretation.

Summary

- Ratio analysis is a part of financial accounting.
- It is used with other financial accounting methods and with management accounting to help in setting and reaching strategic objectives.
- The main ratios concern:
  - efficiency: how effectively a company is using its resources
  - liquidity and gearing: how capable a company is of paying long and short-term debt
  - profitability: how profitable the company is, how this affects shareholders returns.
- Ratios need to be used to compare different time periods and different companies. They ensure that comparisons are meaningful.

People in business — SECTION 4

Specification content

Advanced Supplementary (AS)

AQA

Module 2 is *'People and Operations Management'*. It includes:

- Management structure and organisation
- Organisational design
- Management by objectives
- Delegation and consultation
- Motivation theory and practice
- Management and leadership styles
- Human resource management

OCR

Module 2972 is *'Business Decisions'* and Module 2873 is *'Business Behaviour'*. They include:

- People in organisations
- Management and organisational structures
- Human resource planning
- Motivation and leadership
- Management structure and design, effects on organisational performance

Edexcel

Unit 1 is *'Business in Context'*. It includes:

- Internal organisation
- Communication
- Motivation

Advanced Level (A2)

AQA

Module 5 is *'People and Operations Management'*. It includes:

- Communication
- Employer/employee relations – collective and individual levels
- Employee participation and industrial democracy
- Trades Unions, ACAS and relevant legislation
- Human resource management
- Measuring personnel effectiveness

OCR

Module 2876 is *'Further People in Organisations'* (optional). It includes:

- Communication
- Organising and controlling the activities of people at work
- Motivation
- Organising on a production or systems basis
- Leadership and management styles
- Management of change
- Employer/employee relations including the law, the labour market, the implications of EU
- Employee participation
- Methods of remuneration

Edexcel

Unit 3 is *'Analysis and Decision Making'*. It includes:

- Industrial relations decisions
- Principles of employment law
- EU employment law

Unit 5 is *'Business Planning'*. It includes:

- Human resource planning
- Recruitment and selection
- Appraisal and training
- Leadership and motivation

Chapter 19: Management structure and organisation

PREVIEW

- In this chapter you will revise the way in which companies are organised. You will need to be aware of the advantages and disadvantages of different organisational structures.
- You will need to know why organisational structures are needed and be able to say why a particular organisational structure is appropriate to a particular business.
- If you are an AS student you will need to understand the significance of various management and organisational structures for both businesses and stakeholders in business.
- If you are an A2 student you will need to be able to understand the relationships between organisational structure, leadership style and motivation. You will need to use your skill of synthesis to draw on other areas of your specification if you are to answer questions on this topic fully.
- See if you can answer at least four of these five questions before reading the rest of the chapter.

Questions

1. Explain why all businesses need organisation.
2. What is meant by a hierarchical pyramid?
3. What is the difference between authority and responsibility?
4. What is the difference between informal and formal organisation structure? Which tends to be the more powerful?
5. Why do you think that there are different ways of representing organisational structures?

Check your answers before reading the rest of the chapter. Try answering the questions again when you've finished the chapter.

Mind Map

Start a Mind Map similar to the one shown here. Put a central image of your own in the middle. This image works for me – it makes me think of structures as being the framework within which managers operate. You need to draw an image that works for you! The first 'legs' of the Mind Map have been started for you. Add points to your map as you work through the chapter. At the end of the chapter is an example of what a finished Mind Map might look like. Don't forget, you can – and should – use at least three colours for the central image and different colours for each leg.

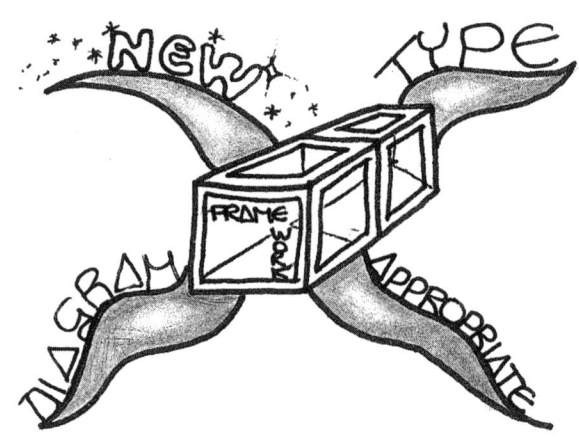

Definition

Organisational structure is needed in a business for planning, communications and efficiency. Management structure can be shown on an organisation chart of a business. This shows the relationships between the parts of an organisation and indicates the authority at each level.

Management structure – why organise?

Organisation is essential for any business. From the smallest sole trader to the biggest multi-national, the questions of who is going to do what, with what resources, how and why, all have to be answered. Without a form of organisation business cannot exist. However, that organisation does not have to be a formal or highly structured one. There are numerous possibilities for organisation structures. The key factor in terms of efficiency, is for a business to choose that form of organisation which best suits its own size and its aims and objectives. Choosing and controlling the organisational structure is thus a vital part of the overall strategy and planning of a firm.

Formal vs informal structures

Formal structures have planned relationships, limited communication channels and carefully delineated

Management structure and organisation

authority. It says who is allowed to do what and how they should pass on and receive instructions.

Informal structures cannot be shown on an organisation chart. They are the relationships and communication channels which exist within and between informal groups of workers in a business, They may be based on common interests, shared aspirations (lottery or pools syndicates) or friendship groups. Communication between such groups (often called the 'grapevine') can be much quicker and more effective than formal channels.

FACTFILE

The more centralised an organisation is, the more unstable it will become on the demise of its central character. Think of the great generals – Napoleon, Alexander, Caesar. Did their organisations outlive them?

Organisational structures

Organisational structures can be shown on organisational diagrams:

- family tree type structures which show each level of an organisation and its links to other levels
- pyramid structures where there are less people with authority at the top of the organisation; more people at the bottom

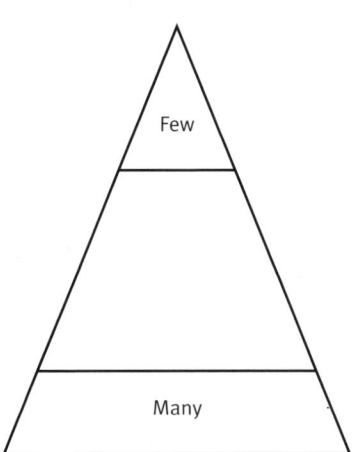

A pyramid structure

- circles – this is a way of trying to show an organisational structure without underlining the hierarchy; people within the same circle are at the same level; the organisation will still be a hierarchical one

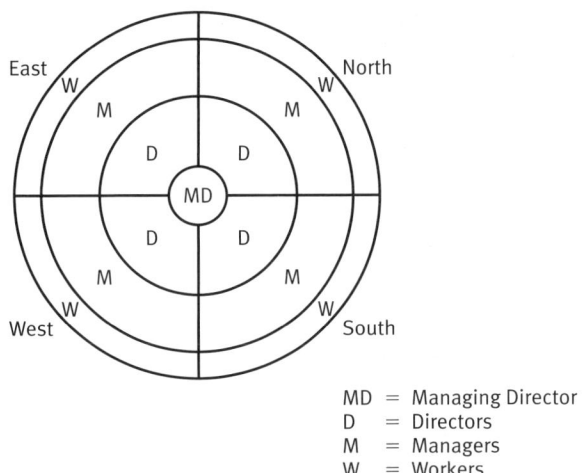

MD = Managing Director
D = Directors
M = Managers
W = Workers

A circle for a firm with a regional structure

- matrices – these 'cat's cradles' show the relationships between individuals or parts of the organisation in a non-hierarchical manner.

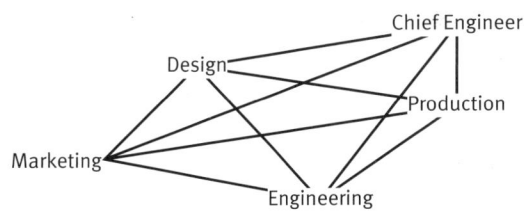

A 'cat's cradle' structure

Organisations may be structured according to a number of different formats:

- by function, i.e. organised according to what a part of the organisation does
- by product, i.e. organised according to what a part of the organisation produces
- by geography, i.e. organised according to where a part of the organisation is situated

Pyramids

Pyramid structures can be tall and thin, with many levels of responsibility. Such pyramids are formally hierarchical and each level of responsibility has a narrow span of control. A typical tall, thin organisation is to be found in the armed forces with many ranks.

Other pyramid structures are wide and flat. These have few layers of hierarchy, each layer having a wide span of control and greater authority than in the tall, thin organisation. There are limited chances of promotion.

People in business

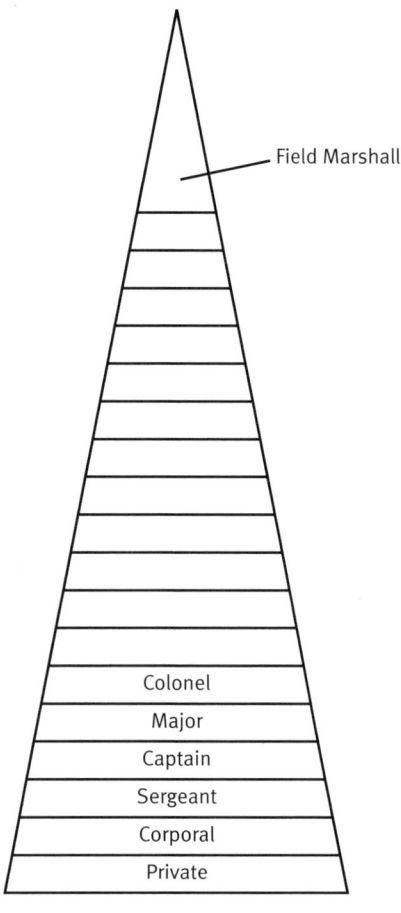

Tall pyramid structure

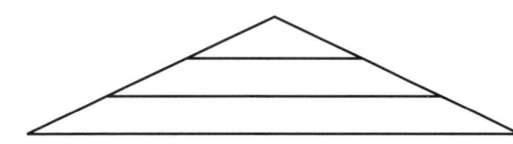

Flat pyramid structure

Terms you need to know

Some of these are shown on the hierarchical pyramid below. A hierarchical pyramid shows that top layers have more authority than bottom layers; there are fewer people at each layer the nearer to the top of the organisation you go.

subordinate: someone who is accountable to someone else, senior to them, in the organisation

authority: the right to tell someone else what to do within the confines of the organisation

span of control: the number of subordinates that a manager has authority over

chain of command: how instructions are passed down the organisation and feedback is passed up

delegation: the power to give a certain amount of authority or responsibility to someone else in the organisation

delayering: the practice of removing managerial layers from an organisation to make it more flexible

line managers: have objectives set, have specific authority and are part of a formal structure

Other staff roles are advisory or of a nature that is non-line, for example, personnel and administrative staff.

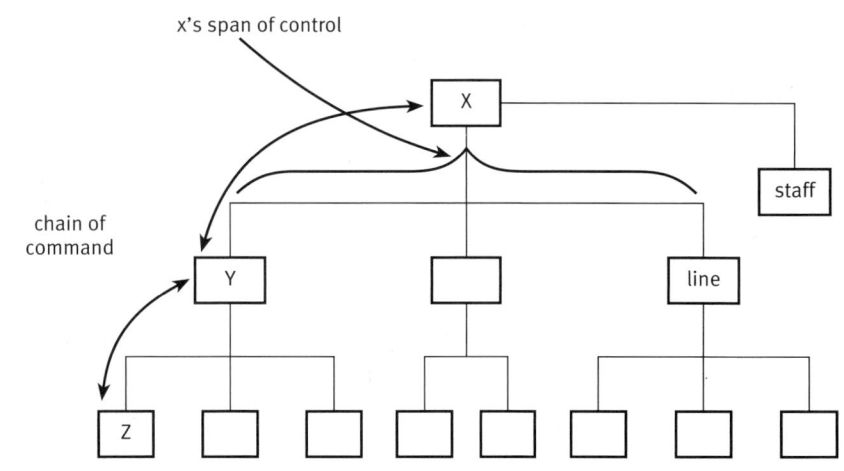

Hierarchical pyramid

Y is subordinate to X
Z is subordinate to Y and X
X has authority over Y and Z
Y has authority over Z
X can delegate to Y or Z
Y can delegate to Z

Management structure and organisation

Matching organisational structure to organisations

Charles Handy undertook some research into the types of organisation structure that might be suitable for a particular type of business. The structure is linked to the culture of the organisation. The culture is the way in which an organisation operates and is perceived by other organisations. Virgin is seen as a young, forward-looking business with a culture of innovation and change. You would not wish your solicitor to have the same values!

In a stable organisation, which is not innovative and not a risk-taker, a bureaucratic or formal hierarchy would be the most fitting.

In an organisation that takes a project-based approach, a matrix structure would be most appropriate. Teams can be recruited from across the organisation with specific specialisms to enable a particular task or project to be completed. In this structure authority levels are blurred; team work means greater motivation and job satisfaction but there can be problems with project team members having more than one superior (e.g. a junior production manager may be on the team for their expertise and reporting to their own senior manager and the project leader). Senior managers are sometimes wary of this approach as it breaks down traditional barriers and moves authority down the organisation. Firms such as Nissan have, however, proved that matrix organisation is an effective way to manage innovation.

Handy suggests that some organisations have a power culture, i.e. they are based around a central, powerful figure. When Mirror Group Newspapers (MGN) was owned by Robert Maxwell, this was certainly true. He had a hand in all parts of the organisation and few decisions could be made without his influence. This web structure shows its inherent weakness when the spider at the centre leaves the organisation. The Maxwell organisation collapsed on his death.

The opposite of a hierarchical structure is one where little formal structure exists at all. The organisation is only there to promote or support a particular individual. Examples of this 'person culture' might be creative organisations such as Saatchi and Saatchi and Jean-Paul Gaultier, where the person is more important than the organisation.

An appropriate organisational structure will deliver many benefits to the business:

- costs can be kept down
- the use of cost centres and profit centres can provide examples for other parts of the business
- good communications and information can help to motivate workers
- inviting workers to participate and encouraging feedback will motivate them
- faster and more accurate decisions will be made, giving the business a commercial edge
- good co-ordination and control means projects will be finished faster and better
- problems will be spotted and solved at an earlier stage
- managers in the right place in the organisation overseeing work will ensure quality and consistency

FACTFILE

You should be able to link these different types of organisational pattern with the factors affecting cost and profit centres. How do you think that they are related to each other?

Who makes the decisions?

If the main decisions are made by senior managers and directors within the organisation, it is also likely that they will retain most of the authority and be reluctant to delegate. This sort of centralised organisation has the advantage that decisions are made by the people with power and experience who should have an overview of the organisation. The disadvantage is that they may be too far removed from the reality of the business to understand the consequences of decisions and that their overview may not be an accurate one – managers further down the hierarchy may have a clearer idea of what effect decisions will have.

Decentralised organisation means that the authority to make decisions is passed down the hierarchy to subordinate layers. This means that parts of the organisation have the authority to act quickly and in response to changing conditions. However, the lack of an overview may be a disadvantage. Decentralised decision-making leads to greater flexibility in organisations.

Bureaucratic vs flexible

The armed forces are a good example of a bureaucratic structure. Bureaucracy means that the organisation follows a clear set of rules and precedents. If a decision has to be made it is made

People in business

'according to the book'. Decisions for which there are no precedents or rules are referred up the hierarchy. Individuals within the organisation are effectively discouraged from being innovative or independent. This leads to an extremely stable organisational structure which is predictable in its responses. The weakness of the system is that it discourages ideas and change.

A flexible organisation is willing to consider its framework and change it if necessary. The strength of this system is the ability to respond to change quickly and efficiently. The weakness is that too much flexibility can lead to disorganisation and chaos.

Managers and management

People in positions of authority within organisational structures are managers. Their job can be summed up in the cycle of management.

Managers:

set targets → plan strategy → communicate strategy → organise → delegate responsibility → co-ordinate and control → motivate → monitor → achieve targets → report to superiors

The way that managers carry out these functions will further affect their efficiency and power. This is discussed in detail in the following chapter on management styles.

Current innovations

Management consultants are always seeking new ways to improve organisational structures to make them more efficient. Innovations in the 1990s include:

Bench marking

This is checking the performance of a department, plant or process against that of a competitor and adopting 'best practice'. The use of cost and profit centres can encourage bench marking within an organisation.

Intrapreneurialism

Organisations in a competitive environment need to balance a set of rules against the ability to be flexible and proactive. This balance is called intrapreneurialism, a play on the word entrepreneur, meaning that the enterprise has to come from within the organisation. Such organisations are market oriented and encourage and reward ideas and innovation.

BPR

This stands for Business Process Re-engineering. BPR encourages people in an organisation to define what they actually do and to share this with colleagues. Positive contributions should be isolated and maintained whilst the rest of the organisation is completely re-structured. The drawbacks of this system are that sometimes this is an excuse for a new manager to impose their own systems; sometimes it is a response to a crisis; sometimes good features are swept away with the rest.

CHECKLIST

✓ Organisational structures are formal or informal.

✓ Formal structures may be:
 – hierarchical
 – pyramidical
 – tall and thin
 – wide and flat.

✓ Decision-making may be centralised or decentralised.

✓ Different cultures lead to different appropriate structures. An appropriate structure is essential.

TEST YOURSELF

Use your Mind Map to see if you can answer the following questions.

AS

1 Apart from the business itself, who else might need to see the business's organisation structure?

2 Define authority, responsibility, delegation.

3 Suggest different ways in which a firm might be organised.

A2

1 Why is it important for a business to have an appropriate structure?

2 Why do organisations 'delayer'?

3 What do you understand by the term 'organisational culture'?

Management structure and organisation

Mind Map

Finish off your Mind Map by adding all the rest of the points mentioned. Don't forget to use word pictures where appropriate. An example of a finished Mind Map is shown below.

Sample question and answer

Suggest what organisational structures would be appropriate for a stable, non-innovative firm or an innovative competitive firm. Discuss the main benefits and drawbacks of each approach.

1. There are numerous possibilities for organisation structures. The key factor is for a business to choose that form of organisation which best suits its own size and its aims and objectives. It is linked into the overall strategy and planning of a firm.
2. Charles Handy: The culture of a firm is the way in which it operates and is perceived by other organisations. Organisational structure needs to be linked to culture.
3. In a stable organisation which is not innovative and not a risk taker a bureaucratic or formal hierarchy would be the most fitting.
   The main benefits of a bureaucratic structure are certainty and stability.
   The main drawbacks are its slowness to operate and its inability to respond to change
4. In an innovative firm a matrix structure would be more appropriate. In this structure, teams can pool expertise and individual projects can be encouraged to go forward.
   The main benefits of a matrix structure are flexibility and adaptability.
   The main drawbacks are the blurring of chains of command and the possible lack of clear direction or overview.
5. Conclusion: an appropriate organisational structure will deliver many benefits to the business. It is essential that organisational structure is linked to business culture and to the objectives and strategies of the firm.

Summary

- Organisation is essential to the efficient running of a business.
- The type of organisation needs to be appropriate to the type of business.
- Organisations may be formal or informal. Informal communication tends to be more powerful.
- Organisations tend to be
  - hierarchical pyramids: authority at the top, more people at the bottom
  - matrices: equal standing for all levels within a project team although drawn from different levels of the organisation
  - webs: based on a central, sometimes charismatic, figure.
- Stable organisations suit bureaucratic structures.
- Innovative businesses need more flexible approaches.

Study and Revise AS and A2 Level Business Studies

Chapter 20: Management styles

PREVIEW

- In this chapter we look at how the organisational structure of a firm is linked to leadership styles and to methods of motivating people. You need to be able to evaluate how different styles and different combinations of styles and leadership can affect the management and planning of human resources within an organisation.
- To do this you will need to not only know the theories involved, but also be able to apply them to situations or cases that you have studied. You will need to know the advantages and disadvantages of various styles of management and leadership and be able to recommend which will be effective in which circumstance.
- You will be expected to show knowledge of the major contributors to particular areas of management study. Remember, management theories do not tend to conflict, but to develop details of previous theories.
- See if you can answer at least four of these five questions before continuing with the rest of the chapter.

Questions

1. What is the nature of the management process?
2. What do Minzberg and Fayol see as the role of the manager?
3. Look at the theories and theorists below. Link the correct theorist with the appropriate theory.

Taylor	Trait theory
Fayol	Autocratic/democratic
Maslow	Systems management
Tannenbaum and Schmidt	People vs Production
Likert	Scientific
Blake Mouton	Administrative
Handy	Human relations

4. Name five of the six recognised leadership styles.
5. Name three modern methods of management.

Check your answers before reading the rest of the chapter. Try answering the questions again when you've finished the chapter.

Mind Map

Start a Mind Map similar to the one shown here. Put a central image of your own in the middle. This image works for me – it makes me think of targets and attempting to reach them; it reminds me that businesses operate within a framework. You need to draw an image that works for you! The first 'legs' of the Mind Map have been started for you. Add points to your map as you work through the chapter. Don't forget, you can – and should – use colour!

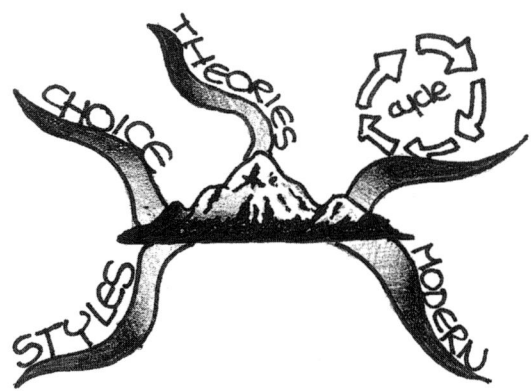

FACTFILE

The cycle of management is part of the strategic planning of a company or organisation. Look at the diagram on page 113 and learn the stages in the cycle of management.

Theories of management

Each school of management theory tends to build on the work of a previous school. The earliest theories are those of F.W. Taylor (1856–1915) with later theories still currently being developed.

Scientific management

This theory states that workers are motivated by monetary rewards and need clear guidance. Taylor sought to increase productivity:

- by breaking down jobs into component parts (specialisation)
- by providing monetary rewards for increased production (piece work)

Management styles

The role of the manager starts with target setting – when a target is achieved, a new one needs to be set. (*Minzberg, Fayol*)

The cycle of management: Set target >> Devise strategy >> Communicate strategy >> Organise >> Delegate responsibility >> Co-ordinate and Control >> Monitor >> Motivate >> Achieve >> Report >>

Administrative management

Fayol defined the higher functions of management as being able to:

- plan
- organise and delegate
- instruct or command
- co-ordinate
- control

Human relations

The human relations school of management looks at psychological needs and how these can be met to improve production and productivity (Maslow, Herzberg, McGregor). This is treated in more detail in the section on motivation on page 126.

Systems management

Likert puts management styles into four systems, ranging from the democratic and participative to the autocratic 'top-down' management style. Each business organisation is seen as a total system, taking in factors of production, processing them and producing goods or services. Each part of the system is dependent on the other parts; the bigger the organisation, the more sub-systems there are and the greater is the potential for breakdown if management is ineffective or inefficient.

- **System 1:** autocratic and exploitative, motivation through threats and punishment
- **System 2:** authoritative but benevolent, allowing some consultation but retaining control
- **System 3:** consultative, motivation through rewards, subordinates' opinions sought
- **System 4:** participative, subordinates fully involved

Contingency theories

These suggest that particular management styles should be chosen to suit particular circumstances. Things that may vary are:

- the job to be done
- the time scale
- the personnel available
- the materials available
- the opinion of the personnel of the manager

An authoritarian style might be appropriate, for example, if:

- the job needs to be well-defined
- the time scale is tight
- personnel and materials need to be organised or commandeered
- the subordinates have a respect for the manager

Modern methods of management

These are based on the involvement and empowerment of workers. Examples include:

Team working

Management decisions are taken by and within teams. Management agree objectives with teams and teams are then empowered to meet those objectives.

Quality circles

Small groups of subordinates meet to discuss problems and/or improvements to working practices. This leads to a consultative process with management, giving subordinates a feeling of greater control over decision-making.

Human Resources Management (HRM)

Introduced from Japan and used by firms such as Marks and Spencer and IBM, Human Resource Management considers the welfare of the worker and involves them in decision-making and the generation of ideas, performance related pay and excellent selection and training systems.

People in business

Management by Objectives (MBO)

Peter Drucker introduced the idea of management by objectives. Managers decide objectives as part of general strategy and specific targets to reach on the way to these objectives. This is part of the planning cycle. The MBO system is based on the manager communicating these objectives to subordinates and agreeing the objectives. In order to measure success, targets must be time limited and quantifiable 'SMART' targets, but the crucial part of the system is for workers and management to agree the objectives. This agreement is seen as 'ownership' (as opposed to imposition) and motivates workers to want to achieve objectives. MBO is seen as being particularly useful in large organisations where effective communications become stretched.

FACTFILE

A SMART target is:
- **SPECIFIC**: you should know when an objective has been reached by making it as definite as possible.
- **MEASURABLE**: it should, where possible, be quantifiable.
- **ATTAINABLE**: it should be a target that it is possible to achieve.
- **RELEVANT**: it should form a logical part of the business's overall strategy.
- **TIME-RELATED**: there should be a time for achievement set.

CHECKLIST

✓ The role of the manager is to:
  - set targets
  - make decisions
  - delegate authority
  - communicate
  - motivate employees.

✓ Minzberg defines the functions of a manager as:
  - entrepreneur: the function of decision-making or risk-taking
  - trouble-shooter: responding to difficult situations as they arise (Minzberg uses the term 'disturbance handler')
  - allocator: of both human and non human resources
  - negotiator: communicator and go-between.

Leadership styles

Managers will operate particular leadership styles. The best managers will vary their style to suit the situation. The main types are:

Authoritarian or autocratic

Central, clearly defined directives. The disadvantage is that there is no room for subordinate input, leading to dissatisfaction, e.g. 'Put it there.'

Laissez faire

The opposite of autocratic, allowing subordinates the freedom to make decisions within broad guidelines. This allows for innovation but may leave subordinates feeling that they have little direction or support, e.g. 'You decide where it goes.'

Democratic

Subordinates participate in decision-making on an equal or apparently equal footing with management. This can be time consuming and undermine management control but does lead to more motivation and job satisfaction, e.g. 'Do you think we should put it there? Let's discuss it and take a vote.'

Bureaucratic

Decisions are made according to the rules – this can be very inflexible and frustrating to subordinates but has the advantage of certainty. Such decision-making may be seen as typical of organisations such as the armed forces, e.g. 'Rule 41b says that it must go there (even if its in the way).'

Paternalistic

Managers consider the welfare of their workers when making a decision. However, the management idea of welfare may conflict with that of the workers. (In the same way that your opinion of what is good for you may conflict with your parents!) e.g. 'I think you'd be much happier if it was put there.'

Hands-on

Managers consider that they will get a better insight into the job and be able to make more informed decisions if they involve themselves with the work of their subordinates, This can have a detrimental effect if it is viewed as interference but a positive effect if it is viewed as 'management mucking in'.

FACTFILE

The best managers will not operate a single leadership style, but will alter their style of leadership to suit the situation.

Management styles

Choice of style

Think about how you could get someone to do a simple job, e.g. to close a door. The way in which you get the job done defines your management style. Look at the alternative possible commands/requests:

- Close the door!
- Close the door if you like.
- Let's see if we all want the door closing.
- The rules say that you must close the door.
- You'll feel better if I close the door.
- I'll close the door for you.

Think about how you would like to be asked. Which styles do you think workers are more comfortable with? With which styles are managers more likely to be comfortable?

Tannenbaum & Schmidt proposed a range of management styles:

					Democratic
					I share
				I consult	
			I test		
		I sell			
	I tell				
Autocratic					

- 'I tell': you will do as I say
- 'I sell': you will do as I say because I have persuaded you as to my reasons
- 'I test:' I allow subordinates to participate in decision-making but reserve the power to take back control if necessary
- 'I consult': I seek the opinions of my subordinates before making a decision, they consult with me before making a decision
- 'I share': decisions are made equally, usually as part of a team

The Blake Mouton grid makes the comparison between those managers who are more concerned with people than production and those more concerned with production than people. The grid shows extremes of management styles.

Concern with production

- 1.1 – little concerned with either people or production, an unlikely and 'impoverished' management style
- 1.9 – very concerned with workers' welfare, possibly to the detriment of the production task – termed 'country club management'
- 5.5 – balancing the concern for people with an equal concern for the task 'middle of the road' management
- 9.1 – very concerned with the production task possibly to the detriment of the workers welfare
- 9.9 – extremely concerned with both people and production – a teamwork approach to management
- All other 'squares;' on the grid are possible. The best managers will vary style to suit situations.

Trait theory

Some people in business seem to have certain 'traits' which make them good leaders or managers, e.g. Rupert Murdoch (News International), Anita Roddick (The Body Shop), Richard Branson (Virgin). Can these traits be identified?

Handy identifies leadership traits as:

- intelligence
- initiative
- self-assurance
- the ability to take an overview (termed the 'helicopter' factor)

People in business

Sample question and answer

'Managers are becoming increasingly obsolete as the role of the manager has been replaced by the role of the team.' Discuss this statement.
Use a mini Mind Map to plan this through a question and answer approach.

1. What is the traditional role of the manager? What is it according to theorists?
   - The role of the manager is to set targets, devise the strategy for reaching those targets, organise a team to meet the targets, delegate responsibility, communicate, monitor and assess when the targets have been reached before setting a new target. Part of the role is to motivate employees.
   - Minzberg defines management functions as entrepreneur, trouble-shooter, allocator and negotiator.
   - Taylor saw the manager as being able to increase productivity by increasing monetary reward.
   - The human relations school sees motivation by other then money as being a bigger factor.
2. What is the role of the team?
   Teams work together towards common goals – either agreed by the team or agreed by management. The functions of communicating, monitoring and evaluating can be taken over within the team. Quality circles.
3. Are managers still needed? If so, why? If not, why?
   - It depends (always a good conclusion – answers are generally not 'right' or 'wrong' and the ability to evaluate both sides of an argument is central to achieving a good grade). Managers are still needed in order to set long-term targets and make strategic decisions; they also need to be able to take responsibility. Teams may end up with authority without responsibility.
   - Some management styles might be obsolete (e.g. autocratic – Likert's System 1) in many situations, but could still be appropriate if the nature of the task demands it.
4. Conclusion
   Teams are replacing traditional styles of management (quote a firm you know) but in certain circumstances, depending on the nature of the task, managers are still necessary. (It doesn't really matter which way your conclusion goes as long as it is presented as a balanced argument.)

TEST YOURSELF

Use your Mind Map to see if you can answer the following questions.

AS

1. What is the role of the manager? What does Minzberg define as management functions?
2. What is the difference between management and leadership?
3. Can you list the main leadership styles?

A2

1. What are the main management theories?
2. Can you explain what is meant by empowerment?
3. Can you outline the main management styles and link them to leadership styles?

Summary

- The management process is defined as 'getting tasks done through motivating or leading others'.
- Managers display different leadership styles:
  - authoritarian
  - laissez faire
  - democratic
  - paternalistic
  - bureaucratic
  - hands-on.
- A manager may only have one style. A good manager will be able to alter his/her style to suit the situation.

Employer/employee relations — CHAPTER 21

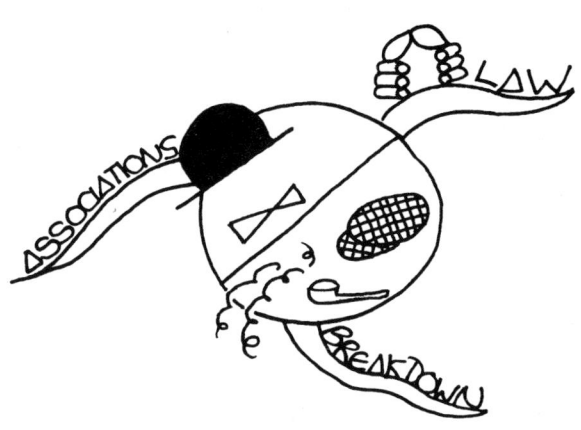

PREVIEW

- In this chapter you will revise the major aspects of employment law. You should understand the importance of good industrial relations and the causes and effects of break downs in those relations.
- You will need to know the framework for collective bargaining and consultation between employee and employer, including the nature and role of institutions such as trades unions and employer associations.
- You should be aware of the importance of communication between employer and employee and within an organisation.
- You should be aware of the changing patterns of employment linked to changes in the economy, the infrastructure and the changing needs of employers.
- See if you can answer at least four of these five questions before continuing with the rest of the chapter.

Questions

1. Can you define industrial relations?
2. What is meant by 'union recognition'?
3. Describe what you understand by 'collective bargaining'.
4. What are the five main areas in which there is employment legislation?
5. How is membership of the EU affecting employer/employee relations?

Check your answers before reading the rest of the chapter. Try answering the questions again when you've finished the chapter.

Mind Map

Start a Mind Map similar to the one shown here. Put a central image of your own in the middle. This image works for me – it makes me think of conflicts that have been resolved. It also reflects my traditional view of workers vs employers – this may not be your view! You need to draw an image that works for you! The first 'legs' of the Mind Map have been started for you. Add points to your map as you work through the chapter. Don't forget, you can – and should – use colour!

Definition

Employee–employer relations are the methods and reasons by which employer and employee communicate with each other. Much of the interaction is governed by legislation. Industrial relations covers the particular communication which relates to possible industrial disputes.

Employment law

The government legislates in five main areas of employment law:

- legislation designed to protect workers from injury and health risks – health and safety legislation
- legislation designed to encourage and promote equal opportunities and make discrimination illegal
- political legislation – laws fulfilling a political agenda regarding trades union power and influence
- legislation designed to help solve disputes between workers and employers including arbitration bodies such as ACAS and other government agencies such as industrial tribunals
- legislation brought about as a result of changes in EU law

You are not expected to know all the details and dates of the major Acts but are expected to have a broad knowledge of the major laws. The major Acts are:

Health and safety legislation

1961 Factories Act

This covers general health and safety issues such as adequate ventilation, fire exits, heating and lighting, guards on machinery, adequate washroom facilities.

Study and Revise AS and A2 Level Business Studies

People in business

1963 Offices Shops and Railway Premises Act

This extended much of the Factory Act regulations into other workplaces.

1974 Health and Safety at Work

This is the major health and safety Act. Many of the other regulations are based on this legislation or amendments to it. Its major features are:

- the working environment must be safe
- employers are obliged to provide necessary safety clothing and equipment
- businesses with five or more employees must display a written safety policy
- it set up the Health and Safety Executive with Inspectors who can check that premises are complying with the Act.
- union-appointed inspectors also have the right to check that employers are complying.

An important provision was to say that employers and employees are equally responsible for health and safety. The employer has a duty to provide a safe working environment. The employee has a duty to carry out his work as safely as possible.

1985 Reporting of Injuries, Diseases and Dangerous Occurrences Regulations

Certain listed diseases must be reported as must any accident occasioning an employee to take more than three days off work.

1988 Control of Substances Hazardous to Health Regulations

This was brought about due to the dangers of asbestos, but covers other harmful substances.

1989 Noise at Work Regulations

Employers should reduce the risk of damage to employees' hearing.

Equal opportunities legislation

Government has legislated to cover four of the five main areas where discrimination has taken place: gender, sex, race and disability. They have not yet tackled age discrimination.

1970 Equal Pay Act

Men and women should receive equal pay for equal work. A worker can make a claim by drawing a direct comparison with someone of a different gender in the organisation doing the same work.

1975 Sex Discrimination Act

Employers may not discriminate on grounds of gender or sexual orientation in employment terms, selection procedures, training, promotion opportunities, selection for redundancy. The Equal Opportunities Commission was set up to enforce the Act. There are three types of discrimination:

- direct discrimination, e.g. stating that a woman would be best for a job that could equally well be done by either sex
- indirect discrimination, e.g. not appointing a woman to a job because she might have children and need a career break
- positive discrimination – where an employer is allowed to discriminate in favour of a minority that has been traditionally discriminated against, e.g. employers with more than 20 workers have been encouraged to have at least 3% of their workforce drawn from the disabled.

Note that there are still some jobs which are allowed to be advertised for 'men only' or 'women only' due to the nature of the job.

1976 Race Relations Act

Discrimination on the grounds of race or colour is illegal.

1995 Disability Discrimination Act

Employers with 20 or more staff cannot discriminate against applicants or employees on grounds of disability, providing that they are capable of doing the job. For example, a firm could not deny someone in a wheelchair a job because there was no wheelchair access – they would be obliged to provide the access rather than refuse the appointment.

Political legislation

As a result of a series of industrial conflicts in the late 1970s and early 1980s, the Conservative government led by Margaret Thatcher decided to legislate to reduce the power of trade unions. The most damaging disputes were the 'winter of discontent' in 1978/79, when council workers went on strike in protest at a 5% ceiling imposed by government on pay rises, and the 1980 national steel strike and the coal miners strike. Further industrial problems, in particular difficulties in introducing new technology into the newspaper industry, led to further legislation.

You need to remember that, up to this point, there had been very little interference by the law in industrial relations. In extreme cases, unions might

Employer/employee relations

be taken to court by employers and there were some spectacular cases of judges ruling one way and then higher courts reversing the ruling. For example, the Law Lords eventually upheld the right of steel strikers to picket plants other than their own in 1980. The main legislation is:

1980 Employment Act

This removed the right of automatic trades union recognition at a place of work, meaning that employers could refuse to recognise and refuse to negotiate with a union. It also stopped the practice of 'flying pickets', limiting action to their 'own place of work'. This Act has led to 'beauty contests' between rival unions who wish to represent a firm or industry when employers have decided to recognise and negotiate with only one union. Single union agreements mean that all workers in a plant or factory are members of one union, which the employer recognises.

1982 Employment Act

This redefined what disputes were lawful. They had to be 'in pursuit of an industrial dispute'. This stopped unions from taking secondary action to support workers in dispute in other parts of their industry. If a dispute was deemed unlawful, union funds were open to sequestration and fines of up to quarter of a million pounds could be levied. The Act also made it easier for strikers to be dismissed.

1984 Trades Union Act

No strike action could take place without a secret ballot, with various rules and restrictions on how these must be carried out. If action was taken without the requisite ballot, employers could sue the union for damages.

1990 Employment Act

This extended the right to sue for losses from unofficial action to customers and suppliers.

1993 Trades Union Reform and Employment Rights Act

Employers must be given seven days notice of official action and a 'citizen's right' to stop unofficial strikes was established. This Act also abolished the remaining wages councils and minimum wage rates. It established a workers right to a Contract of Employment.

The Labour government, which came to power in 1997, has introduced minimum wage legislation but has not proposed any major reforms to trade union legislation.

FACTFILE

Union membership enjoyed a boom in the 1950s but has been decreasing over the last 40 years, this decrease accelerating in the 1980s and 1990s. One reason is the decline of traditional heavy industry such as coal mining, steel and ship building. Another is the increase in the number of women in the work force.

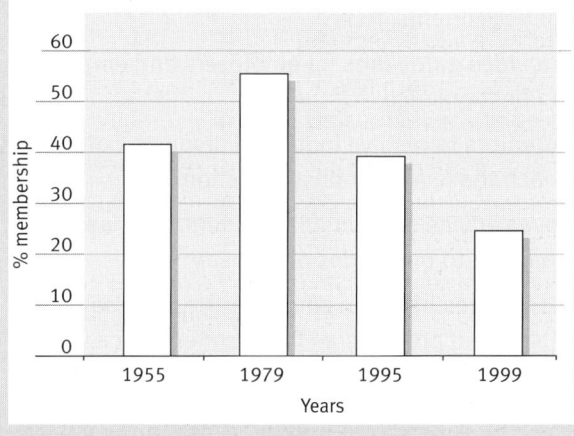

Union membership in the UK since 1955

Industrial relations legislation

Industrial relations involves negotiation and agreement between employers and employees.

The Industrial Relations Act 1971 protected employees against unfair or arbitrary dismissal. It was updated by the 1980 Act. Fair reasons for dismissal are described as:

- **incompetence:** an inability to carry out a task; dismissal is subject to warnings
- **redundancy:** when the job is no longer needed
- **gross misconduct:** dangerous, illegal or offensive conduct can result in immediate or summary dismissal
- continued employment that would break the law, e.g. a lorry driver who has lost his licence
- another substantial reason such as persistent lateness

Dismissal must follow a set dismissal procedure and workers must be aware of this. It usually consists of two verbal warnings and a written warning. Constructive dismissal is where an employer changes working conditions or practices so substantially as to force the employee to leave.

People in business

Industrial Tribunals

These were established to decide whether a dismissal was or was not fair and can order reinstatement, compensation and fines. They are independent judicial bodies.

ACAS

The Advisory Conciliation and Arbitration Service was set up in 1974 with a nine member council drawn equally from trades unions, employers associations and independents. ACAS:

- provides guidelines for employers and employees on best practice
- attempts to resolve industrial disputes before they reach the level of industrial action
- gives advice on industrial matters, such as training, to both sides of industry
- conciliates between employers and employees in dispute; it provides an independent voice which attempts to persuade the parties to negotiate
- mediates: proposes a solution between parties; they are not obliged to accept
- arbitrates between parties; provides an independent voice which proposes a settlement of a dispute. Both sides will agree to accept the result of the arbitration before it is made as ACAS has established a reputation for itself of being fair.

European Union legislation

The major piece of European legislation affecting industrial relations in the UK is the Social Charter. This sets out basic principles regarding workers rights. Minimum standards are directed in:

- health and safety in the workplace
- hours of work
- benefits and pension rights
- equal opportunities
- minimum wages
- worker participation

Because countries within the EU are all at different stages regarding employer/employee legislation, they agreed to the principle of *subsidiarity*. This effectively means that each country can introduce the reforms at its own pace and, to a certain extent, according to its own interpretation.

The Social Charter subsumes the 1993 Health and Safety (General Regulations) Act which brought six EU employment directives into force.

Industrial relations

Simply put, industrial relations involves the channels of communication between the employer and his representatives and between the employee and his representatives. Employee representation is usually by trade union but may be by professional association. These represent employees or the self employed who do not wish to belong to a union. Sometimes they are really trades unions by another name; sometimes (bodies such as the General Medical Council, the Law Society) they carry out functions apart from collective bargaining.

Trades Unions

Trades Unions are collections of workers. Traditionally, the power of the individual worker was limited but if he joined together with fellow workers, then a united or collective front could be established for bargaining with the employer – collective bargaining. The main types of union which developed are:

- **craft:** small trades with highly skilled workers
- **industrial:** representing all the workers in an industry
- **general:** representing workers in different industries
- **white-collar:** representing non industrial workers

Unions represent, educate, help and protect the interests of their members. When collective bargaining breaks down, unions have a number of weapons that they can use: the strike – the withdrawal of the workers labour – is an ultimate resort. Other actions include:

- **overtime bans:** refusing to work more than standard hours
- **work to rule:** following all the rules to the letter
- **go slows:** slowing down work rate

Strike action may be:

- **selective:** key people only strike (for example, if caretakers strike, buildings are not opened)
- one-day strikes
- all out strikes

In support of a strike, workers might try picketing – standing at a place of work and trying to persuade other workers not to break the strike. Those who do so are called 'black-legs'. The law prevents picketing from being intimidatory and has outlawed 'flying pickets' who picketed at other than their own workplace. Official pickets are limited to six people.

Employer/employee relations

The national body which represents most unions is the Trades Union Congress. This is a permanent body with full-time employees. It meets in conference once a year so that its members, nominated from the trades unions to which they belong, can decide on policy. It attempts to influence government and acts as spokesman for the Union movement. Its power and influence has been much diminished by the Conservative legislation of the 1980s.

Employer Associations

Employers may be represented by Employer Associations who represent the collective views and interests of employers in a particular industry. The national body that represents employers is called the Confederation of British Industry or CBI. It also attempts to influence government and acts as spokesman for the employers.

In a dispute, employers have their own set of 'weapons' including lock-outs, dismissal and recourse to the law if a strike looks like damaging their business.

Employee participation

Industrial relations can be improved by inviting employees to participate in the management process. This has the effect of increasing confidence and trust between employer and employee. There are both informal and formal ways to involve workers.

Informal
- Consultative committees where employees are asked their opinions
- Quality circles where groups of employees meet with management to share ideas and iron out problems

Formal
- Works councils: a committee of employee representatives is formed. Works councils have a right to co-determine policy with employers and to appoint a director to the board. These are common in Germany and Scandinavia, rarer in the UK.
- Worker directors: an employee representative on the Board; again, rare in the UK, common in Germany and Scandinavia; encouraged by the Social Charter

When workers have equal power in the policy and strategy making functions of a business this is called industrial democracy.

Mind Map

Finish off your Mind Map by adding all the rest of the points mentioned. Don't forget to use word pictures where appropriate.

FACTFILE

Pendulum arbitration is when two sides agree that, instead of seeking the middle ground, an arbitrator will decide in favour of employer or employee. This tends to make initial demands more reasonable.

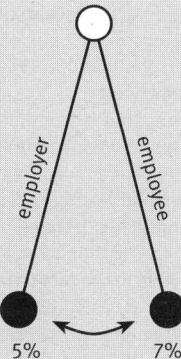

Pendulum arbitration brings opposing claims closer together to begin with

People in business

Sample question and answer

'Strikes are certainly less frequent than they were. The propensity to strike has been greatly reduced'.

Discuss this statement with regard to trends in industrial relations over the last 40 years.

You could use a mini Mind Map for a question and answer approach:

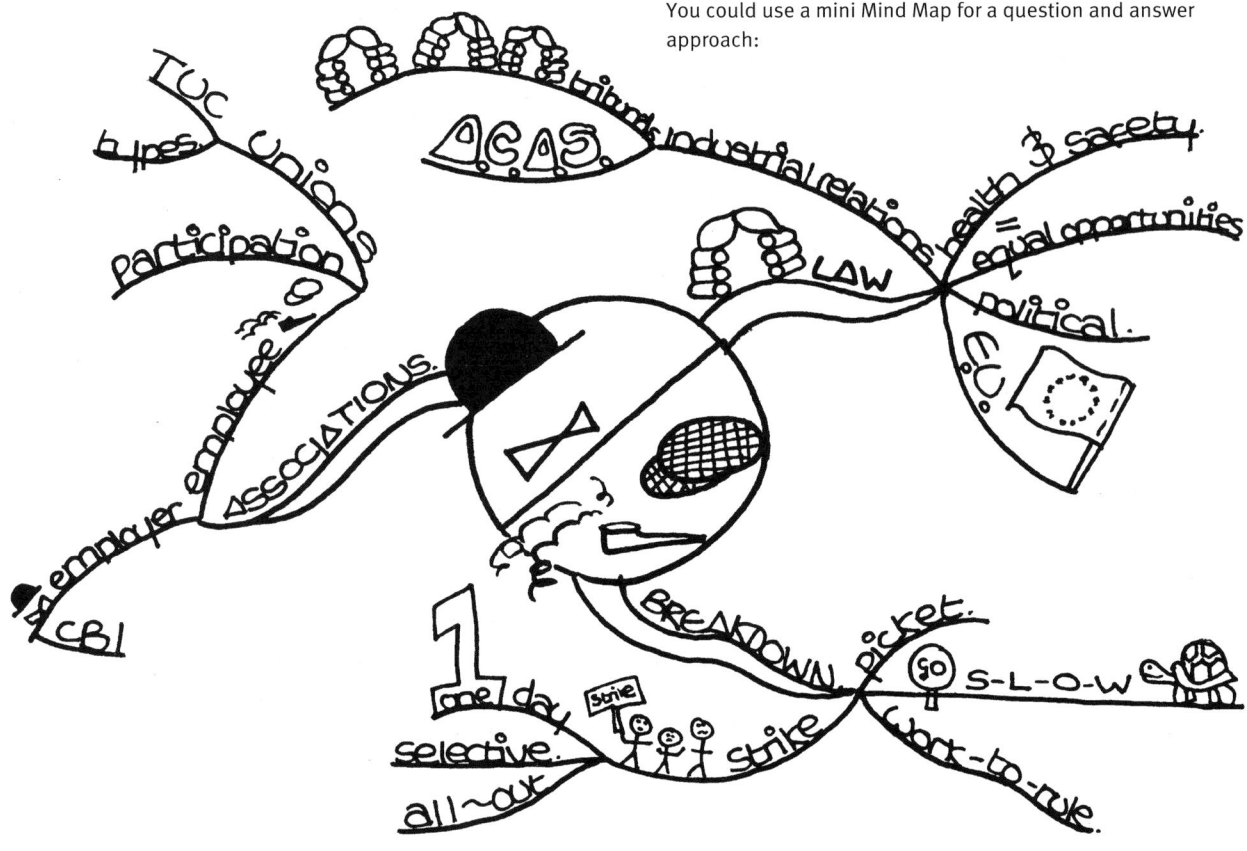

1. What is a strike? The ultimate form of industrial action – the ultimate signal that industrial relations have irrevocably broken down.
2. What are industrial relations? The dialogue between employer and employee.
3. What is an industrial dispute? A disagreement: about pay, working conditions, and working practices such as demarcation.
4. To establish whether strikes are less frequent, we need to compare then and now. The 1960s to mid-1980s saw more strikes. Unions were seen to wield power and brought down governments – Ted Heath's Conservative government and the three day week (1973/74); James Callaghan's labour government and 'the winter of discontent' 1979. Particularly high profile was the 1984 miners' strike. Strikes are less frequent and less high profile today. Why?
5. Changes in working practices.
   - Strikes were concentrated in certain industries, the characteristics of which were labour intensive, male dominated, excellent communications e.g. mining, steel, power workers, shipbuilding, car assembly lines. These traditional industries have declined or changed (e.g. car assembly is more capital than labour intensive now).
   - The amount of women in the labour force has increased; evidence shows they are less likely to strike
   - The amount of part-timers has increased
   - Workers are more multi-skilled and flexible, leading to less disputes over demarcation
6. Changes in labour supply and the economy
   - Strikes occurred in depressions (1920s and 30s; 1970s and 80s)
   - Full employment means no pool of replacement labour therefore stronger unions
   - control of inflation leads to lower pay demands
7. Changes in legislation
   - ACAS established in 1974 – helps solve disputes by mediation and arbitration.
   - Between 1980 and 1993 government legislated to make strike action harder – five major acts:
   - employers could refuse to recognise and negotiate with unions
   - mass and flying picketing outlawed
   - unions could be fined and sued for striking
   - strikes need an official ballot
   - unofficial strikes virtually outlawed
8. Some effects:
   - no-strike agreements made in order to be recognised
   - single union agreements which mean strikes would be more damaging therefore they are avoided
   - strikes must be planned and agreed therefore no 'shock tactics' means less effectiveness.
9. Conclusion
   Industrial action still happens but threat of industrial action may be enough. Non-strike action can be effective e.g. work to rule. Industrial relations may have improved with better working practices and communications channels between employer and employee.

   Do you agree with the statement? It's up to you, but balance your argument!

Employer/employee relations

CHECKLIST

✓ Employer/employee relations concern effective communication between employer and employee.

✓ Industrial relations concerns the facets of those communications channels that refer to possible disputes.

✓ Employers are represented by Employer Associations. The national body is the CBI.

✓ Employees are represented by Trades Unions and Professional Associations. The national body is the TUC.

✓ Legislation is generally enacted under one of the following headings:
- health and safety
- equal opportunities
- industrial relations
- European Union directives
- political motivation.

✓ Disputes are resolved by
- negotiation
- arbitration
- mediation
- industrial action.

✓ Worker participation in decisions leading to industrial democracy can greatly reduce industrial disputes.

TEST YOURSELF

Use your Mind Map to see if you can answer the following questions.

AS

1. What is the process of collective bargaining? Who is likely to be involved in it?
2. What is meant by the process of increased worker participation and industrial democracy?
3. What was the main thrust of the 1980s legislation concerning Trades Unions and workers rights?

A2

1. Why is winning a 'beauty contest' of particular importance to a trade union?
2. What reasons can you give for the power and influence of trades unions declining in recent years?
3. What are the functions of ACAS. How successful do you think it is at carrying out those functions?

Summary

- Employer/employee relations concerns effective communication between employer and employee.
- Industrial relations concerns the sections of that communication regarding the avoidance or resolution of industrial disputes.
- Legislation was traditionally to protect the worker.
- Later legislation tackled discrimination.
- Legislation regarding industrial relations is a fairly new concept but has been used to 'democratise' or 'limit the power of' trades unions (it is a matter of opinion).

Chapter 22: Human resource management

PREVIEW

- You will need to be able to evaluate how changes in the structure of labour supply affect both employer and employee.
- You need to understand how important good and appropriate recruitment strategies are and be able to suggest recruitment and training strategies for businesses.
- You need to understand how employees may be motivated including the rewards other than pay that may be offered. You should have knowledge of the main theories regarding motivation.
- Human resource management is only a part of the strategic management and objective setting of businesses. You need to use your skill of synthesis to draw on other relevant parts of your specification. As an A2 student you will need to be able to discuss the inter-relationship between organisational structure, leadership and motivation.
- See if you can answer at least four of these five questions before continuing with the rest of the chapter.

Questions

1. Can you define HRM? What is the difference between it and personnel management?
2. What external factors does a firm have to take into account when workforce planning?
3. Can you outline the process of recruitment and selection?
4. What different types of training might be offered?
5. Can you explain what is meant by appraisal?

Try answering the questions again when you reach the end of the chapter.

Mind Map

Start a Mind Map similar to the one shown here. Put a central image of your own in the middle. This image works for me – it makes me think of all the people in an organisation and the different things that they might want. You need to draw an image that works for you! The first 'legs' of the Mind Map have been started for you. Add points to your map as you work through the chapter. At the end of the chapter is an example of what a finished Mind Map might look like. Don't forget, you can – and should – use colour!

Definition

Human resource management (HRM) is using staff as a strategic resource to improve the business's performance. This is more than just the personnel function, placing greater emphasis on staff needs, skills and training in order to get the best work force to meet the businesses objectives.

Workforce planning

An employee starts by being recruited to a firm through a process of selection. Induction into the firm follows, then training, appraisal, promotion and finally dismissal, redundancy or retirement. Workforce planning involves a business analysing what workers they need, how many and when. When a vacancy arises managers have to decide firstly whether to fill it – does the business actually need that particular job (just because there has 'always been a senior grockle-squeezer' doesn't mean that there always has to be!) Secondly what calibre of worker it needs and, thirdly, how to attract that particular calibre.

External factors

There are many external factors affecting labour supply which will have an influence on who a firm can employ. These include:

- the changing nature of the economy – less jobs in heavy industry and manufacturing as both decline, more jobs in the service sector
- demography; the size and structure of the population and the way in which it is changing
- changing work patterns – earlier retirement, more part time workers, more teenagers staying on to

Human resource management

higher education; more women joining the labour force etc.
- legislation; factors such as the minimum wage may make a firm reluctant to employ more staff
- European influences such as the Social Charter, the move towards greater worker participation

Recruitment, selection, training

Recruitment

A firm decides what is needed through writing the following:
- **job analysis:** a detailed study of what the job entails,
- **job description:** a brief outline of the job that can be sent to applicants
- **person specification:** outline of exactly the qualities and qualifications needed for the job

A firm seeks applicants by:
- **advertisement:** this needs to be placed in the right medium to attract the right applicants
- **head-hunting:** finding exactly the right person for a job and then enticing them to join the firm
- **agencies:** using government (Job Centres) or private agencies

Application and selection

Application for a position may be by letter of application, filling in a form or sending a CV. An initial selection will then produce a long list, and then a short list of applicants for interview.

The interview may be conducted by a panel, an individual, an agency. Aptitude tests may be used to see if a person can do a job. Psychometric tests may be used to show if an applicant is a team player, or an individualist etc. (these may be unreliable and should be treated with caution).

A technique called situational interviewing may be used in which candidates are put into situations that might occur and the interviewers can observe how they cope.

Appointing

Appointment will be made through written confirmation of appointment. The worker is entitled to a Contract of Employment which states basic details of the post.

Training
- **induction training:** an introduction to the firm, basic information and an introduction to the firm's culture
- **on-the-job training:** training whilst working
- **off-the-job training:** gaining knowledge, experience or qualifications from experts away from the job

Continuous feedback
- measuring effectiveness through observation and analysis
- appraisal is a particular tool, where peers or superiors appraise work, attitudes and progress and use this to build a training programme

Leaving

A person may leave a firm through:
- redundancy (the job no longer exists)
- retirement
- resignation: employee leaves of own accord, usually to move to another job
- dismissal: legal processes must be followed

Communication

Good communication is seen as being a good motivator. Communication within an organisation requires a sender, a medium, a message and a receiver. A two-way channel involves the sender receiving feedback. If any part of this breaks down, the communication channel will not be effective.

Sender–receiver

The sender and receiver may be in different parts of the organisation necessitating:
- vertical communication: superior to subordinate or vice versa
- horizontal communication: at the same level in the organisation
- lateral or matrix communication: within teams

Media include:
- written information: memoranda, reports, figures etc.
- spoken information: verbal reports, telephone, presentations etc.
- electronic information: e-mail, video conferencing etc.

People in business

- formal channels: interviews, memos, reports etc.
- informal channels: conversation, notice boards etc.

Motivating workers

Motivation is the way in which workers can be encouraged to do a good job. It involves much more than just pay. Businesses have discovered that many things may be used – while good levels of pay are a common motivator, other methods work just as well. Many firms now use a whole range of tactics and benefits, from Japanese systems of having single status workforces (Nissan), German and Swedish systems of team working (Volkswagen, Volvo), American systems of lifetime training (IBM, Ford) to British systems of profit sharing (John Lewis Partnership, the Co-operative movement). Anything that encourages people to work better or harder for the firm is a motivator.

Many motivators can be linked to the reasons why people work. You will need to know the main theorists behind motivation theory.

Motivation theory

There are several theories as to what it is that makes people work harder. The most well known are those of Taylor, Mayo, Maslow, McGregor and Herzberg.

F.W. Taylor (1856–1915)

Scientific Management Theory
Taylor was an American who sought greater efficiency in engineering plants. (Henry Ford's production line Model T Ford in Detroit 'any colour you like as long as it's black' was based on Taylor's principles.) He believed that money was the only motivator and pioneered a ' carrot and stick' approach; rewards for those who worked hard enough, penalties for those who didn't. This was embodied in his differential piece rate system. He also introduced time and motion observation to see who worked fastest and how the fast workers methods could be adopted by others. He advocated a high division of labour, meaning that machinery could be used and the production line born.

E. Mayo (1880–1949)

Mayo carried out the Hawthorne Experiments at a plant in Chicago to try to find out how different conditions affected work rate. His conclusion was that the subjects of his study increased their work rate less because of changes in conditions and more because they were being studied – being shown attention. His Relay Assembly Test identified that other motivators included being able to direct their own work, teamwork and good communications between management and team. His conclusions led to the growth of personnel departments in organisational structures.

A.H. Maslow (1908–1970)

An American psychologist who said that people worked in order to gain certain things. He established a 'hierarchy of needs'.

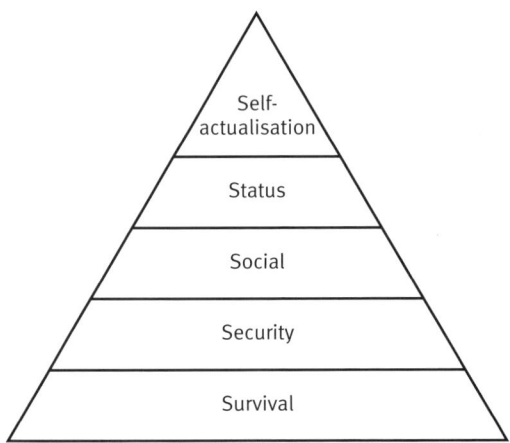

Maslow's hierarchy of needs

- Firstly, they need to satisfy their survival needs; this means that they must either grow their own food or earn sufficient money to be able to buy the basic necessities of food, clothing and shelter.
- Secondly, once these needs are met, people will want to be safe and secure, so the next level of needs was for security.
- Once people feel safe, they then look for friends and social activities; they want to be part of a group or family. People have social needs.
- Higher order needs can then be met. The first of these is for status – people need to feel that they are respected both for who they are and for what they do.
- Finally, there is what Maslow called self-actualisation needs. We might think of it better as ambition or fulfilment.

FACTFILE

Where marketing has the 'Four Ps', Maslow's hierarchy can be thought of as the 'Five Ss': survival, security, social, status, self-actualisation.

Human resource management

D. McGregor (1906–1964)

Looked at the way that employers and employees traditionally viewed work – the employer paid the money, supervised the worker and gave instructions; the worker did the job, didn't ask questions and took the money. This traditional way of working he called Theory X. This he balanced with Theory Y, which was that most people actually enjoyed working and would readily take on responsibility. McGregor believed that the Theory Y worker was the more typical example and that, if people were treated as if they were Theory Y type people, then firms would be more efficient and better managed.

Theory X: Workers . . .	Theory Y: Workers . . .
. . . don't like working	. . . enjoy their work
. . . do as little as they can get away with	. . . will work hard to gain rewards
. . . don't like things to change	. . . want to see new things happening
. . . need to be told what to do	. . . will work independently
. . . can't be trusted to make a decision	. . . can be trusted to make a decision
. . . are only interested in money	. . . are motivated by things other than money
. . . must be closely watched	. . . can work unsupervised
. . . can't be trusted or relied on	. . . are trustworthy and reliable

F. Herzberg (b. 1923)

Came to similar conclusions to Maslow and McGregor. He asked workers what motivated them and found out that the main things were a 'job well done', a feeling of being appreciated, trust, responsibility and promotion. One of the major factors which de-motivated people was if a job was boring. Some conditions, which Herzberg called 'hygiene' factors, were discovered to make people unhappy at work, to de-motivate them if they were missing or poor. Pay and working conditions are two of the main ones. This means that good pay or good working conditions are not necessarily motivators, but bad pay or working conditions are de-motivators.

V. Vroom

Introduced expectancy theory or the path-goal concept. His contention was that motivation was linked to what a worker wanted and how likely they were to achieve it. Workers set themselves goals – such as a promotion, or a certain level of responsibility. If these goals are seen to be attainable, workers will work towards them. If they are seen to be out of reach, workers are de-motivated. (Think of the worker who has been passed over for promotion three times and told that he is 'too old' for the job; will he feel motivated or de-motivated?)

Pay

The amount of money that people earn in their jobs can be adjusted to try to make them work harder. Managers should realise, however, that this is not the sole motivator. There are different ways of paying people:

- time rate
- piece rate
- bonus payments
- fringe benefits or 'perks'. These are extras, other than money, which the person may have in addition to his or her actual pay.
- incentives, such as commission
- performance related pay is linked to the achieving of targets.
- profit related pay
- share options

FACTFILE

Herzberg warned against bonuses saying 'a reward once given becomes a right'.

Motivation in practice

Teamwork

Teams are given the power to make decisions, lead to greater motivation in workers. Many firms have moved towards a culture of project teams as being the most efficient way of working. The key concept is that teams must be empowered – they must have the authority to carry out their remit.

Multi-skilling

This means ensuring that your workers are trained to work in a number of different areas. This has reduced the incidence of demarcation disputes and is also a motivator.

People in business

Developing transferable skills

As traditional jobs and roles rapidly change the flexible worker needs to develop skills which can be easily transferred to a different occupation. The concept of a 'job for life' no longer exists and people will be expected to change occupations several times during a working career.

Strategies to achieve multi-skilling include:

- job enrichment: giving the worker greater responsibility
- job enlargement: widening a worker's range of responsibilities
- job rotation: changing round the jobs that people do at regular intervals

Flexibility

Many firms take a much more flexible approach to their workforce requirements than in the past. They may employ core workers, who are the mainstay of the firm, but contract out specific tasks to specialist firms or individuals. For example, each business may no longer have an accounting department, but contract this function out. Agencies may also be used for functions such as personnel.

Flexible staff (or flexi-workers) are those who have developed transferable skills and can be called in to fill particular gap or address a particular problem or issue.

Effective HRM

The effectiveness of HRM policies and practices can be gauged against the following:

- low labour turnover
- high morale and productivity
- good communications
- good industrial relations
- loyal workforce

Mind Map

Finish off your Mind Map by adding all the rest of the points mentioned. An example of a finished Mind Map is shown on page 129. Don't forget to use word pictures where appropriate.

CHECKLIST

- ✓ Human resource management is using personnel as a strategic resource of the business.
- ✓ It involves analysing the workforce – what skills, qualifications, experience are needed.
- ✓ It involves planning the workforce – taking into account external factors.
- ✓ It involves recruiting, selecting and training the workforce – through a formal process.
- ✓ It involves motivating the workforce – according to several different theorists, most of whom agree that valuing the workforce is a major factor.
- ✓ It involves communicating with the workforce.
- ✓ Problems with any of these can affect a firm's performance through:
  - poor labour relations
  - high staff turnover
  - low staff motivation.

TEST YOURSELF

Use your Mind Map to see if you can answer the following questions.

AS

1. What sort of costs might a firm incur through not training staff?
2. What benefits might a firm gain from appraisal?
3. How could you judge the effectiveness of a firm's HRM policies?

A2

1. What external factors will affect workforce planning?
2. What is meant by motivation?
3. What are the major differences between Taylor, Maslow and Vroom?

Human resource management

Sample question and answer

Explain the purpose of human resource management. How does it differ from personnel management?

1. Human resource management is using staff as a strategic resource to improve the businesses performance. This is more than just the personnel function, placing greater emphasis on staff needs, skills and training in order to get the best work force to meet the businesses objectives.
2. It involves analysing the workforce in terms of their skills, qualifications and experience. It involves planning the workforce, recruiting, selecting and training the workforce and motivating the workforce. There are a number of different theorists with regard to motivation – list the major ones (such as Maslow, Herzberg and McGregor) and outline their theories.) HRM also involves communicating with the workforce through formal or informal channels.
3. Problems with any of these can affect a firms performance. For example, if they suffer from a high staff turnover this will mean a greater proportion of budget will need to be spent on recruitment and training. Poor labour relations could lead to industrial strife and lack of motivation will lead to poor work and negative features such as absenteeism.
4. The main difference between HRM and personnel management is that HRM is seen as being linked into the firm's strategic objectives and is an integral part of its planning.

Summary

- **Human resources management is a strategic tool of management.**
- **Workforce planning involves analysing the existing workforce and deciding what a future workforce should comprise.**
- **External factors affect workforce planning; especially important are economic and demographic factors.**
- **The staff 'life cycle' at a firm consists of:**
  - recruitment: seeking applicants
  - selection: finding the best applicant for the job
  - training: induction and further training
  - appraisal: receiving feedback on performance
  - leaving: resigning, retiring, redundancy or dismissal.
- **Motivating workers means getting them to work harder and/or more efficiently or effectively.**
- **Theories include:**
  - Taylor: scientific management; the 'father' of the production line
  - Mayo: the Hawthorne factor; the 'father' of personnel departments
  - Maslow: hierarchy of needs
  - McGregor: theory X and theory Y workers
  - Herzberg: hygiene factors
  - Vroom – expectancy theory.
- **Pay and pay incentives can be used as motivators.**
- **Good communication is essential to motivation.**
- **The effectiveness of HRM policies can be judged by:**
  - levels of labour turnover
  - staff loyalty to the organisation
  - good industrial relations.

SECTION 5 — Operations management

Specification content

Advanced Supplementary (AS)

AQA
Module 2 is *'People and Operations Management'*. It includes:
- Productive efficiency
- Economies and diseconomies of scale
- Distinguishing quantifiable diseconomies from quality issues.
- Capacity utilisation, including rationalisation and sub-contracting
- Capital intensive vs. Labour intensive production
- Controlling operations
- Stock control
- Quality control, improvement and assurance
- Lean production, cell and JIT production
- Time based management
- Kaizen

OCR
Module 2972 is *'Business Decisions'* and Module 2873 is *'Business Behaviour'*. They include:
- Operations management
- Operational efficiency
- Organising production
- Economies and diseconomies of scale
- Quality : importance, methods and approaches
- Stock control

Edexcel
Unit 2 is *'Marketing and Production'*. It includes:
- Methods of organising production
- Capacity utilisation
- Diseconomies of scale
- Stock control
- JIT
- Quality assurance and quality control
- TQM and Kaizen
- Training and development to improve quality

Advanced Level (A2)

AQA
Module 5 is *'People and Operations Management'*. It includes:
- Productive efficiency
- Research and development
- Critical path analysis
- Controlling operations
- Application of IT within and between organisations
- Facilities
- Locational decision making

OCR
Module 2877 is *'Further Operations Management'* (optional). It includes:
- Management and the production process
- Operations management and its relationship with other functions
- Location of industry
- Production methods
- Constraints on production
- Production and the law
- Ethical constraints and considerations of production
- Costs and costings
- Productive efficiency: productivity, capacity utilisation and critical path analysis
- Stock control
- Quality control
- Value analysis
- Technology and its changing role in production
- Research and development

Edexcel
Unit 4 is *'Analysis and Decision Making'*. It includes:
- Sales forecasting for decision making
- New product decisions
- Probability and decision making techniques
- Project management
- Investment appraisal

Organising production — Chapter 23

PREVIEW

- This chapter deals with the organisation of production – deciding where to produce, what the scale of production should be and how to produce most efficiently.
- You are expected to be able to establish clear links between productive efficiency and people especially where this involves productivity.
- You will need to know the sources and types of economies and diseconomies of scale and to suggest how a firm might maximise the former and minimise the latter.
- You should be able to discuss the problems of location from an organisational viewpoint and show how location affects production.
- You will need to be able to relate operations management to other parts of your specification. Using your skill of synthesis in your answers.
- See if you can answer at least four of these five questions before reading the rest of the chapter.

Questions

1. What is meant by the process of 'transformation'?
2. Can you list the main decisions that an operations manager has to take?
3. Can you give examples of market oriented and supplier oriented businesses?
4. What is the difference between bulk increasing and bulk decreasing industry?
5. What is the difference between a greenfield site and a brown-field site?

Check your answers before reading the rest of the chapter. Try answering the questions again when you've finished the chapter.

Mind Map

Start a Mind Map similar to the one shown here. Put a central image of your own in the middle. This image works for me – it makes me think of cogs and wheels and production in general. You need to draw an image that works for you! The first 'legs' of the Mind Map have been started for you. Add points to your map as you work through the chapter. At the end of the chapter is an example of what a finished Mind Map might look like. Don't forget, you can – and should – use colour! Use three colours at least for your central image and a different colour for each 'leg' of your Mind Map.

Definition

Organising production is part of the decision-making process of a business. It means deciding what to produce, how many to produce, how to produce and where to produce. Production involves the process of transformation – turning one set of materials and inputs into a set of outputs. Traditionally, this means turning raw materials and component parts into finished goods.

Decisions on location

A firm needs to decide on location when it is first starting up or when an expansion in production means it has outgrown its current capacity. Deciding where to produce – industrial location – is influenced by a number of factors, in particular the proximity of its market, factors of production and suppliers.

Market oriented

Some businesses need to be near their customers; those providing a service such as banking or hairdressing for example.

Supplier oriented

Some businesses need to be near a supplier or source of raw materials.

The diagram on page 132 shows the difference between bulk increasing and bulk decreasing industries. A bulk increasing industry will need to do its processing as near to its market as possible, to minimise transport cost. A bulk decreasing industry will carry out refinement or reduction nearer to its source of supply.

Operations management

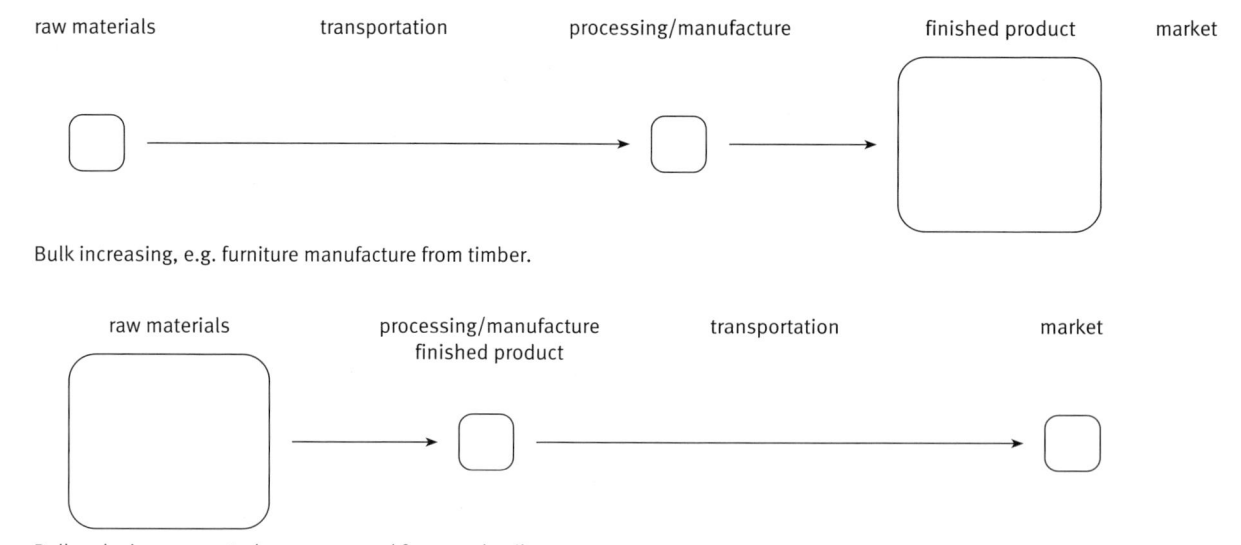

Bulk-increasing and bulk-decreasing industries

Making the decision where to locate involves the firm considering:

- opportunity cost: it can only locate at one site and must therefore forego 'the next best alternative'
- cost benefit analysis
- investment appraisal analysis

These techniques will enable it to judge the costs of a particular location against alternatives. Factors to take into account include:

Land

- natural resources, e.g. a textile mill needs a ready source of water
- quality: greenfield (previously undeveloped sites) may be preferable to brown field ones (a site that has previously had industry on it). Greenfield sites are likely to be more subject to planning restrictions and environmental constraints.
- the nature of the business: this may subject it to planning limitations, e.g. if it is engaged in hazardous processes, it should not be situated in populated areas
- the size of the site: the firm may be considering room for further expansion

Labour

- availability of a local labour force
- size of the labour force
- quality (education, training) of the labour force
- cost of labour

Infrastructure

It is not just the existence but also the efficiency of infrastructure that is important:

- transport: motorway links, ports and airports
- communications
- reputation: some regions or cities have a reputation which is valuable to the business, e.g. Sheffield steel
- labour: if local labour is already skilled and trained then this can be counted as part of the infrastructure

Government help

This may come in the form of grants, subsidies, taxation breaks or help and advice.

- Enterprise Zones and Development Areas: government designated areas of deprivation or decline which attract extra help
- Department of Trade and Industry: helps to attract investment into the UK
- EU Regional Development Fund (improving infrastructure) and European Social Fund (improving quality of labour)
- Local government schemes to attract business and industry, such as lower rates or freedom from planning restrictions

All of these factors will affect the cost of location and – the main measure by which a decision will be made – the potential profitability of the site.

Transnationals

Some businesses operate internationally. Such multinationals or transnationals have production, sales or distribution facilities in more than one country. The main reasons for this are:

- Historical: a sugar refining firm is likely to have owned sugar plantations and processing plant and distributed and marketed worldwide.
- Access to markets. A particular case involves the EU. Firms established inside the EU have access to the whole of the Single Market. Examples include Nissan establishing in Sunderland and Intel in Wales.
- Access to raw materials. The extraction of natural resources must take place where those resources are found, for example oil deposits in Arabia or precious metals in Africa.
- Access to labour. Usually this means access to cheap labour in countries where labour regulations are less strict than western industrialised nations.
- Tax avoidance. Transnationals can avoid paying taxes in countries with high tax rates by declaring profits in those countries with low tax rates. This is called transfer pricing.

Productive efficiency

A further operations decision concerns the scale of production. This may depend on the likely economies and diseconomies of scale that can be earned.

Economies of scale are earned when an increase in output adds a less than proportionate increase in costs. This results in a fall in average costs.

Economies include:

- Financial economies: large firms find it easier and often cheaper to borrow money, they can also gain by being able to purchase goods in bulk, thus lowering the unit price.
- Technical economies: mass production means that unit costs are lower as fixed costs are spread over more units of output. Plant and machinery may be used which would be too expensive or too big for a smaller scale of operation.
- Risk-bearing economies: firms can afford to take risks on new products because other parts of the business are still profitable.
- Marketing economies: advertising and marketing can be carried out extensively, channels such as national TV advertising are no use to small firms.
- Managerial economies: top managers can be employed; these can only be attracted for top salaries

Diseconomies of scale are when an increase in output causes a more than proportionate increase in average costs. Unit costs rise as the business increases in scale.

- Decision-making diseconomies: decision-taking can be slow so that responses to changes take a long time. As firms grow, the record-keeping and bureaucracy grows with them and problems of communication can increase.
- Managerial diseconomies: there may be too many middle managers so that it becomes unclear as to who has authority and difficult to define spans of control.
- Diseconomies of diversification: the firm may be trying to do too many things at once, going in too many directions for anyone to have an overall grasp of its affairs.
- Geographical diseconomies: head office and branch offices may be so far away from each other that branches could be pulling in a different direction to the centre.
- Staff diseconomies: employees may feel remote from a large organisation leading to lower morale and to them being less loyal than they would be to a smaller firm.

> **FACTFILE**
>
> You will need to be able to distinguish the quantifiable aspects of scale economies from the quality aspects. Some economies are measurable (such as financial economies), some are difficult to quantify (such as staff diseconomies).

Capacity

Part of the operations decision will involve how many of a product the firm is able to produce. Capacity defines the maximum amount of a product that a firm is able to produce using the resources that they have. Capacity can be increased through:

- adding more resources
- increasing productivity – getting more output for the same inputs
- rationalisation – reorganising productive inputs to increase efficiency. This often means closure of plants or operations in order to lower fixed costs

Operations management

- **sub contracting** – may be a part of rationalisation. A sub contractor may be able to specialise in terms of skill and/or equipment and produce more efficiently than the firm can itself. Many firms sub-contract services such as cleaning and car parks.

Capacity utilisation measures the proportion of the firm's productive capacity that is actually being used. It is usually expressed as a percentage of the nominal maximum.

Under-utilisation is where the firm has spare capacity. This means that it is able to increase output fairly easily.

Production methods

Managers need to decide on the best method of production. This decision will impact on whether production is capital or labour intensive (job production is labour intensive, the use of machinery in mass production is capital intensive). Methods are:

- **job production:** where a product is a 'one-off' made to individual specifications, for example made-to-measure clothes
- **batch production:** where the same capital equipment and resources can be used to produce different batches or groups of products. For example, a printing press can produce a football programme, a magazine and concert tickets using similar resources.
- **flow production:** also called mass, continuous or process production. This involves a product moving along a line of production with modifications or additions being made along the way, examples include car manufacture (production line) or oil refining (processing).
- **project production:** where a one-off project, needing inputs from many different firms and teams – is made. A good example is the Millennium Dome.

Research and development (R&D)

The decision on what to produce may involve existing products but, if a firm is to stay competitive, should also involve new products. These products are often the result of work by the R&D department. R&D may also be bought in from outside research, in particular at universities.

The important point about R&D is that it should be related to:

- product design: an emphasis on efficiency, style and consumer attraction

- product life cycle: there is little point in putting masses of R&D into a product with a short life cycle
- market research: R&D should be looking at market research findings and directing development accordingly

Simultaneous engineering is the term used to show that product design and development is going hand-in-hand with the production and marketing departments to provide a 'whole picture' for innovation.

CHECKLIST

✓ Organising production involves deciding where to produce – location decisions based on considerations such as raw materials, infrastructure and the cost of a site.

✓ How many to produce also needs to be decided – linked to scale economies and diseconomies and the productive capacity of the business.

✓ Another factor is how to produce – the most efficient or appropriate production methods.

Mind Map

Finish off your Mind Map by adding all the rest of the points mentioned. An example of a finished Mind Map is shown on page 135. Don't forget to use word pictures where appropriate

TEST YOURSELF

Use your Mind Map to see if you can answer the following questions.

AS

1. What is meant by the process of transformation?
2. Describe the location factors that will most influence the oil refining industry.
3. Can you give examples of job, batch and flow production?

A2

1. What are the main economies of scale a firm might gain from growth?
2. What are the main diseconomies of scale?
3. How could a firm use strategic planning to minimise diseconomies and maximise economies of scale?

Organising production

Sample question and answer

'Economies of scale are all quantifiable whereas diseconomies are quality issues.' Discuss this statement with regard to the growth of a business. Define your terms. Explain what is meant by each.

1. Economies are gains from growth, diseconomies are losses. Outline what economies of scale might be i.e:
   - Financial: easier to borrow money, lower interest rates, benefits of bulk purchase
   - Technical: lower unit costs, use of large/expensive machinery
   - Risk-bearing: innovation is possible with the support of other successful lines
   - Marketing: extensive advertising and marketing is practicable
   - Managerial: top managers can be employed
2. Outline what diseconomies of scale might be i.e:
   - Slowness in decision-making due to bureaucratic growth.
   - Too many managers blurring lines of communication and control.
   - Diversification – the firm trying to pull in too many different directions at the same time.
   - Geographical diseconomies if the branches are, for example too far away from the head office. Employees may also feel remote from the centre.
3. Are all scale economies quantifiable? Financial can be measured in money terms and technical in lower costs. However it is difficult to quantify the benefits of managerial, marketing and risk bearing economies. Diseconomies are all quality issues.
4. Conclusion
   All economies and diseconomies have elements of qualitative issues; some economies can also be quantified.

Summary

- **Decisions on organising – the nature, size, location and methods of production – need to be taken as part of the firm's overall strategy decisions.**
- **Location decisions are linked to the cost and availability of land as well as to the state of the local infrastructure and any external help available.**
- **Transnationals can be 'footloose' in that they can establish where they get the best labour rates, tax breaks etc.**
- **Productive efficiency can be improved through growth by a firm gaining economies of scale.**
- **Firms may also suffer diseconomies from growth.**
- **Firms' levels of production are limited by their capacity.**
- **Different production methods are suitable for different types of goods being produced.**
- **Research and development is important if a firm is to continue to produce new products required by the market.**

Study and Revise AS and A2 Level Business Studies

Chapter 24: Controlling operations

PREVIEW

- Operations management is the generic term used to cover the operation and control of the production process. The previous chapter dealt with a major part of this, which is decisions regarding scale, location and methods of production.
- Other management decisions also need to be made regarding production. There are a number of modern production methods for managers to consider which cut down on costs and increase efficiency. Decisions also have to be taken about inventory or stock control.
- Project planning is a major part of controlling operations and includes the technique of critical path analysis.
- You should be able to construct a network from data given and determine the critical path and float times.
- You may be asked to manipulate a network to produce the most efficient or profitable production paths and this could entail the use of Gantt charts.
- As an AS student, the focus of study is on the way organisations use inputs efficiently to satisfy customers.
- As an A2 student you are expected to be able to analyse and evaluate different operations management tools used to enhance decision-making and improve productive efficiency.
- You will need to draw on other parts of your specification to fully answer some questions, for example, some production techniques are closely linked to HRM.
- See if you can answer at least four of these five questions before continuing with the rest of the chapter.

Questions

1. What is meant by 'inventories'?
2. What is meant by 'lead-in' time?
3. What are the main methods of lean production?
4. Can you name the Japanese method of 'stock pulling'?
5. What are the main uses for information technology in business?

Check your answers before reading the rest of the chapter. Try answering the questions again when you've finished the chapter.

Mind Map

Start a Mind Map similar to the one shown here. Put a central image of your own in the middle. This image works for me – it reminds me that production does not just take place – it needs someone to pull the strings! You need to draw an image that works for you! The first 'legs' of the Mind Map have been started for you. Add points to your map as you work through the chapter. At the end of the chapter is an example of what a finished Mind Map might look like. Don't forget, you can – and should – use colour!

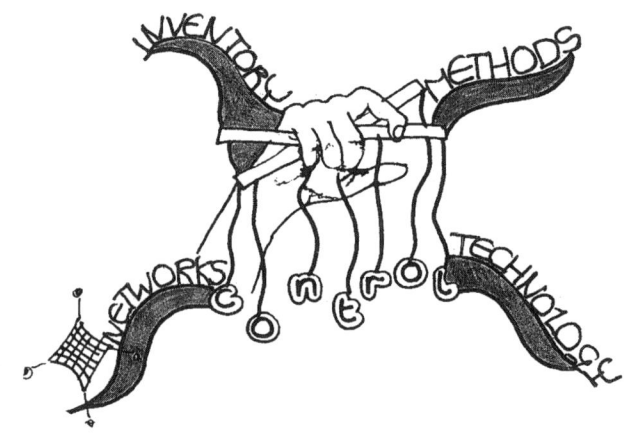

Definition

Control of production operations is essential to the efficient running of a plant. This involves controlling stock, controlling technology and using plans and charts as operational forecast and control tools.

Inventory control

Inventory is another term for stock. Stocks include supplies of raw materials delivered, unfinished production and finished goods that have not yet been sold. On a firm's balance sheet they appear as current assets, making the assumption that they are fairly liquid, i.e. can easily be converted into cash.

It is costly to store stocks and, wherever possible, stock levels are kept to a minimum. The aim is to provide a steady flow of raw materials, component parts etc. in, matched by a steady flow of sales out.

The diagram opposite shows various different stock levels. Maximum stock is when there is room to store no more stock; buffer stock is the amount of stock kept as a safety measure against, for example, a

Controlling operations

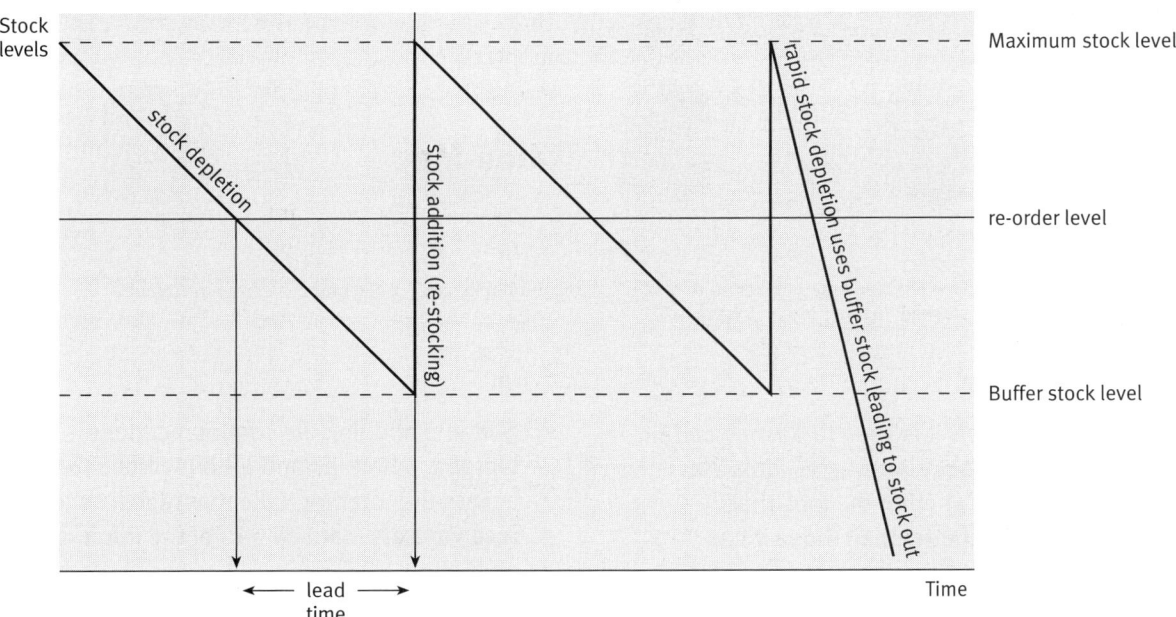

Different stock levels

supply failure. The lead time is the time it takes from the ordering of the stock to its arrival.

Problems with stock include:

- stock rotation: firms should be careful to use older stock first; this is particularly important with perishable stock
- wastage: stocks that are damaged or destroyed in storage
- storage costs: these can be high if stocks are of a large volume, expensive and therefore need to be kept secure; perishable
- opportunity cost: money tied up in stocks cannot be used to more gainful purpose elsewhere

Modern production methods

Lean production is any system that attempts to keep stock levels at a minimum, lead in and development times as short as possible. The main versions of lean production are:

- Just In Time (JIT) production. This involves stock arriving just in time to be used in the production process. This has obvious advantages in terms of not holding stock but disadvantages if suppliers are unreliable. JIT needs to be closely linked with flexible working and the people centred management that is at the heart of Human Relations Management. For example, if stock arrives, a number of different employees should be able to deal with it.
- Cell production in which teams work in separate bays or cells, each producing a component or adding a particular aspect to production. This is then passed on to the next part of the process. This encourages efficiency, competition and team spirit.

FACTFILE

A Nissan Primera car takes approximately three hours to manufacture. As the production process for the car starts, so does that for the car seats (manufactured by a different company); the seats are timed to arrive at the correct point on the production line less than ten minutes before they are needed.

Kanban

Kanban is a Japanese system of stock control. It is a practical application of just-in-time, in that stocks are only ordered as they are needed by the production process. Managers can therefore visibly see what stocks are needed and in operation and stocks are 'pulled through' the system as they are needed. This system depends on a short and/or reliable 'lead-in' time – the time it takes for stock to be delivered. The system is often run on a simple 'two bin' system.

Technology

Technology, in particular information and communications technology, is now a vital adjunct to efficient control of operations. Staff may see

Operations management

1 Bins full   2 First bin empty, taken to re-stock.   3 Second bin in use.   4 Second bin empty as first bin arrives stocked 'just in time'.   5 Back to '2'.

technology as a threat as it is seen to destroy certain jobs, however, technology also creates jobs. You may be asked to judge whether the jobs that technology creates are better than those it has destroyed.

Information technology

IT within and between organisations cuts down on communications problems, cuts down on costs; speeds communications. The main business tools are:

- spreadsheets enable forecasting and modelling, in particular 'what if' statements such as 'what if a new supplier reduced costs by 5%'
- databases enable better data management and storage
- expert systems store expertise and can be used to provide expert support, for example in helping a doctor to diagnose

Communications technology

- conference calls enable several people to hold a single telephone discussion
- video-conferencing in which people can 'meet' without leaving their offices; this cuts down on time and on travel costs
- e-mail allows instant communication of text, graphics, figures etc. in the exact format required so that the receiver is able to work on them
- network systems in which computers are linked to one another over a network; this may be used for sharing software or files, or for communication in general
- Internet: websites can be used to advertise the firm and offers the facility to buy direct over the net; e-commerce is a fast-growing business sector

- portable and flexible communications – laptops, palmtops and mobile phones which can access the Internet, take messages, send and receive faxes – are all part of the information revolution
- teleworking enables workers to work from home as efficiently as in an office, cutting down on the firms costs

Control technology

Specific computer based production or control systems include:

- Computer Aided Design (CAD)
- Computer Aided Manufacture (CAM)
- Computer Integrated Manufacture (CIM): IT used to integrate one or more parts of the manufacturing process
- Manufacturing Resource Planning (MRP): Essentially a spreadsheet tool that can plan production by taking forecast figures as a base and giving figures and times for stock and actual production. It can be used to model scenarios.
- Operations research (OR): although designed before the advent of computers OR is an ideal technique to use on them. It involves predicting probabilities and risks within constraining factors in order to plan the optimum efficiency for an operation.

Simultaneous engineering

Time-based management integrates many aspects of control in order to cut down the time it takes for a process. One example is simultaneous engineering which involves the integration of the design and manufacturing processes. With designers working with engineers and production controllers, designs which could cause production problems are ironed out at the development stage.

Controlling operations

Critical path analysis

The following example illustrates critical path analysis.

Jonathan has decided that there are a number of tasks to complete for his Business Studies coursework and has worked out how much time he will need for each. This is the list that he has come up with:

- **A** check that task is OK with tutor – 3 days
- **B** check task out with friends – 5 days
- **C** plan research techniques – 7 days
- **D** plan field research – questionnaire
- **E** do library research – 5 days
- **F** do postal research – 14 days
- **G** do Internet research – 2 days
- **H** write up library notes – 7 days
- **I** write up postal information notes – 7 days
- **J** write up Internet notes – 7 days
- **K** carry out field research – 7 days
- **L** analyse field research – 7 days
- **M** write up field research notes – 7 days
- **N** check notes with friends – 5 days
- **O** check notes with tutor – 2 days
- **P** write in neat – 7 days

A network analysis will help him to see how long the task should actually take and which are the critical or exceptional activities to which he should give his management attention (called managing by exception).

The diagram below shows how this information could be networked. The time needed to complete the project is 52 days. The critical path – the shortest time in which the project can be completed – is shown by the two short lines which cross the arrows. This line joins the longest time periods between each node and crosses the nodes with equal EST and LFT times.

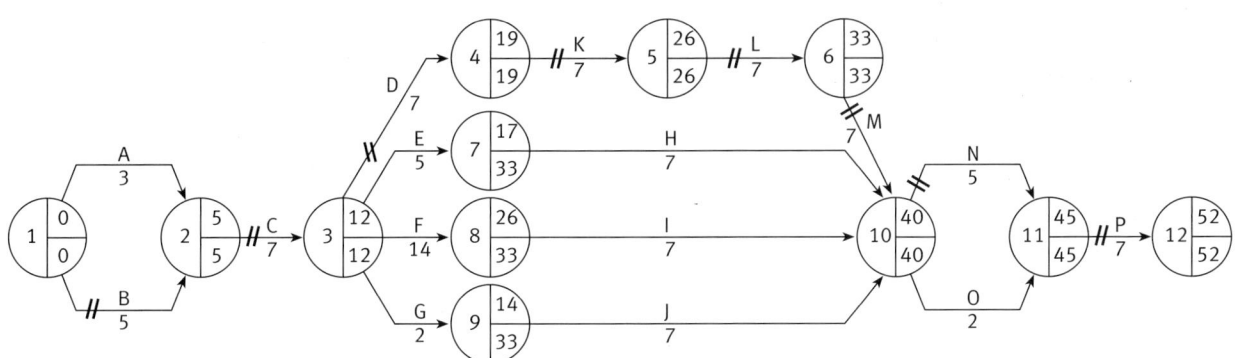

Within each circle is shown the EST – the estimated soonest time after the project is started that this operation can take place – and the LFT – the latest finishing time for an operation leaving enough time to complete the project.

Where these are not equal there is 'float time'. Activities with float time can take more days to complete without affecting the overall timing of the project. It is therefore not crucial for these activities to be completed on time and they can be tackled at a more leisurely pace – in business terms using less resources or allocating resources at more convenient times.

The exceptional operations in this example are B, C, D, K, L, M. Operations E, F, G all have float time.

Total float is the spare time available so that the project completion date is kept. For any activity this is measured as LFT of operation minus duration of operation minus EST of operation.

Free float is a tighter measurement; this is the spare time available so that the next activity is not delayed. It is EST for the next activity minus time minus EST for this activity.

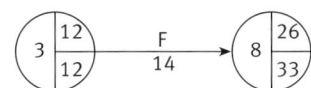

For activity F this is reduced to 26 – 14 – 12 = 0

Operations management

Networks

Networks are used to show what tasks need to be done, the order they should be done in and the time taken for each task. They can also show what is the earliest time that the next stage can start or the latest time that a stage can finish.

- Nodes or circles are used to show the start or end of an activity
- Arrows are used to show an activity taking place
- A node is drawn as a divided circle like so to show the number of the operation, the Earliest Start Time for that operation and the Latest Finish Time (EST and LFT).

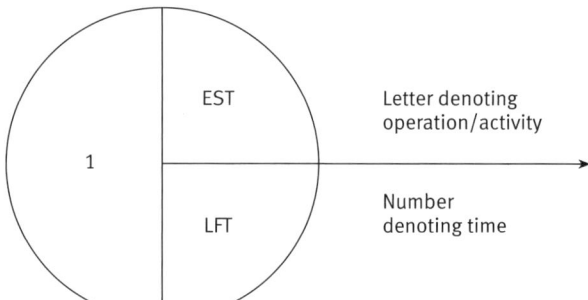

Gantt charts

Devised by management scientist Henry Gantt, these are drawn as a horizontal bar chart. They are used as a visual addition to networks and can show how far a task has actually progressed compared with its target.

Mind Map

Finish off your Mind Map by adding all the rest of the points mentioned. An example of a finished Mind Map can be found on page 142. Don't forget to use word pictures where appropriate, for example the spider's web for 'networks'.

CHECKLIST

✓ Operations control is part of operations management, the contemporary term for production management. It involves controlling:
 – stock
 – production methods
 – technology.

✓ Lean production methods include:
 – Just In time (JIT)
 – Cell
 – Kanban.

✓ Networks are used to show:
 – tasks to be done
 – the order of the tasks
 – time to be taken.

✓ Critical paths identify:
 – essential or exceptional tasks
 – the shortest time that an operation can be completed.

TEST YOURSELF

Use your Mind Map to see if you can answer the following questions.

AS

1 Which information technology tools are most useful to business?
2 Define simultaneous engineering. What are its main advantages?
3 Describe the operation and advantages of Kanban.

A2

1 How could a small business make use of a spreadsheet application?
2 Describe the main features of networks.
3 Give three advantages of using Critical Path analysis.

Controlling operations

Sample question and answer

Activity	Time needed (days)
A – first activity	2
B – dependent on completion of A	4
C – dependent on completion of A	2
D – dependent on completion of B	2
E – dependent on completion of C	5
F – dependent on completion of E	3
G – dependent on completion of D and F	2

	Time	EST	LFT	float	free float
A	2	0	0	0	0
B	4	2	10	4	0
C	2	2	4	0	0
D	2	6	12	4	4
E	5	4	9	0	0
F	3	9	12	0	0
G	2	12	14	0	0
			Total	8	4

Use the table to complete a network to show EST (earliest start times) and LFT (latest finish times) at each node. Mark on the critical path. Which operations have float times and which are critical or exceptional? Calculate total float and free float times. What are the advantages and disadvantages of using a network like this one?

1. Networks are used to show what tasks need to be done, the order of the tasks and the time taken for each task. They can also show what is the earliest time that the next stage can start or the latest time that a stage can finish.
2. Advantages include:
   - overall view of planned project
   - managers see which operations are dependent and which can be carried out simultaneously
   - resources can be ordered to arrive just in time
3. Disadvantages include:
   - large networks becoming so complex as to be meaningless
   - timings and calculations all assume compliance with possibilities; some aspects can not be included on the chart (such as staff motivation).

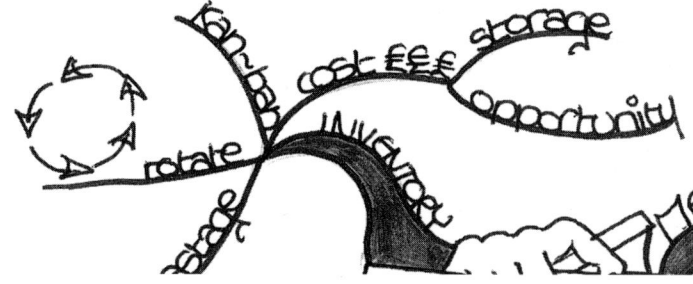

Study and Revise AS and A2 Level Business Studies

Operations management

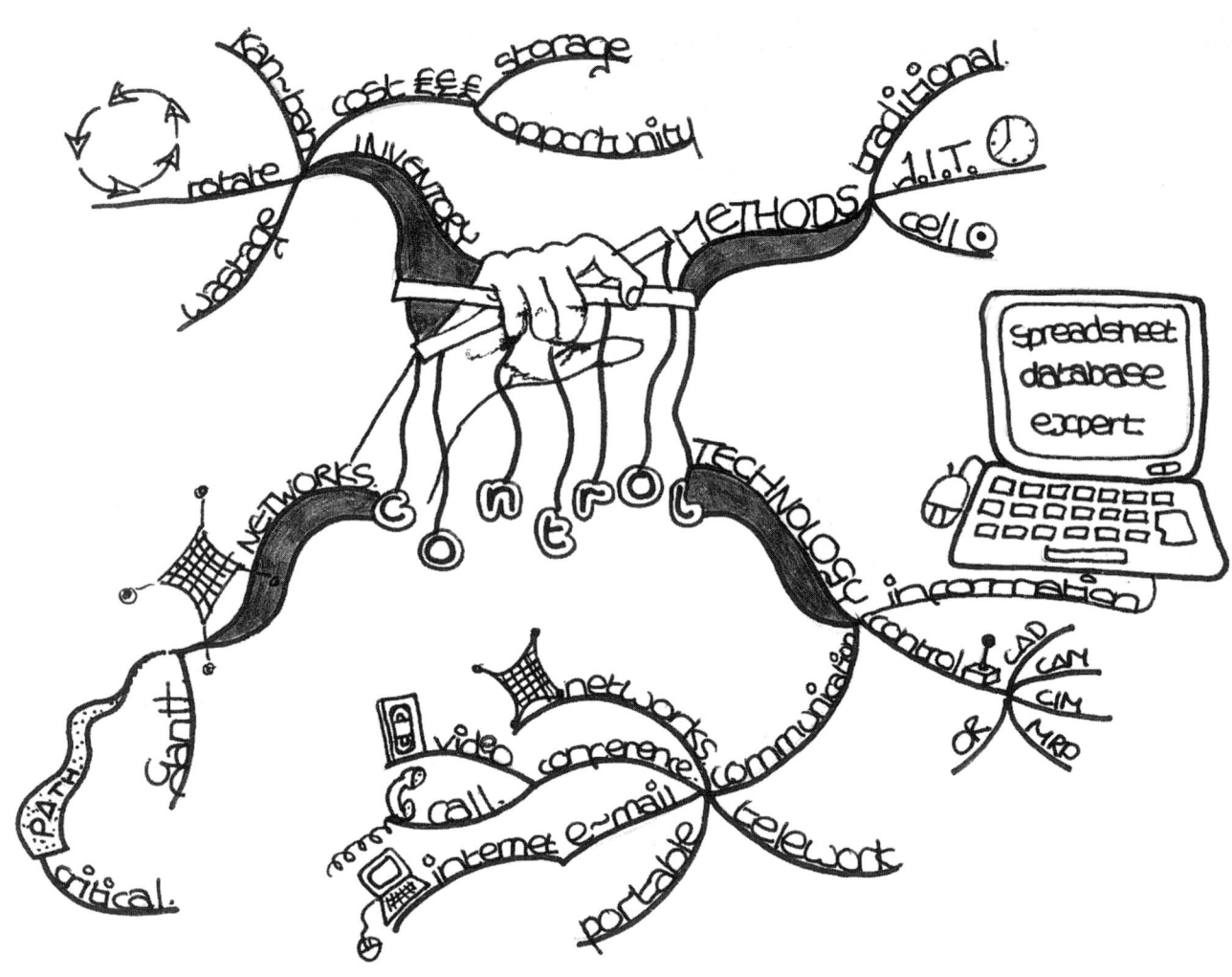

Summary

- Production management is now more usually termed operations management and includes all aspects of production and resource management and control.
- Control of stock levels is important in keeping costs down.
- Control of production now involves lean production methods. These include Just In Time, where stock arrives as it is needed and Kanban, which is the practical operation of this.
- Cell production is closely linked to HRM and team working.
- Networks are used as planning, forecasting and management tools.
- Critical path analysis involves finding the most efficient route to the completion of an operation.
- Gantt charts are used as a visual help to interpreting networks.
- Many of these techniques would not be possible or practical without new technology.

Maintaining quality — Chapter 25

PREVIEW

- In this chapter we look at the definition of quality – fit for purpose – and at how a business attempts to establish and maintain quality.
- Quality management has moved from a 'you check' approach to one of 'I check, we all check'. It also includes machine and computer based checks.
- You should be aware of the development of total quality management and understand its advantages. You should be able to discuss other systems of quality control.
- You should be able to show knowledge of British and international standards and understand why firms would wish to gain them.
- You should be aware of how quality issues link in with other parts of strategic management and be able to use your skill of synthesis to draw from other parts of your specification.
- AS students are expected to discuss the way organisations satisfy customers through quality control.
- A2 students are expected to be able to analyse the operations management techniques used to improve quality.
- See if you can answer at least four of these five questions before continuing with the rest of the chapter.

Questions

1. Can you define quality?
2. What was the traditional method of quality control?
3. What are the main points of total quality management?
4. What is Kaizen?
5. What systems might companies use to maintain quality?

Check your answers before reading the rest of the chapter. Try answering the questions again when you've finished the chapter.

Mind Map

Start a Mind Map similar to the one shown here. Put a central image of your own in the middle. This image works for me – it reminds me of a certain product associated with the word 'quality'! You need to draw an image that works for you! The first 'legs' of the Mind Map have been started for you. Add points to your map as you work through the chapter. At the end of the chapter is an example of what a finished Mind Map might look like. Don't forget, you can – and should – use colour!

Definition

Quality control is the set of techniques which ensures that a business is providing goods or services that meet the needs and wants of its consumers. A 'quality' item is one which is perfectly fitted to its purpose; the purpose for which the customer has bought it. There is no absolute measure of 'quality'.

Historical quality control systems: 'you check'

Historically quality control involved a check or series of checks at or towards the end of the production process. If any faults were detected, the goods would be rejected. This was an expensive method as it meant that:

- finished goods were rejected due to early faults
- some components or materials could not be recovered
- the whole manufacturing time was wasted

Contemporary quality control systems: 'I check/we check'

Contemporary systems emphasise continuous quality control i.e. defects should be detected as early as

Operations management

possible and anyone who detects them should have the power to report and rectify them.

Total Quality Managemen (TQM)

The major thrust of TQM is that quality is everyone's responsibility. Faults, if they do occur, should be detected and rectified as soon as possible. Preferably, attention should be such that defects do not occur. In TQM, only employees are not customers; anyone the business deals with, including suppliers and sub contractors, should be treated as customers. The main parts of TQM are:

- quality is everyone's responsibility
- there should be no defects
- all employees are empowered to take action to maintain quality
- team work and training is encouraged so that skills and experience are shared
- procedures are as important as production and must be constantly monitored

Deming

W.E. Deming is considered to be the 'father' of TQM. He came up with a 14-point plan for senior management which covered aspects of HRM, production and operations management. The 14 points include:

- there should be continual improvement in the workplace
- workers are responsible for ensuring that products are 'right first time'
- quality is as important as price when choosing a supplier
- improvement and change should have no limits; it should go on for ever

Deming admired Japanese production management methods and recommended that these be adopted wherever possible. One of these is Kaizen.

> **FACTFILE**
>
> Deming said that organisations should be customer driven. He claimed that the customer was 'the most important part of the production line'.

Kaizen

In management terms, this has become known as 'the Japanese way'. *Kaizen* means 'continuous improvement' and involves evolution rather than revolution. Western companies have tended to expand or re-tool in 'leaps', using new or improved technology. This was termed Business Process Engineering (BPR) in the 1990s. Kaizen is a process of gradual improvement. It involves the workforce in generating ideas for small improvements, sometimes in Kaizen groups and has, as its biggest advantage, none of the 'shocks' of revolutionary change. Whereas sudden change may involve costs, redundancies and other problems, gradual change does not. Kaizen can be seen as part of quality management.

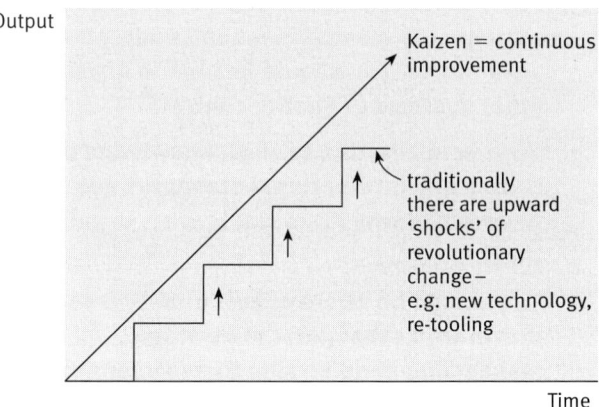

Managing change

Other systems or variations on systems include:

Zero faults

A system whereby employees are rewarded for production that is perfect from start to finish. Often the rewards are paid out of the savings made.

Quality Assurance (QA)

Quality assurance means that a business has quality systems in place to ensure that quality standards are met. Some firms set their own strict quality standards. Marks and Spencer, for example, ensure that any product which carries the St Michael label is perfect. They will reject entire batches of products, particularly clothes, if they spot even one defect in the batch. Other examples of QA include firms introducing systems of continuous quality checking of processes as well as products.

Quality circles

Another Japanese management concept, developed first by Toyota, this is an extension of TQM and team working. Groups of employees meet in the firm's time to discuss and resolve quality issues, with the viewpoints of management, design, production and customer represented. Its success depends on workers sharing knowledge and expertise with managers and managers being willing to take note.

Maintaining quality

> **Questions**
>
> 1. Can you explain how statistical process control works?
> 2. Why have Western companies adopted benchmarking?
> 3. How would a firm register for the BS5750/ISO9000 standard? What does it tell other firms?

Statistical process control

A machine, part of a production process, can be set to automatically shut down or notify an operative if, for example, a component is outside tolerance. A component may have a tolerance of plus or minus 2mm so the machine would be set up to detect if anything was outside tolerance. Computer assisted manufacturing methods can mean that the computer checks the tolerances and resets the machine automatically to achieve maximum quality and efficiency (see the diagram below).

Improving through copying – benchmarking

In the late 1970s and early 1980s traditional Western markets were penetrated by Japanese companies who produced good quality but lower priced products. Much of this was due to Japanese management techniques and new approaches to process and operations control. Western companies lagged behind their Japanese counterparts and wanted to benefit from their advances.

One way to do this is through benchmarking. Companies measure their own performance aginst that of a competitor and see where they might improve. The best practices in other companies are studied and applied to your own business.

The process involves:

- identify best competitor – a suitable benchmark partner
- measure performance in key areas (wastage, productivity, lead-in times, supplier reliance) against them
- compare performance in these areas
- improve those areas that fall short by adopting competitors systems or processes
- re-measure your performance
- start again

The main drawback of benchmarking is that companies don't develop their own systems, which might be better than those being copied. The main advantage is that the systems they do adopt have been successfully trialled.

Companies can improve bench marking by 'piggy backing' – adopting the successful process or system and then adapting it to suit their own requirements.

Standards

BS5750 (ISO 9000)

The British Standards Institute (BSI) and International Standards Organisation (ISO) have agreed on the BS5750 standard. To obtain the standard and exhibit the BSI kite-mark, an organisation must open its procedures to scrutiny regarding quality. It must produce a document detailing its quality procedures and quality management systems which show how it ensures quality from the beginning of the production process to the end. This includes process, management and human relations quality systems.

It is independently checked by an external assessor who will return at regular intervals to ensure that the business continues to comply with the standard. The

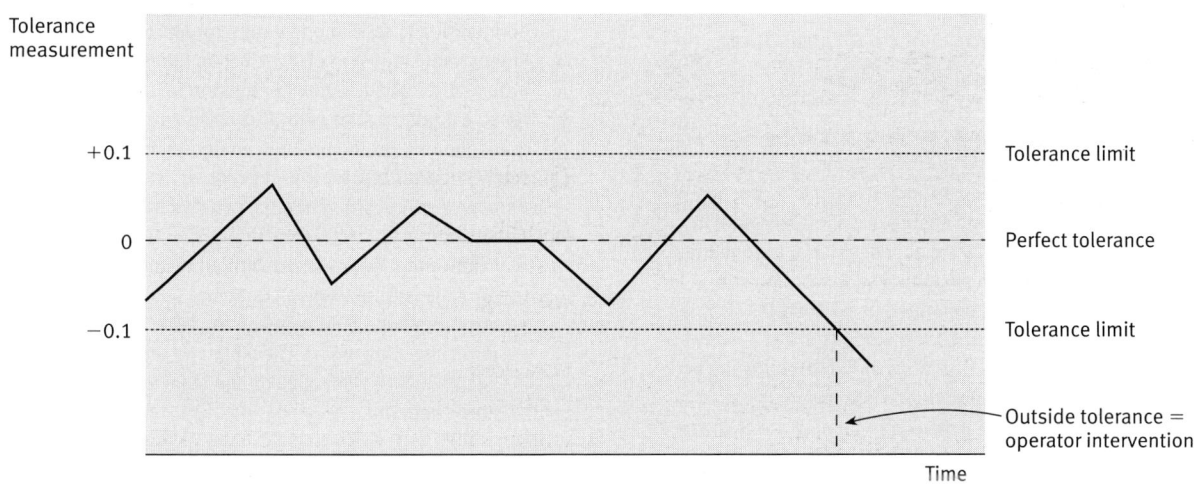

Operations management

standard does not ensure the quality of goods or services produced; it does ensure that acceptable quality systems are in place.

Firms use the BS5750/ISO9000 standard to ensure that they are dealing with firms who take quality seriously. Some firms would not deal with other firms without the mark.

Quality and consumer law

The main laws regarding consumers and quality (Sale of Goods Acts, Supply of Goods and Services Act) state that:

- goods must be fit for the purpose for which they are sold
- goods must be of 'satisfactory quality'
- services must be of a reasonable standard

Mind Map

Finish off your Mind Map by adding all the rest of the points mentioned. An example of a finished Mind Map can found on page 147. Don't forget to use word pictures where appropriate.

CHECKLIST

- ✓ Historically quality control was 'you check'. A quality control inspector rejected defective products.
- ✓ Modern methods rely on: 'I check' – workers have responsibility for ensuring that defects do not occur; 'We all check' – quality is everyone's responsibility.
- ✓ The main aspects of modern quality control are:
  - TQM
  - Kaizen
  - Zero faults
  - QA
  - Quality circles.
- ✓ Machine based quality control includes statistical process control and CAM.
- ✓ Companies copy best practice from competitors in order to improve.
- ✓ BS5750/ISO9000 ensures good quality systems.

TEST YOURSELF

Use your Mind Map to see if you can answer the following questions.

AS
1. Why might a firm use benchmarking?
2. How would a firm go about benchmarking?
3. What is BS5750/ISO9000?

A2
1. Can you explain what is meant by total quality management?
2. Can you list the main techniques used by firms to maintain quality?
3. What drawbacks are there to benchmarking?

Sample question and answer

TQM is, by definition, the responsibility of everyone in an organisation. Discuss this statement with regard to the use of teams in an organisation.

1. Define your terms.
   - TQM means that quality is everyone's responsibility (total quality management). Problems should be detected and rectified as early as possible. The aim will be zero faults – i.e. no mistakes if at all possible. In TQM, only employees are not customers; anyone the business deals with, including suppliers and sub contractors, should be treated as customers.
   - Another major part of TQM is empowerment – every member of the organisation is empowered to take action if they see any deterioration in quality.
2. This also means that teamwork and training are encouraged so that skills and experience are shared. Teamworking involves each member sharing responsibility within their team. It also allows for rivalry between teams – such competition is said to encourage continuous improvement.
3. The natural extension of TQM is in to quality circles where groups of employees meet in the firm's time to discuss and resolve quality issues, with the viewpoints of design, management, production and customer represented. The really important factor is that everyone, except the employee, is considered to be a customer.
4. Conclusion
   - TQM cannot be achieved without teamworking – the two are mutually inclusive.
   - Why? Because TQM relies on the team ethos, the whole team checking and re-checking and on empowerment. Teamworking also relies on the team ethos and empowerment.

Maintaining quality

Summary

- Quality is defined as 'fitness for purpose' – the purpose for which the consumer purchases.
- Historically quality was maintained by a separate department who checked and accepted or rejected at the end of the production process.
- Modern systems rely on everyone being responsible for quality. They are thus linked to team working, motivation theory and human relations management.
- W.E. Deming introduced the notion of Total Quality Management – quality is everyone's responsibility and everyone is empowered to do something about it.
- Modern systems include offering rewards for no defects, using shop floor expertise and advice and continuous improvement.
- Marks such as BS5750/ISO9000 and QA exist to indicate that firms are maintaining quality.
- Firms can improve quality by learning from competitors and benchmarking.

Index

absorption costing 82
ACAS 120
accelerator 32
accounting 79–83, 95–100
acid test ratio 101, 102
acquisition/integration 16–17
activity ratios 101, 102
administrative management 113
adverse variances 80, 81
advertising media 69–70
aggregate demand 31
AIDA 69
Ansoff matrix 39, 53
applications/appointments 125
assets 29, 97, 98, 102
authority 108, 113, 114
average costs 79
average rate of return 91, 92

balance of payments 33
balance sheet 97
benchmarking 110, 145
best practice 5, 81, 110
Boston matrix 51, 52
brands/branding 40, 51, 66
break-even analysis 84–9
broadcast media 70
budgets/budgeting 30, 51, 80
buffer stock 136–7
bureaucratic leadership style 114
bureaucratic structure 109–10
business cycle 31–2
business process re-engineering (BPR) 110, 144
business strategy/objectives 2–7

cannibalism (market share) 67
capacity/capacity utilisation 133–4
capital employed 97, 102–3
capital goods 44
cash flow 66, 86
CBI 121
cell production 137
ceteris paribus 22
chain of command 108
circles (organisation structure) 107
co-operatives 15, 76
communications 18, 125–6, 137–8
Companies Acts (1985, 1989) 96
competition 18, 25, 29, 40, 60
competitors 51, 101
complements 22
computers 138
conflict avoidance 11
consultative committees 121
consumer goods/durables 44, 63
consumers 10, 53, 71, 75, 146
contingency theories 113
contribution methods 82, 88
control technology 138
controlled economy 29
controlling operations 136–42
corporate culture 4
correlation 57
cost-based pricing 60

cost benefit analysis 93, 132
cost centres 81–2, 109, 110
costs 79, 84–8
creaming (price) 60
creditors 10, 101
critical path analysis 139
cross elasticity of demand 23–4, 61
current assets/liabilities 97, 102

data sources (investments) 93
databases 138
debentures 97
decisions/decision-making 5–6, 109, 133
delayering 108
delegation 108
Delphi technique 55
demand 22–4, 31, 61
demand management 32
Deming, W.E. 144
democratic leadership 114
depreciation 98
deregulation 29
direct costs 79, 82
direct selling 71, 76
disability discrimination 118
discount rate 91
diseconomies of scale 133
dismissal procedures 119
distribution 56, 74, 75–6
diversification diseconomies 133
dividend yield 103
downsizing 17
Drucker, Peter 114
duopoly 61

e-commerce 18–19, 76, 138
earnings per share 103
economies of scale 16, 133
elasticity of demand 23–4, 61
employees 9, 117–23, 126
employers 117–23
employment law 117–20
endorsement 71
Enterprise Investment Scheme 14
equal opportunities 117, 118
equity 97
ethics 34–5, 40
European Union 33–4, 120
exchange rate 30–1, 33, 34
expectations 32
expert systems 138
external bodies (social responsibility) 11
external data sources 47, 55
external factors (labour) 124–5
external finance (sources) 96
external influences (business) 21–36
extrapolation 55, 57

factoring 97
family tree type structures 107
favourable variances 80, 81
finance sources 96–7
financial accounting 95–100, 103

financial assets 97
financial economies of scale 16, 133
financial planning 14
fiscal policy 30, 32
fixed assets 97, 98
fixed costs 79, 82, 84, 85–8
flexibility 109–10, 128
forecasting/prediction 55–8
formal structures 106–7, 109
franchises 15, 76
free market system 28–9
full costing 82

Gantt charts 140
gap analysis 5
GATT 33
gearing 101, 102
geographical diseconomies 133
globalisation 18–19
goods 44, 63
goodwill 97
government policies 29–31, 34, 132
graphs 22–3, 85–6
gross profit margin 102
growth 16, 39–40, 66

'halo effect' 66
hands-on-leadership 114
Handy, Charles 18, 66, 109, 115
Hawthorne Experiments 126
health and safety legislation 117–18
Herzberg, F. 113, 127
hierarchical structure 109–10
hierarchy of needs 26
human relations 113
human resource management 113, 124–9

imperfect competition 25
income elasticity of demand 23–4, 61
incremental budgeting 51
indirect costs 79, 82
industrial goods 63
industrial marketing 44
industrial relations 117–19, 120
industrial tribunals 117, 120
infinite series 32
inflation 32
informal structures 106–7, 109
information technology 18, 137–8
infrastructure (location decision) 132
intangibles 44
integration 16–17
inter-quartile range 56
intermediaries 75
internal constraints 40
internal data sources 46, 55
internal finance (sources) 96
internal markets 29
internal rate of return 91, 92
international influences 33–4
intrapreneurialism 110
inventory control 136–7
investment appraisal 6, 90–4, 132
investors 101

Index

joint stock companies 8, 9
Just In Time system 76, 137

Kaizen 144
Kanban 137
Keynes, John Maynard 31

labour/labour supply 81, 124–5, 132
laissez-faire leadership 114
land (location decision) 132
law (external constraints) 40
leadership styles 114–15
lean production 137
leasing 96
legislation/legal constraints 34
liabilities 97
liability (limited/unlimited) 15
limited liability 15
line managers 108
liquidity ratios 101, 102
loans 14, 96
local government 30
location decisions 131–2
loss leaders 60

McGregor, D. 113, 127
macro-factors (influences) 28–36, 40
management accounting 79–83
Management Buy-Ins (MBIs) 17
Management Buy-Outs (MBOs) 17
management of change 17–18
Management by Objectives (MBO) 114
management structure 106–11
management styles 112–16
managerial diseconomies of scale 133
managerial economies of scale 16, 133
managers 9, 101, 110
Manufacturing Resource Planning 138
marginal costs 79, 82
marginal pricing 60
market 39, 131
    adjustments 23
    analysis/research 43–9
    domination 45
    failure 25–6
    forces 22–3, 29
    -led development 67
    organisation 24–5
    price 60
    research 45–7, 70, 134
    segmentation 44–5, 66–7
    share 22, 45, 67
    size 43–4
    types 44
marketing
    economies of scale 133
    needs (price-based) 60–1
    objectives/planning 38–43
    plans 50–4
marketing mix 50
    place 74–7
    price 59–62
    product 63–8
    promotion 69–73
Maslow, A.H. 113, 126
mass markets 43–4
master budget 80
material assets 97
material variances 81
maximising objectives 3
Mayo, E. 126
mean 56
media advertising 69–70
median 56
mergers 17
micro-factors (influences) 21–7
middlemen (intermediaries) 75
minimising objectives 3
minimum wage 33, 119
mission/mission statement 2, 8, 38
mode 56
monetary policy 30
monopolistic competition 25
monopoly 24, 25, 26
mortgages 97
motivation theory 126–8
multi-skilling 127, 128
multiplier 32

national government 30
net assets 97
net present value (NPV) 91, 92
net profit margin 102
networks 140
niche markets 44

objectives 2–7, 38–42
Office of Fair Trading 25
oligopoly 24–5, 61
operations management
    controlling operations 136–42
    maintaining quality 143–7
    organising production 131–5
operations research 138
opportunity cost 59, 91–2, 132, 137
organic growth 16, 39, 66
organisational structure 106–11
organising production 131–5
outlets (distribution) 75–6
output 84, 85–8
owners/ownership 8–9, 96

partnerships 8–9, 15
patents/Patent Office 14
paternalistic leadership 114
pay (as motivator) 127
payback 91
pendulum arbitration 121
penetration price 60
perceptual map 52
perfect competition 25
personnel (internal constraints) 40
PEST analysis 5
place (in marketing mix) 74–7
planned economy 29
planning, marketing 38–42, 50–4
planning cycle 6, 38–9, 50

political legislation 117, 118–19
positional analysis 4
pressure groups 11, 35
price
    discrimination 61
    -earnings ratio 103
    elasticity of demand 23–4, 61
    in marketing mix 59–62
    variance 81
pricing in practice 60–1
pricing in theory 59
primary research 45–6
Private Finance Initiative 15, 30
private limited company 15
private sector businesses 15
privatisation 25, 29
probability 55, 57
producer, distribution channel and 75
product
    design 134
    development 40, 67
    differentiation 40
    diversification 40
    features 66
    levels 63–4
    life cycle 51, 64–6, 134
    in marketing mix 63–8
    mix 67
    placement 71
    positioning 66–7
    range 67
product portfolio analysis 52
production methods 134, 137–8
productive efficiency 133
profit 9, 29, 98
profit centres 81–2, 109, 110
profit and loss account 98
profitability ratios 102
promotion (in marketing mix) 69–73
promotional pricing 60
psychological point pricing 60
public limited company 15, 16
public relations 71
Public Sector Borrowing Requirement (PSBR) 30, 31
public sector businesses 14–15
published media (advertisements) 70
pull/push strategies 75
pure monopoly 24
pyramids/pyramid structures 107–8

qualitative research 46
quality (maintenance) 143–7
quality assurance 144
quality circles 113, 121, 144
quality control 143–4
quantitative research 46
quota sample 46

Race Relations Act (1976) 118
random sample 46
range of distribution 56
ratio analysis 101–4
recruitment 125
reputation 10

Index

research and development 70, 134
retail outlets 76
Return on Capital Employed 102–3
return on equity 103
revenues 80, 84, 85–8
risk 13–14, 16, 90–1, 133

Sale of Goods Acts 146
sales related budgeting 51
satisficing objectives 3
scientific management 112, 126
secondary research 45, 46–7
selection techniques 125
semi-variable costs 79
sender–receiver (in HRM) 125–6
sevices 44, 63
Sex Discrimination Act (1975) 118
shareholder ratios 102, 103
shareholders 9
Sigmoid curve 18
simultaneous engineering 134, 138
single European currency 33, 34
skills 127–8
skimming (price) 60
small businesses 14, 16, 97
SMART scheme 14
SMART targets 3, 114
Social Charter 120, 121
social costs/benefits 93
social environment 34
social marketing 71
social responsibilities 10–11
sole traders 8–9, 15, 16
span of control 108
sponsorship 71
spreadsheets 91, 92, 138
staff diseconomies 133

stakeholders 8–12
standard deviation 56
standards (of BSI/ISO) 145–6
statistical process control 145
statistics 55–7
stock levels 136–7
stock turnover 102
strategic economies of scale 16
strategic management 17–18
strategic planning 4
strategies (push/pull) 75
strategy 2–7
stratified random sample 46
stratified sample 46
subcontracting 134
subordinate 108
subsidiarity principle 120
substitutes 22
suppliers 10, 101, 131–2
supply 22–3
Supply of Goods and Services Act 146
survival (of business) 14
SWOT analysis 4, 53
synergy 17
systems management 113

take-overs 17
target market 45
targeted sample 46
targets 3, 114
taxation 30, 133
Taylor, F.W. 112, 126
teamworking 9, 10, 113, 127
technical economies of scale 16, 133
technology 137–8
Theory X/Theory Y 127
time-lags 32–3

tolerance measurement/limit 145
total quality management (TQM) 144
trade barriers 33
trade credit 96
trade cycle 31–2
trade pattern 33
Trades Descriptions Act (1968) 70
Trades Union Congress 121
trade unions 119, 120–1
training 125
trait theory 115
transferable skills 128
transnationals 133

undercutting (predatory pricing) 61
unemployment 32
unlimited liability 15

variable costs 79, 82, 84, 85–8
variance analysis 80–1
variance interpretation 57, 80
venture capital 97
Vroom, V. 127

wage rate variance 81
window dressing (accounts) 98–9
worker directors 121
workers (motivation) 126
workforce planning 124
working capital 97, 102
works councils 121
World Trade Organisation 33

zero budgeting 80
zero faults 144